TWO TRADITIONS, ONE SPACE

TWO TRADITIONS, ONE SPACE

Orthodox Christians and Muslims in Dialogue

George C. Papademetriou, *Editor*

SOMERSET HALL PRESS
Boston, Massachusetts

Published by Somerset Hall Press
416 Commonwealth Avenue, Suite 612
Boston, Massachusetts 02215
www.somersethallpress.com

ISBN: 978-1-935244-06-6

LIBRARY OF CONGRESS CATALOGING-IN-PUBLICATION DATA

Two traditions, one space : Orthodox Christians and Muslims in dialogue / George C. Papademetriou, editor.
    p. cm.
  Includes bibliographical references (p.   ).
  ISBN 978-1-935244-06-6
  1. Islam--Relations--Christianity. 2. Christianity and other re-ligions--Islam. 3. Jesus Christ--Islamic interpretations. I. Papa-demetriou, George C.
  BP172.T89 2010
  261.2'7--dc22   2010033205

CONTENTS

Historical, Philosophical, and Theological Encounters

Contemporary Dialogue

Reference

Acknowledgments

The front cover image is a contemporary mosaic (ca. 1980s) depicting Patriarch Gennadios in dialogue with Sultan Mehmed II the Conqueror after the capture of Constantinople in 1453. It is located at the Orthodox Christian Ecumenical Patriarchate in Istanbul, Turkey. By permission of the Ecumenical Patriarchate. Photo courtesy of Dr. Tom Papademetriou.

The following were used by permission:

"Contemporary Dialogue between Orthodox Christians and Muslims," by George C. Papademetriou, previously appeared in *Islam & Christian-Muslim Relations* 15:1 (January 2004).

"Saint Gregory Palamas: Three Dialogues with the Muslims," by George C. Papademetriou, previously appeared in a Festschrift for Gregorios D. Ziakas in *Philia and Koinonia* (Thessalonike: Editions Vanias, 2008).

"Byzantine and Contemporary Greek Orthodox Approaches to Islam," by Anastasios Yannoulatos, translation by George C. Papademetriou previously appeared in *Journal of Ecumenical Studies*, vol. 33, no. 4 (Fall, 1996).

"The Ecumenical Patriarchate of Constantinople and Recent Dialogue with Islam," by Gregorios D. Ziakas, previously appeared in *Threskiologika Meleti-*

mata (Religious Studies), vol. 1 (Thessalonike: Editions Vanias, 2004) and also *Phanari: 400th Anniversary* (Istanbul: Ecumenical Patriarchate).

"Islamic Aristotelian Philosophy," by Gregorios D. Ziakas, previously appeared in *Aristotle in Arabic Tradition* (Thessalonike: Aristotelian University of Thessalonike Press, 1980).

The editor wishes to thank the following: The Most Reverend Emmanuel Adamakis, Metropolitan Archbishop of France, and his assistant at his Brussels office, Archimandrite Aimilianos Boginou, for providing documents from the Ecumenical Patriarchate demonstrating recent efforts at dialogue; Deacon Nephon at the Ecumenical Patriarchate for facilitating the rights to the front cover image; Brother Michael Philips for typing and entering some of the articles into computer format; Dr. Cynthia Col for preparing the index; Herald Gjura for designing the layout; and Professor Mahmoud M. Ayoub for encouraging me to complete the project." I especially wish to thank the publisher, Dean Papademetriou, for all his hard work in preparing this book for publication. Without his help, this book would not have seen the light of day.

Foreword from an Orthodox Perspective

Bartholomew I
Archbishop of Constantinople, New Rome
and Ecumenical Patriarch

It is with joy and interest that we received and read the book entitled *Two Traditions, One Space: Orthodox Christians and Muslims in Dialogue*.

There is no doubt that the interface between Christians and Muslims is an issue of critical importance, which will shape the one world that we inhabit as one human race, albeit as many faith communities, traditional cultures, and distinct nationalities.

As our Ecumenical Patriarchate initiated its Christian-Muslim Dialogue 23 years ago, we believe that this important undertaking will prove crucial and formative for the sake of peace, understanding, and respect between the two religions.

Foreword from a Muslim Perspective

Mahmoud M. Ayoub

Muslim-Christian dialogue is as old as Islam itself. It began with the Prophet of Islam and the Christian delegation of Najran who went to Medina from southern Arabia to make peace with the Muslims. The immense significance of this encounter for contemporary Christian-Muslim dialogue lies in the fact that Christians and Muslims shared one house of worship when, in spite of the protestations of some of his companions, the Prophet allowed the Christians to use his mosque to pray to the God they both worship.[1] Thus the Prophet established as *Sunnah* the validity of prayers in all of God's houses. This is in accordance with the *Qur'anic* principle that the houses of God include churches, synagogues, mosques, and monasteries – any place where His name is glorified.[2]

Until recent times, Muslims engaged Eastern Orthodox Christians of the Fertile Crescent – Iraq and Syria-Palestine – and Egypt in direct and often constructive and fruitful dialogue. With Muslim immigration to the West – Europe and North America – since the mid-nineteenth century, Muslim-Christian dialogue entered a new phase. It must, however, be observed that the full spiritual and cultural potential of Eastern

3

Orthodox Christian-Muslim dialogue is yet to be realized. It is hoped that the present volume will be a small but decisive step in this direction.

Although Christians and Muslims hold sharply distinct views of God and His attributes, of Christ and his relationship with God, and of sin and salvation, they share many common moral, spiritual, and theological values. These shared values can, and should, serve as a framework of a dialogue between the two faith-communities.

Eastern Orthodox Christians and Muslims have much to dialogue about. First, they share a rich civilization, which was heir to ancient Greek science and philosophy. With the help of other Christians, Jews, Sabaeans, and Zoroastrians they built an enduring philosophical, theological, and scientific heritage that substantially contributed to the Western Renaissance and Enlightenment. Therefore, Islamic civilization should be properly regarded as Islamic-Eastern Christian Civilization.

The mystical theologies of the two traditions provide still another fertile ground for interfaith dialogue. To be sure, the Christian doctrine of the trinity will in itself remain problematic for Muslims. Nonetheless, the apophatic theology of the absolute ineffability of the Godhead of the Orthodox Church and the Islamic mystical theology of absolute oneness of God (*tawhid*) provide yet another rich field of meaningful spiritual dialogue. In fact this spiritual dialogue began with St. Gregory Palamas and his Muslim captors centuries ago, as discussed in the essay on Palamas in this volume.

A third area of theological-humanistic engagement is the Christological theologies of the two traditions.

For both communities of faith Christ is a prophet, and much more than a prophet. He is, according to the *Qur'an*, "high-honored (*wajihan*) in this and the next world, and one who is brought near to God."[3] Christ was, according to the Gospel, conceived by the "holy spirit," and according to the *Qur'an*, by God breathing of His spirit into Mary's generative organ.[4] Some of these sensitive issues will be touched upon in this volume. Of course, they will not be resolved, but explored, and hopefully received by Christian and Muslim readers in a spirit of prayerful humility and openness.

The spirit as well as the primary purpose of the present volume are captured in its title: *Two Traditions, One Space*. It is essentially an Eastern Orthodox Christian attempt to reach out for dialogue with Muslims. It also aims at explaining Islam to Orthodox Christian readers. It explores points of contacts between individuals and groups in both communities with honesty and candor.

On the level of mystical contacts, the essay on St. Gregory Palamas and his encounters with Islam, and the comparative article on the Sufi Dhikr and the Jesus Prayer, show clearly the creative potentials of dialogue. It is important to observe that these two spiritual exercises developed in mutual social interactions rather than direct influences by either of the two communities over the other. These and other points of spiritual contacts happened despite the hostilities and warfare between the Byzantine and Muslim empires.

It is noteworthy that the first Christian theologian to be engaged in dialogue with Islam, but not with Muslims, was St. John of Damascus. His views of Islam are presented and closely analyzed. It is significant that St. John of Damascus regarded Islam as a Christian heresy, and not a pagan religion, as was the case in Western Europe, particularly during and after the Crusades.

It must finally be observed that this volume is the fruit of the effort of Father George C. Papademetriou. Throughout, it breathes his deep spirituality and dedication to Christian-Muslim dialogue. This is Father Papademetriou's second contribution to this important and sorely needed area of interfaith dialogue. The first was a lively exchange between Muslim and Christian scholars and clerics on Orthodox Christian-Muslim dialogue. Father Papademetriou edited a useful volume of the proceedings of that conference.[5] One can only pray that the faithful of both communities will continue the work that the reverend Father has so admirably begun.

NOTES

1 See *Qur'an* 29:46, which declares, "our God and your God is one."
2 "Had God not restrained some people by others, monastic cells, churches, synagogues and mosques in which God's name is remembered much would have been demolished." (*Qur'an* 22:40.)
3 *Qur'an* 3:45.
4 See Luke 1:35. The *Qur'an* asserts, "And Mary daughter of 'Imran who guarded well her generative organ, and thus We breathed into it of our spirit." (*Qur'an* 66: 12.)
5 The conference took place at Hellenic College/Holy Cross Greek Orthodox School of Theology in Brookline, Massachusetts in May 1985. The volume of proceedings appeared a year later: *Muslim-Greek Orthodox Relations* (Brookline: Holy Cross Orthodox Press, 1986).

Introduction

George C. Papademetriou

Orthodox Christians and Muslims have a long history of contacts and encounters in the Byzantine and Ottoman Empires and currently in the Middle East and Turkey. Yet, ignorance of each other's faith and culture has resulted in great misunderstandings and conflicts. As a result of these past and present misunderstandings, there is need for mutual enlightenment. We need to avoid dangerous misconceptions and unfounded myths about each of these two great faiths. To do this, each religion needs to examine and honestly discuss the fundamentals of the "other." In the present volume we will examine the encounters and dialogues of these two religions.

In the past it was not possible for Orthodox Christians and Muslims to sit together to dialogue and honestly, freely, discuss their respective faiths. Various scholars, and notably the erudite professor-archbishop of Tirana, Albania, Anastasios Yannoulatos have described the Orthodox inability to see Islam clearly.[1] Although Orthodox Christians have lived alongside Muslims for many centuries, and in many areas still do, they could not interpret Islam objectively. The Byzantines were engaged in polemics, pointing out the weaknesses and contradictions of the Islamic religion and of its founder

7

Muhammad. Later, during the Ottoman period, it was impossible for the subjugated Orthodox to accept a true picture of the religion of their overlord. Even later, when Greece was independent, Greek scholars did not give the religion of their neighbor, Turkey, an objective presentation.

For their part, the Muslims also were unable to interpret objectively the Christian faith even though they had a sketchy knowledge of Jesus through the *Qur'an*. Although it is true that the Muslims have a special place in the *Qur'an* for Jesus as a prophet and have praise for his mother Mary, there is a misunderstanding even in the Qur'an, which says, "Allah is the Messiah and the Son of Mary."[2] Nowhere do Christians claim that "God is Jesus," only that Jesus Christ is God.[3] In the present volume Professor George Patronos treats the Muslim view of Christ in his study on Jesus as prophet.

Despite these differences, popular religious expressions of Christian Orthodoxy and Islam were closely connected, and it is interesting to note the commonality of their ascetic practices and mystical experience of God's presence.[4] There was also a philosophical sharing: The West owes a debt for the recovery of classical philosophy, especially Aristotelian, to Islamic scholars who received it from the Byzantine heirs of classical Greek philosophy,[5] as demonstrated by Professor Gregory Ziakas in his study included in this volume. In the Middle Ages, instead of conversations, numerous disputes took place in Islamic centers between Christians and Muslims, including one in which Saint Gregory Palamas was the Orthodox Christian spokesperson at Bursa.[6] It seems the overall picture of the medieval and later contacts were polemical in nature.

In the contemporary setting of religious tolerance

and cooperation, we choose dialogue rather than debate. A contemporary American scholar states, "A new dimension is added to the experience of religion—the understanding in love of the religion of one's neighbor. And once this dimension is opened, it becomes clear that a living faith implies the obligation to open one's mind and heart to a sincere perception of the faiths of others."[7]

The late Ecumenical Patriarch Athenagoras lived in his early youth with Muslims in Epiros, Greece, then under Ottomans rule, and talked about it in his later years as follows:

> The area where I was born had been occupied by the Turks a century before the fall of Constantinople. In my village there were both Turks and Christians, but we lived peacefully together; the Moslems were invited to christenings and in turn the Christians were the guests at circumcision feasts.
>
> It was a sort of biblical coexistence and we all felt that we were children of Abraham. The Muslims ate mutton and lamb during the festival of Baihram and we Christians ate the Easter lamb. The dervishes were very good to me; they were very tolerant toward the Christians and some of them were well known for their intelligence. We had one dervish in my village by the name of Jamil. He often came to visit us at home and dine with us. My mother and sister, in particular, were very fond of him and kept no secrets from him. Jamil knew their innermost thoughts better than our village priest.[8]

In this "age of dialogue," we must confess our painful past, and begin the road of mutual respect, recognizing our common heritage in the faith in the one God, the God of Abraham, Isaac, and Jacob. This common experience is beyond any other reward. The present collection of studies brings together the work of prominent Orthodox Christians in thoughtful discussion on theological, historical, and philosophical topics of interest. Its objective is to present the views of committed believers who offer scholarly studies based on philosophical and theological positions. It is not limited to any particular period of history or any specific doctrine. It hopes to offer challenges and new directions in the relations of Orthodox Christians and Muslims and, furthermore, to emphasize the Orthodox existential religious experience of interreligious dialogue. The authors do not overlook the essential differences between Muslims and Christians; but they do want to stress – as a common element – the supreme importance of personal belief-commitment for the future of both religions. Their hope is that these studies will be a testimony to the trust and hope in the one God and his unfathomed purpose for humanity. By clarifying some murky issues between the two religions, they open a way toward further understanding and peaceful coexistence in our constantly shrinking world.

I hope that you, the reader, will benefit spiritually and especially that you will expand your religious knowledge and will enrich your experience in the spirit of understanding in the world religious community.

NOTES

1 Anastasios Yannoulatos, Archbishop of Albania. *Islam: A General Survey* (in Greek). Athens, Greece (1979), p. 9. See also the Islamic aggressionist policies in Francis E. Peters, "The Early Muslim Empires: Umayyads, Abbasids, Fatimids," *Islam: The Religious and Political Life of a World Community*, ed. Mar-

jorie Kelly (New York, 1984), pp. 73-93.

2 *The Holy Qur'an: Text, Translation, and Commentary*, by Abdulla Yusuf Ali (Doha-Qatar: Qatar National Printing Press, 1946; Washington, D.C.: The Islamic Center, 1946), Sura 5: 75, p. 266.

3 Gerard S. Sloyan, *Jesus in Focus: A Life in its Setting* (Mystic, Connecticut, 1983), pp. 192-93. For a Muslim understanding of Jesus, see the excellent chapter, "The Jesus of the Qur'an," pp. 188-96. See also *We Believe in One God: The Experience of God in Christianity and Islam*, ed. Anne Mario Schimmel and Abdoldjavad Falaturi (New York, 1979).

4 H.A.R. Gibb, *Mohammedanism: A Historical Survey*, 2nd. ed. (London, 1953), pp. 128-29.

5 Alfred Guillaume, *The Legacy of Islam* (London, 1968), p. 249. See also Robert M. Haddad, *Syrian Christians in Muslim Societies: An Interpretation* (Princeton, 1970).

6 Dialexis, *Soter*, 15 (1892), pp. 140-46. George C. Papademetriou, "Judaism and Greek Orthodoxy in Historical Perspective," *The Greek Orthodox Theological Review*, 21 (1976), pp. 105-07.

7 Jacob B. Agus, "Foreword," *Jewish Monotheism and Christian Trinitarian Doctrine*, Dialogue by Pinchas Lapides and Jurgen Moltmann, trans. Leonard Swidler (Philadelphia, 1981), p. 17.

8 Demetrios Tsakonas, *A Man Sent by God: The Life of Patriarch Athenagoras of Constantinople* (Brookline, 1977), pp. 9-10.

Historical, Philosophical, and Theological Encounters

Jesus as a Prophet of Islam

George Patronos

Translated by George C. Papademetriou

Introduction

In recent years, there has been a noticeable growth of interest in the dialogue between Christianity and Islam, in the East as well as in the West. Though I am not aware of the specific fruits of this interest, I would like to suggest that dialogue between Orthodox Christianity and Islam may offer a particularly fruitful opportunity. Despite the historical conflicts between ancient Greece and Persia, then Byzantium and the Arab world, we have had luminous interactions, especially on the spiritual and cultural levels.

It is well known how fruitful for both sides the exchange of philosophical views and scientific achievements was between these two worlds. Aristotle, for instance, was not seen only as a great philosopher of ancient Greece but was also accepted by the thinkers of the Arab world as their "first teacher." Moreover, among the great theologians and doctrinal Fathers of the Eastern Church there were not only Greeks, but also Arabs such as the Syrian Fathers.[1]

Jesus appeared and ministered in Palestine. Islam was

15

also originated in the East, in places where the Eastern Orthodox Church had been active for centuries. Thus, they share a common ground and an identical context for mutual understanding and essential dialogue.

We also know that the encounter and conflict between Hellenism and Judaism happened in the same area of the Middle East, followed by the great differences and rupture between Judaism and Christianity. Indeed, Judaism had a negative attitude toward Jesus, both because of his dissent from the hermeneutical schools of his time, such as *Hillel* and *Ben Zakkai*, and because of criticism of traditional messianic thought by his disciples. The same negative view characterizes later Talmudic Judaism, in which Jesus is more seriously engaged. Talmudic Judaism, in its turn, differs from the main points of the Christian gospel tradition.[2]

Only later, toward the end of the first and the beginning of the second centuries, do we find extended references to the history and personality of Jesus but, again, in absolute contradiction to the tradition of the canonical Gospels. This Apocryphal literature concerning Jesus (the so-called *pseudepigrapha* Gospels) treats the life and career of the prophet of Galilee in a secular spirit and through the perspective of a Gnostic soteriology. During the post-apostolic era, the *Nazarene Gospel* and the *Gospel of the Hebrews* in particular, formulated a strong tradition concerning Jesus as a prophet of Judaism from Nazareth. Even though these treatises accept the prophetic and messianic aspects of Jesus, they agree neither with the idea of his virginal conception nor with a doctrinal faith in his divine nature as the

Son of God on earth.

For more than six centuries after Jesus's birth, the Apocryphal literature played a decisive and formative part in various Jesus traditions within the region of Anatolia, especially in the territories around Syria and Mesopotamia. This Semitic tradition, which differed from the Judeo-Christian faith, developed primarily around the Euphrates valley. Conversely, Hellenistic Christianity, with Antioch and Alexandria as its centers – and later Constantinople as the main seat – was far removed from the formation of the peculiar Jesus tradition of the Far East.

When Islam appeared in the beginning of the seventh century, in the regions of South Arabia there were Jewish and Christian communities (isolated from Jerusalem and Constantinople) with their own characteristic traditions that attempted to influence the local Arab population toward a monotheistic faith.

The *Qur'an*, the holy book of Islam (believed to have been revealed to Muhammad in segments over a period of 23 years), demonstrated the profound influence of these efforts.[3] This is why the study of the *Qur'an* is very important for an understanding of Jesus's personality, not only for Muslims, but also for Christians, with the awareness that the source material and details of information do not come only from the canonical tradition of the four Gospels of the New Testament, but primarily from the apocryphal literature. This reveals to us the particularity of the Arabic Christianity that Muhammad, along with the first generation of his faithful, came to know.[4]

One who studies the *Qur'an* and the history of Islam gets the impression of an historical, religious evolution. In this evolutionary course, three basic stages can be identified.

Judaism, with its great patriarchs, prophets, and God's first Testament with his people (that of the Mosaic Law and the Old Testament), represents the first stage. According to the *Qur'anic* history of Islam, this people rebelled, lost its faith in God, and the Old Covenant became non-valid.

During the second stage, God decided to send a new Prophet, Jesus, to reorganize the people of God from the beginning and to establish through Jesus a new covenant, that of the New Testament. Unfortunately, though, the Christian world was led into wars and heretical conflicts that were extremely intense around the sixth century, especially in the portions of the Arab world. There, a feeling that this second covenant between God and humanity was leading to a dead-end became more and more intense.

Consequently, a third testament, that of the *Qur'an*, and the mission of a final prophet – Muhammad – became necessary. According to this perspective and in light of the *Qur'an*, Islam appeared as a new, historical alternative to the spiritual and religious dead-end into which Judaism and Christianity had led humanity.

A modern Islamic scholar, Muhammad Ata ur-Rahim, in his work, *Jesus, A Prophet of Islam*, in the foreword to the tenth chapter, entitled "Jesus in the *Qur'an*," cites, in order and without comment, all the verses that refer to the person of Jesus and his teaching.

Interestingly, he then writes:

> The *Qur'an*, the last of the sacred books, which were re-
> vealed by the Creator to the last of his delegated, is a source
> of knowledge for Jesus that is being essentially ignored by
> most scholars of Christianity.
>
> The *Qur'an* not only helps us toward a more complete un-
> derstanding of Jesus's personality but, through that, makes
> possible a gradually growing respect and love for him. The
> last Apocalypse, which was revealed 600 years after Jesus's
> birth, tells us what is important for us to know concerning
> his life and teaching and places his role as prophet in the
> extreme perspective of his prophecy, which the Ενωτικοί
> wish to see in history. The *Qur'an* advances that perspective
> more than any other source.
>
> In fact, the *Qur'an* does not cover Jesus's life in detail, but
> it does refer to its key events. Miracles and powers, which
> are attributed to Him, are mentioned with general expres-
> sions. In the same way, the Bible that was given from God
> to Jesus, namely the Gospel, is mentioned several times
> although we do not have a detailed exposition of its con-
> tent. Certainly, the *Qur'an* is interested in his mission to the
> world, how he appeared on earth, who he was and who he
> was not and, finally, how he accomplished his mission.
>
> Before one looks at [Jesus's] life, it would be very useful to
> examine what his mission on earth was, and how he har-
> monized his work with what came before him and what
> would follow him. It is repeated once more that Jesus was
> a prophet in the long line of those prophets sent by God
> to the people of earth. As the delegated of God, he taught
> and led his people and his preaching was, on the one hand,
> a confirmation and extension of the preaching of the oth-
> er prophets who preceded him and, on the other hand,
> a preparation and guide for the teaching brought by the
> Prophet [Muhammad] after him.[5]

General Christological Outline

'Isa is the name of Jesus in the *Qur'an*.[6] The *Qur'an* refers to 'Isa in 15 chapters and 93 verses, through which it is possible for someone to build up a *Quranic* story concerning Jesus and a related Christology. This *Qur'anic* Christology parallels that of the New Testament, but is intensely influenced by material drawn from the apocryphal Gospels concerning Jesus's childhood, as well as by elements of a hermeneutical approach based on Christian mystery texts of the early centuries. In addition to the name " 'Isa," the *Qur'an* attributes other titles to Jesus, demonstrating an Islamic Christology: "Messiah" (twelve times); "Prophet"; "delegated of God"; "son of Mary" (thirty times, whereas in the Gospels it is found only once); "blessed"; "word of truth"; "servant of God" (several times); and so forth. With these facts in mind, it is possible for us to build up not only an historical outline concerning Jesus, but also a clear Christological picture and theology, based on similar *Qur'anic* references. Indeed, in the sacred text of Islam we find references coming from the New Testament Gospel tradition, which demonstrate an acceptance of basic events of Christian faith and history, such as the Annunciation of Mary, the virginal conception, Jesus's birth from the Virgin Mary, and so forth up to Jesus's Ascension. However, this does not mean that Islam accepts either the Christian doctrine that the Virgin Mary is the Mother of God or that Jesus is by nature divine.[7]

In particular, we should examine the *Qur'anic* understanding of the following basic events of Jesus's history.

THE ANNUNCIATION OF MARY AND JESUS'S BIRTH

The *Quranic* picture of Jesus is a composite that presupposes the acceptance of his Jewish background and of the efforts to fill in the gaps in the gospel story of the New Testament with material from apocryphal literature. It includes important events preceding Jesus's birth, such as Mary's Presentation in the Temple, the announcement of the marvelous birth of the Prophet and Baptist John to his father, the priest Zechariah, and also similar references to the line of prophets and "delegated of God," from Abraham to Christ. Then comes the Annunciation of the Virgin, Jesus's mother.

The Annunciation is described in the *Qur'an* with a wonderful simplicity and human freshness, which amazes us and reminds us of elements in parallel with evangelical descriptions. As we have already mentioned, here we have references to Mary's Presentation to the Temple, her preparation and sanctification by the Spirit of God, her ennoblement through accepting the Archangel Gabriel and his annunciation of the miraculous birth of Jesus. This birth is considered miraculous, because the *Qur'an* accepts that Mary was a virgin since "no mortal had approached her" and her intention was to preserve her virginity also after her son's birth. This possibility is assured by the Angel with the words: "Such is the will of your Lord," he (the angel) replied, "that is no difficult thing for Him. He shall be a sign to mankind," the Lord, "and a blessing from Ourself. This is Our decree" (*Qur'an* 19:21).

Just as in Luke there is a clear distinction between the Annunciation and the event of conception, in the

same way this distinction is obvious in the *Qur'an*.
God's Angel, who appeared to Mary at the Annunciation, is differentiated from the Holy Spirit, who performed the miracle of conception. The belief that the
Archangel Gabriel performs both the Annunciation
and the conception (as some interpret the *Qur'an*) is in-
correct, as can be seen if we examine all the references
made to these events. The *Qur'an's* assertion that Gabriel is sent to the Virgin under "human form" (*Qur'an*
19: 27) neither rejects a conception by the power of the
Holy Spirit nor projects the Archangel as the father of
Jesus, as has been argued by some *Qur'anic* scholars.[8]
On the contrary, Jesus's conception is put forth as a result of God's creative will. As God created Adam from
the beginning, so in the same way Jesus is created directly by God. The wonderful creation of Adam prepares us for that of Jesus by a virgin, despite the fact
that "To God Jesus is man, like Adam," and "is created
from earth" (*Qur'an* 3:52).

Despite this, "Jesus, the true son of Mary," has become a "doubting issue for many" and again, according to the *Qur'an*, he himself was fully conscious, even
from his childhood, of his special relationship with
God and his great mission:

> Whereupon he [the child] spoke and said: "I am the ser-
> vant of Allah. He has given me the Gospel and ordained
> me a prophet. His blessing is upon me wherever I go, and
> He has commanded me to be steadfast in prayer and to go
> and to give alms to the poor as long as I shall live. He has
> exhorted me to honor my mother has purged me of vanity
> and wickedness. I was blessed on the day I was born, and
> blessed I shall be on the day of my death; and may peace be
> upon me on the day when I shall be raised to life." (Sura 19,
> 31-35, *Qur'an*, p. 34.)

It is known that Islam does not accept the Christian doctrine concerning an "original sin" that Adam transmitted to his descendants.[9] Islam does, however, clearly distinguish between Jesus' birth from the Virgin Mary and the birth of other people, since "every son of Adam" is a fruit of sin and relation with Satan, "except the son of Mary and his mother." This distinction is intended to emphasize the particularity of Jesus's personality from the first moment of his conception and birth, which is why Islam puts forth interesting elements of Christology in the *Qur'anic* theology.[10]

JESUS AS PROPHET AND APOSTLE OF GOD

Jesus clearly appears in the *Qur'an* as a prophet and especially as an Old Testament one, but also as "a servant" (*Qur'an* 19:31) and "delegated (apostle) of God" (*Qur'an* 4:156), or "delegated of the Highest" (*Qur'an* 4:169), and as an "apostle of God" (*Qur'an* 61:6). Like the other prophets, Jesus has his own, divine, mission to accomplish among the people of God. The proof of his divine mission is his "miraculous birth" attested by the fact that he proved his mission by performing miracles, despite the fact that the Jews called him a "deceiver" (*Qur'an* 61:6).

Indeed, "Jesus, son of Mary" was given "special gifts." He had "the power of miracles" and "the spirit of sanctity" (*Qur'an* 2:81; 2:54). The "holy miracles will testify his mission" (*Qur'an* 3:43). This is not merely a general reference to the power of Jesus' miracles; we also have a record of specific miraculous interventions, exactly as in the gospel narratives. The *Qur'an* reminds us, for example, of the healing of the blind man by Jesus, the catharsis of the leper, the healing of the deaf, and the resurrections of the dead "from their graves" (*Qur'an* 5:110), always "with the leave of God" (*Qur'an* 3:43).

Another proof of Jesus's prophetic mission is that he spoke and preached in the world with the authority and power of a mature man even from his childhood (*Qur'an* 3:41; 19:30), exactly as in the New Testament synoptic tradition.

The *Qur'an* makes frequent reference to the miraculous abilities of Jesus and the authority of his speech, drawn directly from the apocryphal literature, particularly from the Gnostic Gospel of Thomas. The well known narrative about Jesus's creation of young birds from clay, in front of his friends' eyes, while he was a child, to which birds, "under God's leave," he gave "breath of life" (*Qur'an* 3:43; 5:110), reminds us of the creation narrative in the Old Testament book of Genesis.

JESUS AS MESSIAH AND SERVANT OF GOD

It is particularly interesting to note that in the *Qur'an* we have references to one of the most basic Christological concepts of the New Testament, that of Jesus as Messiah and Servant of God. The title "Messiah" does not appear as a result of a relevant theological evolution, but is attributed to Jesus from the first moment of his birth.

The term Messiah, of course, in the *Qur'an*, declares that Jesus belongs to the line of great prophets who were sent to humanity by God. This wonderful line, which includes Jesus, ends with the prophet Muhammad. For this reason, as all prophets are human, in the same way Jesus is a natural man. From this it can be concluded that the *Qur'an* does not accept the biblical idea of Messiah with the Christian doctrinal meaning of Son of God (*Qur'an* 9:30-31.)

The term Messiah is used in the *Qur'an* about twelve times and, despite its Jewish origin, was very well known in different areas of Arabia during the pre-Islamic era; it is always attributed exclusively to Jesus and no other person in human history.[11]

The *Qur'an* also preserves references to the biblical term "servant of God," derived originally from the Old Testament, particularly from the prophet Isaiah (Is 42:1; 52:13; 53:12), and picked up in the New Testament (Phil 2:7). As angels are "servants of God," Jesus likewise is a servant too (*Qur'an* 4:170).

It is true though, that despite these important Christological references, the *Qur'an* insists, and this needs to be underlined here, that Jesus "son of Mary" is nothing more than the "servant of God," namely "a prototype" to the Jews (*Qur'an* 43:59). The *Qur'an* insists that Jesus is an exceptional man but still human.

Thus, the *Qur'an* opposes the divinity of Jesus. This is why the use of Christological terms such as "Messiah" and "Servant of God" in the Qur'an should not be interpreted according to the Jewish and Christian traditions and practices. Again, according to the *Qur'an*, "to God, Jesus is man, like Adam" (*Qur'an* 3:52 and 3:73). Jesus is merely a servant of God and he is completely under God's authority.

Jesus, the Word of God and the Trinitarian God

For Islam, the expression *kalima*, "God's word," includes a great number of notions and meanings. Linguistically speaking, *kalima* means simply a word, a speech, or even a poem. However, when used in reference to God, *kalima* means a certain law or provision, a source of blessing, or even a marvelous and essential revelation. In many parts of the *Qur'an* we meet all these variations of meanings (see *Qur'an* 2:37 and 124; 7:137 and 172; 10:34).[12]

The *Qur'anic* textual exegesis provides some interesting approaches to the problem of Jesus's relation to God's word and to the general Christian Trinitarian theology.[13] Indeed, in the *Qur'an* we have many references to the "Word," which comes from God to Jesus. Thus, Jesus appears as the fulfillment of God's creative word, which is offered to him from the first moment of his conception. This however does not imply that he is the incarnate divine Word of the Gospel of John the Evangelist and the Christian doctrine of the Trinity.

The *Qur'an* clearly establishes that "Jesus is the son of Mary, delegated of God and his Word. He sent him to Mary. He is his breath." This is why [Muhammad] invites his faithful, on the one hand, to believe "in God and his apostles," and on the other not to accept "that the Trinity exists in God." God for Islam "is one" and "does not have a son." God is "self-sufficient" and "rules heaven and earth on his own" (*Qur'an* 4:169). And yet, Jesus is not simply a Messiah – namely delegated and servant of God – in the present world but, as the "reliable of God," he will be "Great" in "this world and the other" (*Qur'an* 3:40). Even those angels who surround God's throne will be at His disposal (*Qur'an* 4:170).

While this eschatological view of Jesus's mission is especially interesting, it does not mean that God's unity and uniqueness is being threatened. For the *Qur'an*, God is and will always be one: "There is only one God ... powerful and wise." The *Qur'an* emphasizes that this must be understood by all, including the "Jews and Christians." This is the reason why the ending for the *Qur'an* has a notable clarity in the rejection of every Trinitarian notion of God and emphasizes, "Let us end our differences (with them), we worship only one God, let us worship no one else; Let no one of us have another Lord than him" (*Qur'an* 3:55-57). Thus, Christians are gravely erroneous to say, "that Christ, son of Mary, is God." This belief alone is enough to prove them "unbelievers" (*Qur'an* 5:19).

From these interesting formulations it can be concluded that the *Qur'an* opposes the doctrine of a Trinitarian God. But the Trinity, as it is defined in the *Qur'an*, is not the same as that defined by the Ecumenical Councils of the Christian East. It is a different doctrine altogether. The *Qur'anic* trinity consists of God, Jesus, and Mary. In the *Qur'an*, we read, "God asked Jesus, son of Mary, if he had ordered men to worship him and his mother as gods." Of course Jesus denied it, saying, "Lord, how could I order such a sacrilegious thing" (*Qur'an* 5:116).[14]

Thus the *Qur'an*, by rejecting polytheism, aims to

insist on the preservation of the strictly monotheistic structure of Islam. However, this is true also in Christianity. Any deviation from monotheism is characterized by Christianity as an unacceptable heresy. The Trinity in Orthodox Christian doctrine consists of, and is known in, three consubstantial persons, the Father, the Son, and the Holy Spirit. In other words, one God in substance, who is revealed in history and world as three consubstantial hypostases. This Trinitarian God, the three consubstantial persons, is the center of the Christian revelation.

Jesus's Return and the Last Judgment

The *Qur'an* emphatically refutes that the death of the Messiah was real, and posits that Jesus experienced an eventual, natural, and bodily death. To the belief that the Jews, after the trial, killed "Jesus, the Messiah, son of Mary, the delegated of God," the *Qur'an's* reaction is direct and absolute: No, "they did not kill him. They did not crucify him. An imaginary body deceived their barbarity ... They did not kill Jesus. God exalted him and placed him next to Him, for he is powerful and wise" (*Qur'an* 4:156).

Here, Islam is essentially moving toward a Docetist conception and opens the way for an eschatological view of Jesus's "hypothetical" death and his return. Jesus's return "will be the certain sign that the Last Judgment is coming." For this reason, the *Qur'an* commands: "do not doubt the coming of Judgment." This is the required "path of salvation" (*Qur'an* 43:61). Besides, the idea of Jesus's exaltation by God ("God said to Jesus ... I will exalt you like me") contains this strong faith of returning again (*Qur'an* 3:48).

This does not, however, mean that the judge of all after the final resurrection will be Jesus, as is the case in Christian teaching. In the *Qur'an*, God will always be the judge (*Qur'an* 3:48-49). In any case, the return of Jesus, the chosen prophet, is today considered by many prominent interpreters of the *Qur'an* as a basic element of Islamic eschatology.[15]

Particular to Islamic tradition, after his second coming on earth Jesus will go to the Holy Land, to a place called *Afik*, holding a spear in his hand. There he will kill the Antichrist (a person in Islamic eschatology), then he will go to Jerusalem during the time of Morning Prayer. The Imam will try to relinquish his place to Jesus, who will refuse and pray behind the Imam, according to Muhammad's command. After these events, Jesus will slay the pigs, break the cross to pieces, destroy the synagogues and churches, and vanquish all Christians except those who will believe in him (*Qur'an* 4:159).

After the killing of the pseudo-messiah Antichrist, all "People of the Book" (namely Jews and Christians) will believe in [the Islamic Jesus] and will constitute one flock, that of Islam. Afterwards, Jesus will establish justice and will reign for forty years and then he will die. During his reign there will be peace among the beasts and also among the nations. In the end, he will be buried in Medina next to Muhammad, in an empty tomb between Abū Bakr and Omar. Thus, Jesus is considered a true Messiah of Islam.

JESUS AND MUHAMMAD

According to Islamic theologians and commentators on the Qur'an, verse 61:6, while Jesus "son of Mary" as "apostle of God," was on earth carrying out his mission to the Jews, at the same time he announced the coming of Muhammad as a prophet of God on earth: "I come to confirm the truth of the Pentateuch, which came before me and to announce to you the happy coming of the prophet after me, whose name is Ahmed" (one of three names of Muhammad).

It is well known that the *Qur'an* presents Jesus as one of the prophets who were, from time to time, sent by God to the world. This marvelous line begins with Adam and ends with Muhammad's mission. It is no surprise therefore, that the *Qur'an* presents both prophets, Jesus and Muhammad, as having many common traits. Both of them are called prophets, delegated, and servants of God. Both of them express God's mercy to men. Jesus accepted the revelation that is called "Gospel," and Muhammad, likewise, received the *Qur'an* in an apocalyptic way. Jesus's teaching and Gospel are characterized by wisdom, truth, light, admonition, and guidance, terms that are likewise attributed to the *Qur'anic* message. Jesus declared some things to be legal, which were otherwise prohibited by the Jews, exactly as Muhammad did with certain foods that were prohibited by the Jews, because of their sins (*Qur'an* 3:50; 6:146f).[16]

We can see that the emphasis on Jesus in the *Qur'an* serves, among other things, to legitimate Muhammad's actions, since Jesus acted similarly before him. We read in the *Qur'an*:

> Oh faithful! Be servants of God, as Jesus would say, son of Mary, to the apostles, when he asked them: Who is going to help me to spread the sacred religion? We will become your servants, they answered. A part from the children of Israel adopted the faith, whereas the rest remained unfaithful. We supported the faithful against their enemies and they won them" (*Qur'an* 61:14).

The general historical data that we noted earlier, relevant to the areas where Islam was originated, point to a certain commonality in basic and structural elements of faith in God, then later became religious differences. It is a fact that, for several centuries before the appearance of Islam, the competition between Byzantium and Persia was very intense in the Near East. These two political and cultural forces (Byzantium and Persia) influenced the development of the religious and ecclesiastical (community) spheres.

Though the Byzantine Empire was basically Christian, there was competition among Greek philosophical trends and Christological theological reflection that caused two major heresies around the time of Muhammad's appearance. The first was the heresy of Nestorius, an Arab Patriarch of Constantinople, and expanded as "Nestorianism" in the Syriac Christian world. The second was the heresy of "Monophysitism," expanded through Egypt and Abyssinia where today the great Coptic Orthodox Christian community is located.

External testimony, together with the testimony of the *Qur'an* itself, reveals the prevailing heterodox influence in the original environment of Islam. If the external testimonies do indicate Nestorianism and Monophysitism to be the spiritual background of Islam, the internal testimony is equally indicative of a particular form of religious syncretism, with Judaic and Christian elements or, as could be said, a historical evolution of a "Christian" Judaism.

Epilogue

In conclusion, we could say that the *Qur'an* considers Jesus as a prophet and delegated of God who, like all prophets, has his own mission in this world. The proof of his gracious power, besides his words and actions, is found in the "signs" or miracles that he conducted from the first moment of his birth until his exaltation to God. His mission was to become "great in this world," but also "in the other world" and, finally, become "the reliable of God" (*Qur'an* 3:40). At the same time, the *Qur'an* emphasizes Jesus as a "forerunner" of the other great prophet for Islam, Muhammad, as a demonstration of a historical evolution of divine revelation. For this reason, as mentioned in the introduction of this brief paper, by studying the *Qur'an* as well as the history of Islam in general, one gets the feeling of the "necessity" of an historical, religious evolution through Islam of God's revelation, for the accomplishment of the plan of divine providence.

In the same way, we could say that in our day any religion that harbors negative attitudes toward life, history, and civilization (namely the historical evolution of human affairs, from a spiritual and sotereological perspective) faces the danger of destruction and extinction. The great Newman once said: "One of the causes of the decay in a religion is its resistance to follow the evolution of doctrine and the stubborn desire to remain attached to the perceptions of the past."[17] Religions – in their human dimension – run the danger of decay in history.

That which is essential for religion and its permanent impact on society is the consistent living of the *faithful* and their *faith*. Perhaps, here, it is appropriate to mention Fr. Georges Florovsky, a great Orthodox theologian of the twentieth century, who said: "In the last analysis Christianity can be better understood as real life experience within the framework of history." I would like to believe that the same is true of Islam. Regarding the attitude of the *Qur'an* toward the person of Jesus Christ, perhaps it is proper to remind us here what Gandhi, the great Hindu politician and philosopher of the "non-violence doctrine" in India, said: "It's a pity that Christians appropriated Christ only for themselves and thus minimized his importance. Jesus Christ belongs to the whole world."

In light of what has been said, the premise of this paper, namely that Jesus is also a prophet of Islam, is not at all strange.

Appendix

The *Qur'anic* references to the person and history of Jesus may be categorized as follows:
a. First mention of Jesus (*Qur'an* 2:87);
b. Jesus in the line of God's ministers from Abraham (*Qur'an* 3:84; 4:164; 6:84-86);
c. All the Prophets and Jesus are sent from God for the same purpose (*Qur'an* 23:51-52; 33:7-8; 42:13);

d. Jesus comes with his Gospel to complete the Mosaic Law (*Qur'an* 5:46; 61:6);

e. The conception and virginal birth of Jesus in God's plan (*Qur'an* 3:35-41);

f. John, the forerunner of Jesus, and his wonderful birth (*Qur'an* 19:2-1);

g. The history of Jesus's virginal birth in detail (*Qur'an* 3:42-53; 19:16-36);

h. The place of Jesus's virginal birth (*Qur'an* 23:50);

i. The disciples of Jesus (*Qur'an* 61:14; 5:111-115);

j. The beginning of Jesus's teaching (*Qur'an* 43:57-59; 57:27);

k. Jesus's preaching (*Qur'an* 43:63-64);

1. Jesus's miracles (*Qur'an* 5:110);

m. Christian misunderstanding of Jesus, as "son of God" (*Qur'an* 10:69; 19:88-93; 3:55-59; 2:110; 21:26-30; 5:19; 5:116-118; 9:30-32);

n. The denial of God's Trinity (*Qur'an* 4:169-170; 5:76-79);

o. Jesus was not crucified, but raised (*Qur'an* 4:157-158; 2:253);

p. The second coming of Jesus and the final Judgment (*Qur'an* 3:48-49; 43:61);

Also, see Neal Robinson, *Christ in Islam and Christianity* (New York, 1991). p. 3: about Jesus, the Christians, the Gospel of Christ and the "people of the Book," see Suras and verses: 2:26,62,87,111-141,253; 3:1-84, 113-15; 4:44-57,142,156-175; 5:14-18,46-120; 6:84-90,106; 7:40-49, 156-59, 179,186; 9:29-35,80,111-114; 10:68; 16:103; 18:9-26; 19:1-40,92; 21:74-94; 22:17; 23:45-55; 24:34-40; 33:7-27; 36:13-32; 39:4, 29; 42:13-16; 43:57-65,81; 44: 14;

48:29; 57:12-13,25-29; 58:7; 61:1-14; 66:1-12; 85:1-9; 98:1-8; 105:1-5; 112:1-4.

For an analysis of these formulae, see P. Hayek, *Le Christ de l'Islam* (Paris, 1959), p. 5; Parrinder, *Jesus in the Qur'an* (London, 1965); H. Michaud, *Jésus selon le Coran* (Neuchatel, 1960); and F.L. Bakker, *Jésus en Islam* (The Hague, 1955).

NOTES

1 See A. Th. Khoury, *Les théologiens Byzantins et l'Islam* (Paris, 1969); also, J.D. Sahas, *John of Damascus on Islam* (Brill-Leiden, 1972).

2 See for instance G. Patronos, *Istorike poriea tou theou, apo te fatne os ton keno tafo* (Athens: Domos, 1992), p. 51f.

3 Cf. R. Bell and W.M. Watt, *Introduction to the Qur'an* (Edinburgh, 1970), and J. Wansbrough, *Qur'anic Studies* (Oxford, 1977).

4 For an interesting exposition of this type of *forma* see Gerard S. Sloyan, *Jesus in Focus, A Life in its Setting*, Twenty-Third Publications. For an approach to Christianity through the *Qur'an*, see Chap. 25, and "The Jesus of the *Qur'an*," pp. 188-196; see also K. Cragg, *Jesus and the Muslim* (London, 1985).

5 M.'Ata ur-Rahim, *Jesus, A Prophet of Islam* (London, 1979), p. 207.

6 Cf. G. C. Anawati, *"Isa,"* in *The Encyclopedia of Islam*, ed. E. Van Donzel, B. Lewis, Ch. Pellat, vol. IV (Leiden: E.J. Brill, 1978), pp. 81-86.

7 *Qur'anic* references to the person and history of Jesus are summarized in the Appendix at the end of this article. References to the *Qur'an* in this study are from N. J. Dawood, *The Koran*, translated with notes (New York: Penguin Books, 1974).

8 See for instance H. Michaud, *Jésus selon le Coran* (Neuchatel, 1960), p. 20.

9 See G. Anawati, "Islam and the Immaculate Conception," in *The Dogma of the Immaculate Conception*, ed. E.D. O'Connor (University of Notre Dame Press, 1958), pp. 447-461.

10 See M. Manneval, *La Christologie du Coran* (Toulouse, 1867); G.C. Anawati, *Introduction à la théologie musulmane* (Paris, 1948); and A.A. Sachedina, *Islamic Messianism* (State University of New York Press).

11 See especially *Qur'an* 3: 40; 4:1-56, 169-170; 5:19, 76, and 79; 9:30-31.

12 For an excellent exposition of "the Word of God" in *Qur'an*, see the perceptive article by Mahmoud Mustafa Ayoub, "The Word of God in Islam," in *Orthodox Christians and Muslims*, ed. N.M. Vaporis (Brookline, Massachusetts: Holy Cross Orthodox Press, 1986), pp. 79-78. Cf. N. Robinson, "The *Qur'an* as the Word of God," ed. A. Linzey and P. Wexler, *Heaven and Earth: Essex Essays in Theology and Ethics* (Worthing, 1986).

13 For more details, see Th. O'Shaughnessy, *The Koranic Concept of the Word of God* (Rome, 1948); G.C. Anawati, *Introduction à la théologie musulmane* (Paris, 1948); and M.M. Ayoub, *The Qur'an and its Interpreters* (Albany, 1984).

14 See the interesting article by H. A. Wolfson, "The Muslin Attributes and the Christian Trinity," in *Harvard Theological Review*, 49 (1956), pp. 1-18.

15 See F.W. von Herbert, "The Moslem tradition of Jesus's second visit on earth," *Hibbert Journal*, 7 (1909), pp. 27-28. Also, for a more recent discussion on the topic see Abdulaziz Abdulhussein Sachedina, *Islamic Messianism* (State University of New York Press), p. 171f.

16 For an extensive discussion of the similarities and differences between Jesus and Muhammad, see N. Robinson, *Christ in Islam and Christianity* (New York, 1991), pp. 36-38; for details on the theological differences between Sunnis and Shiites, see A.A. Sachedina, *Islamic Messianism*.

17 Quoted by Paul de Breuil, Ζωροαστρισμός, Greek translation by G. Mauroudes (Athens: M. Kardamitsas, 1993), p. 157.

Inter-Religious Dialogue in Byzantine Thought: The Philosophical and Theological Contribution of John of Damascus

Marios P. Begzos

Translated by George C. Papademetriou

History of Religions and Cultures

The encounter of cultures is best expressed as a dialogue of religions. It is impossible to establish communication between two cultural traditions without the active intervention of their religious expression. Whoever ignores these elements makes a great error. No encounter can expect to succeed in its efforts unless one takes into serious consideration the dynamic and the efficacy of the religious factor in cultural dialogue, particularly today, and especially in the Mediterranean basin, which is the cradle of the monotheistic religions (Judaism, Christianity, Islam). The validity of such a starting point is much emphatically confirmed and clearly revealed simply by glancing at the religions themselves and if we apply it particularly to Greek-Arabic relations within the Christian-Islamic dialogue. The contact of Hellenism with Arabic culture presup-

poses a dialogue of Christianity with Islam. As in the
past, so in the present and even much more in the future, it is clear that the way of Greek-Arabic relations
passes through the gate of Christian-Islamic dialogue.
The history of Greek-Arabic relations cannot be written
without taking into consideration such a decisive and
significant factor as the Christian-Islamic dialogue.[1]

However, is it possible for a cultural contact to receive flesh and bones unless there is an active presence of religious traditions? Culture is the body of the
nation and religion constitutes its soul. Wherever the
body goes there is found also the soul. A soul without
body resembles a ghost; as otherwise, a body without
soul is a corpse. An irreligious culture is dead, as is an
uncivilized religion. Can anyone ever think of the Arabs without Islam? What remains from the Greek culture of the Middle Ages if Christianity is eliminated?

With such concepts, therefore, the encounter presupposes an inter-religious dialogue. Certainly at this
point a justified objection is raised that must not be permitted either to be ignored or to remain unanswered:
the question concerns the rupturing role[2] of religious
fanaticism. Religious leadership can incite the masses
to become fanatics and cause division among people
by their religious convictions. How, therefore, is it ever
possible to accomplish a cultural encounter through
the mediation of religion? In the eyes of some – and
perhaps not a few – of our fellow human beings, religion appears to split and break apart people, while culture unites them. For this reason, many honorable and
sensitive people confronted with such circumstances,

do not hesitate to demand that religion be put aside and only culture be projected.

At first glance, one must confess that this honest accusation is arrived at through accurate phenomenological observation. However, if one looks closely at this view and reflects somewhat more on these phenomena, one forms a different image, one that corresponds closely to reality. We will mention only a few points without developing a theme that is beyond our present discussion.

Religion plays some role in the conflicts of peoples but not, however, the primary role. It is not the faith that divides people, but the special interests such as political, economic, social, etc. Leaders use the pretext of religious differences in order to conceal, under the mantle of faith, their own ideological or economic differences. In this way they more easily influence the popular masses, recruiting warriors in the service of their ambitions. Religion by itself is not sufficient to divide two peoples. Socio-economic and political or national-racial differences always lie beneath its divisive appearance. Religion is involved in order to justify, after-the-fact, the collision that takes on the luminous glow, in appearance only, and becomes a holy cause.

Moreover, we are compelled to distinguish and separate religion from fanaticism with every possible clarification, as well as faith from superstition. Religion is entirely different from fanaticism. And this becomes clear in the case of Jesus Christ who was the victim of intolerance and fanaticism. Christ preached a new faith that challenged the political, economic, and aristocratic priestly class, which was the religious leadership of his time, which incited the masses to fanaticism, and which turned Him over to the Romans to be executed. In this case it seems clear what the qualitative and essential difference between religion and fanaticism is.

It is not religion that divides people, but rather fanaticism and intolerance. We also encounter such cases outside of religion. The concentration camps of fascism, Nazism, Stalinism, and other anti-religious, secular, political systems are monumental monstrosities of fanaticism and intolerance. Their existence is proof that religion is not responsible for the lawlessness of history in spite of the fact that in numerous cases the religious element contributed. Additionally fanaticism is generally accompanied by superstition and ignorance. Enlightened personalities and educated religious leaders, always discern authentic, true faith from superstition and fanaticism. For this same reason, they become leaders in the dialogue between religions, in order to attain peace among people.

John of Damascus in Dialogue with Islam

John of Damascus (650-750) is an exemplary personality in religious dialogue in the area of the Mediterranean basin and especially in the field of Islamic-Christian dialogue. He was a Christian, of Greek descent, from an educated, aristocratic family of Damascus with political ties to Arab leaders. John of Damascus lived the greater part of almost a century as a monk in

Jerusalem where he distinguished himself as a theologian and poet. He is the greatest systematic theologian of Orthodoxy whom the Western Christians compare with their own colossus, Thomas Aquinas (thirteenth century). At the same time, John of Damascus was a distinguished poet and one of the most important hymnographers of the Eastern Church. This rare combination of poetic sensitivity and reflective theological and philosophical precision lend to John of Damascus an unrivaled superiority and uniqueness.

John of Damascus was distinguished for having philosophical and theological erudition. His writings consist of systematic handbooks such as his famous dogmatic theology entitled *Exact Exposition of the Orthodox Faith*; his philosophical handbook, the renowned *Dialectics*; other writings of apologetic character against the iconoclasts and the Manicheans; as well as discourses, hymns, and other writings.

In addition, John of Damascus is credited with the inspiration for a text with a special interest in the Islamic-Christian dialogue. Its title is *Dialogue Between a Saracen and a Christian,* and it exists in two different texts.[3]

Critical research had concluded that, of the two texts recording an oral conversation, one consisted of a synopsis or summary of the other. The version of the text that is included in volume 96 of Migne and the critical edition published by Bonifatius Kotter in 1981,[4] is judged to be more authentic.

From the perspective of philological criticism, the following points are of interest. We do not offer proofs that John of Damascus actually wrote this text, but we are fairly certain that it is comprised of stenographical notes from his speeches. Even though it cannot be stated with scholarly assurance that this text has come from his pen, still, it is absolutely certain that the inspiration of the text belongs to John of Damascus, and it is genuinely his spiritual child. With this understanding, therefore, we hold in our hands the text of an Islamic-Christian dialogue, which expresses the spirit of the greatest systematic theologian of Orthodoxy in an early phase of Greek-Arabic relations. Based on this, there appears, from the beginning, to have been special interest in this document.[5]

The importance of this work and our preoccupation with it centers on the following data:

1. The antiquity of the text. This is one of the oldest documents of Islamic-Christian dialogue, dated at the turn of the seventh century toward the eighth. On the other hand, it is not accidental that in this text all of the topics of early Islamic theology are included.[6] Therefore, we are presenting an exposition of the most ancient list of topics of the Islamic-Christian dialogue.

2. The importance of its inspirer. John of Damascus remains to this day the leading systematic theologian of Orthodoxy. Consequently, his views on the Islamic-Christian dialogue, which are included in this text, remain valuable for conducting a similar dialogue from the side of Orthodox theology. Indeed, within the framework of a Greek-Arabic cultural dialogue, which would embody the Islamic-Christian dialogue, the aforementioned text of John of Damascus would play a leading role.

3. The content of the work. It is not only for historical reasons that we have respect for the antiquity of the
text, or is it the personality of John of Damascus that
draws our attention, but something more important:
the text itself contains thoughts of momentous significance for the topic of the Islamic-Christian dialogue
from that time until today. These thoughts may play a
leading role in the future indirectly, but clearly, influencing Greek-Arabic relations.

As for the content of this text, now we must turn
our attention to evaluate it better within the framework
of our topic. It is about a dialogue between a Saracen
and a Christian. Its title reveals the philological form
of the text: "Dialogue (*Dialexis*) Between a Saracen and
a Christian."[7] The Saracen sets forth the questions and
the Christian gives the answers. The questions of the
Saracen appear to be rhetorical, aiming to prove the
contradictions within the Christian faith. The Christian
answers the questions by explaining the consequences
of faith in a manner that evokes, at the end of the dialogue, great marvel and perplexity in the Saracen who,
having no reply, departs without further attack.[8]

An initial glance at the philological nature of the
text confirms that it is not an antagonistic or polemical text, but a discussion or dialogue that reminds the
reader, more than anything else, of the setting of a Pla-
tonic academy. Indeed, this occurs in an era (seventh
to eighth centuries) and in an area (the Middle East)
where the religious traditions of Christianity and Islam are found to be particularly intense.

PHILOSOPHY OF RELIGION AND ANTHROPOLOGY

In the text, two issues dominate the Islamic-Christian dialogue: human freedom and the problem of evil. The dialogue between the Saracen and the Christian begins with this twofold question. One is impressed with the opening because, in an inter-religious dialogue, one would expect to refer exclusively to theological issues. Instead, it is posited that the dialogue is inaugurated with the serious anthropological questions of freedom and evil. The theological development of the text progresses in order to illuminate the anthropological questions stated from the beginning of the text.

The Saracen sets forth the question: "What do you say is the cause of good and evil?"[9] The classical Christian answer is: "Good has no other cause except God, and of evil, God is not the cause;"[10] while it is taught that evil is caused by "the devil and by us human beings."[11] To the further question of his interlocutor about the reasoning as to where evil comes from in history, the Christian answer is: "From freedom of the will."[12] The theological curiosity of the Saracen regarding freedom of the will gave John of Damascus the opportunity to expand on the Christian theology of freedom, through the mouth of the Christian interlocutor in the dialogue with the Saracen. In this way, we enjoy a small, simple, and very characteristic exposition of the Christian concept of human freedom and the problem of evil in history.

The remaining text, from approximately the middle to the end of the dialogues, is related to Christology, but always within the perspective of the anthropologi-

cal question of evil and freedom. In this way, therefore, freedom remains the pivotal issue around which
the Islamic-Christian dialogue is developed. Even the
Christological theme is approached from the point of
view of freedom: "Did Christ suffered willingly or un-
willingly?"[13] The freedom of the will is examined within the Christological framework.

Through this text, John of Damascus contributes
an example of Islamic-Christian dialogue, which can
and must be utilized today by Christian theology in its
encounter with the Islamic tradition and especially in
Greek-Arabic relations. We will try to summarize, as
briefly as possible, only a few of the most important
points of this text in reference to our topic.

Anthropology and Theology

The inter-religious dialogue is not a goal in itself,
but service to God and humanity. Precisely because of
this, the list of topics for a dialogue such as the one
between Islam and Christianity begins from, is nurtured on, and is guided by anthropological questions.
Human freedom and the problem of evil are the two
leading, vital issues that occupy humanity, both collec-
tively and individually.

One would expect to see a one-sided theological
agenda in a dialogue of religions. Surprisingly, one
discovers that there is a plethora of anthropological
issues. This happened because a dialogue, which em-
braces the human being in his/her totality, cannot be
limited only to one aspect of humanity, that is, the religious. On the other hand, faith is an event of universal

character and for this reason it does not leave anthropology outside its interest. In this way, we see the interweaving of theology and anthropology in the Islamic-Christian dialogue according to John of Damascus.

The religions hold this dialogue in order to bring viable answers to the burning problems of humanity. Truth is the criterion for the success of dialogue. The motive for every dialogical encounter cannot be other than to witness to the truth. Theology sheds light on anthropology and the latter tests the endurance of religious answers to existential questions of everyday life of the human being always and everywhere.

The Problem of Evil

The first vital experience of every human being is directly associated with the presence of evil[14] in the world. The irrationality of history, the pain in human life, natural evil (calamities, destruction), social injustice, political oppression, economic exploitation, death, old age, and sickness. All these constitute the problem of evil. The modern Eastern European philosopher N. Berdyaev defines the human being as follows: "I suffer, therefore, I exist."[15] Suffering is innate in humanity. The first cry, the first sound, the first sign of life the human being makes as soon as one is born is a cry, that is, a sign of suffering.

The significance of this for the inter-religious dialogue and the anthropological starting point is that one cannot, and must not be permitted to ignore human suffering, daily problems, and historical hardships. How can it ever be possible for the religions to dialogue for the salvation of humanity and for the truth of the faith and forget these immediate problems? How reliable can the theological discourse of interlocutors ever be if they close their eyes to the burning daily problems and are indifferent to the tragedies of history? Can an Islamic-Christian dialogue ever be trustworthy if it attempts to circumvent the existential problems of historical justice in the inflammatory zones of Islamic nations where Christians live, such as, for example, the Greeks in Turkey or the Copts in Egypt?

Inter-religious dialogue is not an abstract, theoretical, vague speaking, and destined for inner distribution between some narrow, closed circle of experts in theology. It is, rather, a question of vital reckoning with the burning historical reality, as much of the past as of the present, as well as for the future. The problem of evil and the answers given to it, will judge the sincerity and trustworthiness of the partners in dialogue.

Human Freedom

If cultural contacts include the inter-religious dialogue and inasmuch as the latter moves toward the horizon of anthropology, then, in accordance with the example of John of Damascus, the end result will be that human freedom[16] becomes the number-one topic. Therefore, if one adheres to such terms, every encounter of religions with cultures becomes a very difficult undertaking, especially dangerous inasmuch as it touches upon burning problems of historical justice, as aforementioned. At the same time, however, one such undertaking becomes a vital necessity, an act of truth, a matter of a living and not a dead or anemic preoccupation in the marginal surface of current historical reality.

In an inter-religious dialogue, one must never show indifference to the fate of humanity today. Loss of individual rights, the violation of social freedoms, conditions in which there is no freedom and in which numerous fellow human beings are condemned to live under oppression by the inhumanity of humans today, and obscuring the image of God in the world. All these issues come under the absolute but certainly not exclusive jurisdiction of theology. The concerns are not merely "sociological" issues, but are essentially theological topics.

Something of the above appears in John of Damascus's text, which addresses the "self-determination" (*autexousion*) of the human being, from the beginning of his text in the dialogue with the Saracen. As his interlocutor appears to doubt human freedom, John of Damascus defends "self-determination" and becomes the apologist for human freedom, which he views to as given by God and secured by Christ.

In an Islamic-Christian dialogue, theology is obliged to bear witness and present its own contribution in support of human freedom. For example, the Christian side has to develop the theological category of the person, which embodies the concept of freedom and theologically connects the human person with historical reality.

On the Islamic side, theology has to exercise its criticism of the Western Christian tradition of cultivating individualism. Also, each religious tradition, Christian and Islamic, can pursue critical inquiry into their joint historical responsibility for the emergence of absoluteness, the cultivation of fanaticism, the hatching of sick phenomena such as hypocrisy and intolerance, and so many more.

In each instance, however, the selected partners are judged by the truth of history and are subjected to one criterion: freedom. Every violation of freedom is condemned as being without justification, from whomever it comes.

Religion is a two-sided reality. It can divide human beings but it can unite them as well.

A glimpse at the map of the Middle East, or of India with its many varieties of religious divisions is sufficient to convince the doubter as to the divisive role the religious phenomenon plays in the history of humanity. In contrast, religion is a binding link and unifying element in numerous situations. The inter-religious dialogue is a proof of this.

The reason for a dialogue of religions is to attain harmony. A further goal is truth of life that religion serves. Through dialogue it is possible to attain unity and harmony, to learn of the truth of the other, and in this way to preserve human freedom, dignity and civility. Only in this way can the integrity of the image of God in the world be maintained, which according to the Christian tradition is found in the human person. In other words, theology in its practical application is realized on the anthropological level, and every inter-religious dialogue presupposes the existence of the firm anthropological questions and serious existential dilemmas.

Times change, places vary, and traditions are diverse. The one thing that remains constant, however, is the human being with his/her struggle and anguish and, above all, the anguish about life. And life means harmony, relationships, communion, and dialogue. In this sense and from this perspective, inter-religious dialogue and cultural contact appear to belong to the same phenomenon of life. They are about different aspects of the same phenomenon, though anthropology remains the common denominator.

It is not accidental that such a conviction is confirmed in one of the oldest texts of Islamic-Christian dialogue, inspired by the leader in theology: John of Damascus, great thinker and great poet. His literary sensitivity sharpened even more his theological antenna to receive immediately the serious anthropological implications of the Islamic-Christian dialogue, that continuous to exist even today, and which we, by making this small contribution to the topic at hand, purposely review in order to recall its current relevance.

NOTES

1 Relative to scholarly familiarity of the Greek-speaking world with Islam, the following are important studies by professors of comparative religions at the universities of Athens and Thessalonike: Professor Metropolitan of Androusa, Anastasios Yannoulatos (present Archbishop of Albania) and Professor Gregory Ziakas. I indicate the overview of A. Yannoulatos, *Islam* (in Greek) (Athens, 1975), as well as the studies relative to the dialogue of religions, such as: *The Place of Christians in Contrast to Other Religions* (in Greek) (Athens, 1975); *Toward a Global Community* (Athens, 1975) (reprint, EETPA, vol. 20); "Toward World Commu-

nity," *Ecumenical Review* 26 (1974), pp. 619-636 or with the title "Toward a Koinonia agapes," *Towards World Community*, ed. S. J. Samantha (Geneva, 1957), pp. 45-64. Particularly, Professor Gregory Ziakas offers a series of detailed Islamic studies, including the following: "*The meaning of Freedom of the Will and Evil in later Islamic Mysticism,*" (in Greek) EETPA (1973), pp. 449-4201; *Prophecy Revelation and Salvation in Accordance to the Qur'an* (Thessalonike: Pournaras Press, 1976); "*On the Islamic Teaching of the Eschata,*" (in Greek) EETPA 20 (1976), pp. 319-420; *Faith, Hope, and Salvation According to Islam* (in Greek) (Thessalonike, 1979); as well as *Aristotle in the Arabic Tradition* (in Greek) (Thessalonike: Kyriakides Pub., 1980). The most significant are the publications of the World Council of Churches since 1970 under the direction of S.J. Samantha, under whose editorship were published the collections: *Towards World Community. The Colombo Papers* (Geneva: WCC, 1975) and *Faith in the Midst of Faiths: Reflections on Dialogue in Community* (Geneva: WCC, 1977).

2 For the function of religion, the distinction between religion-Church and other such terms, we presuppose references to our previous publications where we make appropriate references in order to remove any reservations the critical reader of the present text might have. See particularly, M. Begzos, *Handbook of Philosophy of Religion* (in Greek) (Athens: Gregorios Pub., 1991), pp. 75-122; *Freedom of Religion* (in Greek) (Athens: Gregorios Pub., 1991), pp. 44-51 and 161-173; *Phenomenology of the Holy Values and Civilization* (Festschrift, E. Theodorou) (Athens: Tenos, 1991), pp. 39-63. See also A. Yannoulatos, *Introduction The Christian Stand in the Encounter with Other Religions* (from his University Lectures) (in Greek) (Athens, 1989), p. 14. He states: "We would prefer in the theological language to distinguish between 'Christianity' and 'Church' and to propose the formulation that 'the Church is not religion. It is beyond the event of religion.' But such discussion belongs to the province of the problematics of theological language. From the aspect of comparative religion, it is difficult to doubt that Christianity in its historical evolution presented numerous 'religious' characteristics."

3 John of Damascus, *Dialogue of a Saracen and a Christian*, PG 94, 1585-1598 and *PG* 96, 1335-1348 and a critical edition: B. Kotter, *Die Schriften des Johannes von Damaskos* (Berlin: Gruyter, 1981), Bd. IV (*Liber de haeresibus Opera polemica*), pp. 420-438. More in G. Ziakas. *Prophesy, Revelation and History of Salvation According to the Qur'an* (in Greek) (Thessalonike, 1975), p. 169, where a bibliography is given. Cf. the good summary in A. Yannoulatos, *The Place of Christians in Encounter with Other Religions* (Athens, 1975), p. 34 ff.

4 Kotter, pp. 420-438. For the theology of John of Damascus, see N. Matsoukas, *Introduction* 11-25, in the edition John of Damascus, *Exact Exposition of the Orthodox Faith* (in Greek) (Thessalonike: Pournaras Press, 1976). For a philosophical evaluation of John of Damascus, see Ch. Yannaras, *Introductory Note* in a report: John of Damascus, *Dialectics* (in Greek) (Athens: Papazeses Press, 1978), pp. 7-16, where a bibliography is given. L. Siasos, *Patristic Criticism of Philosophical Method* (in Greek) (Thessalonike: Pournaras Press, 1989), pp. 11-56, and B. Tatakes, *Byzantine Philosophy*, trans. into Greek, E. Kalpourtzes (Athens: Studies of Neohellenic Civilization, 1977), pp. 109-128, with an updated bibliography by Linos Benakes.

5 Kotter, pp. 420-422: *ware J D als Autor fur unser streitgesprach sehr wohl moglich* (p. 422).

6 Kotter, p. 422 (includes bibliography).

7 *PG* 94c.1598, *PG* 96c.1335 and Kotter, p. 427.

8 *PG* 96c.1348, Kotter, p. 438.

9 *PG* 96, c1336, Kotter, p. 427.

10 Kotter, p. 427.

11 Kotter, p. 427.

12 Kotter, p. 427.

13 *PG* 96c.1340, Kotter, p. 431.

14 Relative to the problem of evil, see J. Hick, "The Problem of Evil," *Encyclopedia of Philosophy* 3 (1972), pp. 136-141 (with rich bibliography). See also, N. Matsoukas, *The Problem of Evil: Handbook of Patristic Theology* (In Greek) (Reprinted from EETSPT, Annual of the Theological School of the University of Thessalonike), vol. 20 (Thessalonike: Pournaras

Press, 1976). Cf. G. Florovsky, *Collected Works* (Belmont, Massachusetts: Nordland, 1973), III, pp. 81-91. V. Lossky, *Orthodox Theology* (New York: St. Vladimir's Press, 1978), pp. 74-94. C. Tresmontant, *La Métaphysique du Christianisme et la Naissance de la Philosophie Chrétienne* (Paris: Seuil, 1961), pp. 650-691. B. Welte, *Uber das Bose* (Frieburg: Herder, 1959). Ugo Bianchi, *Prometeo Orfeo Adamo Temetiche religiose sul destino ii male la salvezza* (Roma: edizione deli' ateneo & bizzari, 1976). "Ii male nel dualismo gnostico," *Liberarci dal male* (Pavolo Spirito e Vita. Quaderni dialettura biblica, 19) (Bologna, 1989), pp. 199-208.

15 N. Berdyaev, *Existentielle Dialektik des Gottlichen und Menschlichen* (Munich: Beck, 1951), p. 64.

16 On the problem of freedom, more generally than from the philosophical point of view and approaching the newer natural science theories, see works with bibliography in M. Begzos, *Dialectical Physics and Eschatological Theology* (in Greek) (Athens, 1985), pp. 80-97, 157-166, and 222-227. More specifically, on Islam, see G. Ziakas, "The Meaning of Freedom of the Will and Evil in Later Islamic Mysticism," (in Greek) EETSPT (1973), pp. 449-512.

Saint Gregory Palamas:
Three Dialogues with Muslims

George C. Papademetriou

Introduction

Saint Gregory Palamas was the most significant theologian in the last two centuries of the Byzantine Empire. His theological acumen enabled him to elucidate the theological teachings of the Church, successfully defend the Orthodox Christian theological positions, and proclaim the truth of the Gospel to his contemporaries.

Divine providence brought Palamas face-to-face with Islam. When he was Archbishop of Thessalonike, he was on his way to Constantinople in March 1354 when a fierce storm overcame the ship on which he was a passenger. The captain was forced to take refuge in the city of Gallipoli, which had recently suffered from an earthquake that left it in ruins, allowing the Osmanli Turks to capture it. The ship, unable to depart, was captured by the Turks who demanded ransom for the passengers. When they realized they were holding a person of such importance, the amount of ransom was increased substantially.

Palamas and his fellow prisoners were moved around to several cities in Asia Minor. His captivity lasted over a year, from March 1354 to July 1355. While a prisoner, Palamas was able to perform pastoral work and had the opportunity to visit Orthodox Christians in Asia Minor and offer them spiritual care. He also had the opportunity to meet Muslim intellectuals who engaged him in dialogue. Three such dialogues took place: one with Ishmael the grandson of Emir Orcham; the second with the Chiones; and the third with an imam, whose name has not come down to us.

These dialogues were face-to-face conversations rather than imaginary discussions on the similarities and differences of the two religions.[1] Palamas entered into them with all the zeal of an apologist for his Christian convictions. He defended Christian doctrine, especially the Trinitarian dogma, with great erudition. His answers to the questions posed to him were carefully based on reason and the Scriptures.

The First Dialogue

The first dialogue was with Ishmael, the grandson of Emir Orcham. Palamas was brought to the city of Bursa on June 25, 1345. From there, he and his fellow hostages were taken to the emir's palace, about 100 km or two days march from Bursa. When Orcham captured Bursa in 1326 it was declared a Muslim holy city. All the Christian Greeks were displaced and the churches were transformed into mosques. The palace itself was located in what had been a Christian monastery.

While staying at the palace, Ishmael invited Palamas (separate from other prisoners) to engage in dialogue. This dialogue took place in the open air, as Palamas himself inform us. The two men sat down on the soft grass, together with several other leaders. Palamas also notes that, even though Ishmael was known for persecuting the Christians, on this occasion he was moderate in his discussion and demeanor. It is apparent that Ishmael spoke Greek, since the conversation took place without an interpreter.[2]

After everyone sat down, Palamas was offered fruits and Ishmael was offered meat. As they were eating, Ishmael suddenly addressed a question to Palamas, asking if he always abstains from meat and why. Ishmael was interested in comparing the practices of the two faiths. As Palamas finished his answer, someone came and apologized for being tardy. He explained that he just finished distributing alms as Emir Orchan had ordered should be done every Friday.

Now Ishmael directed the discussion to the act of almsgiving by asking Palamas if the Christians practice "charity" or "almsgiving." Palamas answered that charity or almsgiving is at the heart of the Christian faith and is "derived from the love of God." The more one loves God, the more one is truly benevolent. Ishmael then turned the discussion toward the person of Muhammad by asking if Christians accept and love Muhammad. Palamas answered in the negative. Ishmael asked why they did not. Palamas answered that he who does not believe in the teachings of the Master does not love him.

Ishmael noted that Christians claim to love Jesus,

but also believe he was crucified. He wanted to know why Orthodox Christians venerate the cross. Palamas explained that, as an example, a government accepts those who honor its insignia and punishes those who dishonor it. The insignia of Christ's victory over the devil is the cross, and therefore Christians honor it.

Ishmael sought to ridicule Christianity, saying that Christians claim that God has a wife and that he gave birth to a son. Palamas defended the Christian faith by pointing out that the Turks accept that Christ is the Word of God and was born of the Virgin Mary. Mary gave birth to Christ as man without a husband, God begat the Word in a divine manner. God neither had, nor needed, a wife, as Muslims falsely accuse Christians of believing.

Even though those who knew him said that Ishmael was a ferocious persecutor of Christians, but he never became angry during the conversation. When a heavy rainstorm began, Ishmael hurriedly left. Palamas was left sitting in the rain, becoming drenched to the bones. Eventually, he returned to where the other prisoners were. By order of the "tyrant" the prisoners, after the rain stopped, were brought to a neighboring district where they were fed.[3]

The Second Dialogue

Palamas's next dialogue while a prisoner in Asia Minor was with a group of Islamic theologians known to history as the "Chiones." Emir Orcham himself commended this dialogue, but chose not to be present in order not to intimidate the participants.

Who were the Chiones? The name is found in three forms: *Chionios, Chionides, and Chiones*. According to Professor George Arnakis, the name is derived from the Turkish *Akhis*, a society of artisans.[4] P. Wittek disagrees with Arnakis and insists it is derived from *Khodja*, which denotes the Muslim theologian.[5] Fr. John Meyendorff connects it with the Jewish synagogue of Bursa.[6] G.M.Prohorov connects it with the branch of Karaite Judaism, Abeli-Siyyo.[7] H.A.Philippides–Braat supports the derivation from the Persian *akhond*, which means a teacher of philosophy.[8]

According Professor P. Chrestou, scholars also disagree as to the origin and activities of these people. He notes that M. Jugie espoused the view that the Chiones were Jews who were converted to Islam.[9] He further points out that Fr. J. Meyendorff is the first to connect the Chiones to a family of the same name in Thessalonike. This Christian family was converted to Judaism in Thessalonike and, from Judaism, subsequently converted to Islam.[10] Chrestou supports this as the most possible explanation of the origin of the Chiones. Palamas states that he heard that they were Jews. He, however, preferred to dialogue only with Muslims.[11] The Chiones, themselves, insisted that they were Turks.[12] Also, Philotheos, in his praise of Palamas, refers to the Chiones as "apostates from Christianity."[13]

The dialogue with the Chiones[14] began with their statement: "We heard the Ten Commandments (*logous*) written on stone plates and brought down from the mountain by Moses. We know these; the Turks hold them as sacred. We left behind whatever we believed before and we became Turks."

The Ottoman rulers overseeing the dialogue between Palamas and the Chiones demanded that Palamas answer. He began by giving three reasons why he was reluctant to speak. He first said that, "I am not worthy to offer a defense of the lofty and great catholic and apostolic Church of my Christ, since I am the least and almost nothing." Second, he said, "The rulers are sitting as judges supporting my opponents," and felt that it is, "not "appropriate for me to contradict them in defense of piety." Third, he said, "Because I am surrendered as a prisoner and I know from my Lord and God and Savior Jesus Christ that after He surrendered, He did not answer any questions." Palamas then went on to say, "However, because the great Emir has ordered and I understand that God wills for him to have authentic knowledge—and as ruler he needs to know all the faiths with precision—for that reason I will speak about my faith and whatever word God inspires me to say when I open my mouth. I will do this not to defend my faith to the Chiones. I heard they are Jews and this is confirmed through their own words. Now, I am not having a conversation with Jews but with Turks. I shall now speak on the mystery of our faith."

Palamas began to explain the Christian understanding of God. He stated that God always exists and remains in eternity without beginning (*anarchos*), endless (*ateleutetos*), unchangeable (*atreptos*), unaltered (*analloiotos*), unbroken (*atmetos*), unconfused (*asynchytos*), and unlimited or infinite (*aperioristos*). However, all creatures are corruptible or perishable and changeable (*trepto*). Even the beginning (*arche*) of creation is a change, which is derived from non-being into being. Only God is unchangeable. God is not without reason (*alogos*) and He is not without wisdom (*asophos*). Therefore, the word of God is also the Wisdom of God, because the Wisdom (*Sophia*) is with Reason (*Logos*), and, without Reason, Wisdom does not exist. If, therefore, we supposed there were a time when the Reason or the Wisdom of God did not exist, we would have to conclude that there was a time when God was without reason (*alogos*) and without wisdom (*asophos*). This is the ultimate impiety. Therefore, the Reason of God is without beginning and the Wisdom of God is never separated from Him.

Furthermore, neither is the Logos or Reason ever without Spirit (*Pneuma*). Muslims also believe this. By saying that Christ is the Logos of God, Christians also say that God is Spirit and is not separate from the Holy Spirit. Accordingly, God has Reason and Spirit, which exist and remain with Him without beginning (*anarchos*) and inseparable from Him (*achoristos*), because God never was, nor ever shall be without Spirit (*apnous*) and without Reason (*alogos*). Therefore, the one is in three and the three are in one. In God are the Reason (*Logos*) and Spirit (*Pneuma*), not in the same way as we have them dissolved in the air, but in a divine manner (*theoprepos*). For example, the splendor of the sun has its origin in the sun, and the sunrays emanate from sun and descend down to us. At the same time the sun disc is never separated from its splendor, or from its rays. When we make reference to these realities about the sun, we speak of only one sun and not of another sun. In the same way, when we speak of the one God and the Reason of God and the Holy Spirit of God, we do not speak of multiple Gods, but of the one God whom we envision as beginningless and eternally together with the beginningless Spirit. We were taught to believe this way and to confess this faith by Christ, the Logos of God.

Palamas went on to say that not only Christ but also Moses (whom the Chiones themselves respect) spoke this truth in the Decalogue. Moses said, "Hear, O Israel: The Lord our God is one Lord and you shall love the Lord your God with all your heart, and with all your soul, and with all your might." (Deut 6:4). The word of God makes mention three times of "Lord," twice as "Lord," and once as "Lord is God." This indicates that the three are one, and the one is three. Also, in the beginning of the Scriptures, Moses taught that God has Reason and Spirit and, in these and with these, there is but one God, who is the creator of all creation. According to the word of God: "And God said, let there be light; and there was light" (Gen 1:3); and, "…God said, let the earth put forth vegetation; and there was vegetation" (Gen 1:12). Palamas said that he need not mention each creation of God separately, but would rather make reference to David who said: "For God spoke, and it came to be" (Ps 33:9); and, "For God commanded and they were created" (Ps 148:5).

Palamas asserted that the Scripture, "God spoke and it came to be," indicates that God has reason, because no one can speak without word-reason. Thus, through the word all things were created. The Logos-Reason-Word of God existed before all creatures and is uncreated. Since the Logos is uncreated, how could He not be God? Do not reason and the Scriptures instruct us that God is the only uncreated being?

Palamas continued to explain, regarding the creation of the human person, that Moses teaches: "God breathed into his nostrils the breath of life; and man became a living being" (Gen 2:7). Obviously, it is with His reason-word that "God breathed and created living man." This indicates that God has Spirit and this Spirit is creative. The Creator of human souls is God. Thus Job says, "The Spirit of God has made me and the breath of the Almighty gives me life" (Job 33:4).

Palamas was ready to add additional proofs from the Prophets, especially those indicating that God accomplishes the renewal of the human person and the entire world through the Incarnation of His Logos and the manifestation of His Spirit. He turned again to David, who states: "God sent forth His word (Logos) and delivered them from destruction" (Ps 107:20), and elsewhere, "I will send my Spirit and will create and renew the face of the earth" (Ps 103:30).

The Chiones, however, stopped him, and said that all these things were true and could not be challenged. So, Palamas said to them, "Therefore God is three and the three are one God the Creator."

The Chiones either moved by divine power or simply unable to give a reasonable objection, said that what Palamas had spoken had been proven to be the truth, which they also believed.

Palamas said, "Glory be to our God."

The Chiones then said, "But tell us this: how do you speak of Christ as God since he is a human being who was born as a human being?"

Palamas responded that God is not only Ruler of all and Almighty but also righteous and just. David says: "and there is no unrighteousness in the Lord" (Ps 92:15). All the acts of God are righteous and, in a manner similar to how sunrays have life-giving power and the light has heat, even so the energy of God has divine power and righteousness. God created the human being to live in accordance to the divine commandments, but the human being disobeyed God's commandments and, through sin, brought about death. God desired to deliver humanity, but it was inappropriate for Him to violate human freedom. There was a need for a human being without sin in order to assist humanity that willfully sinned. The word of God says, "no one is without sin" (Job 14:4-5). David says: "I was brought forth in iniquity and in sin my mother conceived me" (Ps 51:5).

The only sinless one, the Logos of God, became the son of man. He was born from a virgin as is witnessed from heaven by the voice of the Father (Mt 3:17; Mk 1:11; Lk 3:22). The devil fought against Him, but Christ became victorious over the tempter with His acts, words, preaching, and miracles. In this way, He accomplished salvation. Christ, who is without sin, undertook our passions unto death. He even descended into Hades and saved those of the dead who believed in Him.

At this point, Palamas was preparing to speak of the resurrection and ascension of Christ, but the Turks interrupted him. They asked, "How can you say that the Logos was contained in the woman's womb?" They said that God spoke and Christ became man.

"God is not a massive body who cannot be contained in a small place," said Palamas, "... He is incorporeal and can be present everywhere: in small places, great spaces, above and below. God is not limited." Again the Chiones made a great noise and interrupted Palamas, insisting that God spoke and Christ became man.

Palamas responded patiently: "You say that Christ is the Logos-Word of God. How can the Word 'become' by another word? That would mean that the Logos is not coeternal with God. It was pointed out at the beginning of our dialogue, and you agreed, that God has coeternally the Logos and the Spirit. For that reason, you say that Christ is not only Logos but also Spirit of God. God spoke and the stone was created and similarly, He spoke and the 'plants' (Gen 1:11) and the 'creeping things' were made (Gen 1:24). If, we say that the Logos and Spirit were created by the word, by the word, then by the same token the stone, the plant and every creeping thing created by a word would be Logos and Spirit. The eternal Word of God, as Spirit and Word, was without body. He later took on human nature for our sake; however, He remained coeternal with God, Who also created time."

Now Palapanos, who was presiding, interrupted Palamas. He said that the Emir directed Palamas to answer the following: "We accept Christ, we love Him, and we know Him. He is the Word and breath of God. But you do not accept our prophet and you do not accept him." Palamas replied that one who does not believe in the words of the teacher cannot love him and, for this reason, Christians cannot accept Muhammad. Our Lord and God Jesus Christ said that He will return to judge the entire world and commands us not to accept any other prophet until He returns again. To those who rejected Him, Christ said, "I have come in my Father's name, and you did not receive me; if another comes in his own name, him you will receive" (Jn 5:43). Thus, the disciple of Christ wrote: "But even if we, or an angel from heaven, should preach to you a gospel contrary to that which we preach to you, let him be accursed" (Gal 1:8).

The Chiones and the Turks changed to a new subject, that of circumcision. They asserted that God gave circumcision from the beginning and Christ Himself was circumcised; why, they therefore asked, do not Christians practice it?

Palamas responded: "Since you make references to the comments of the Law given by God to the Hebrews—there were other commandments that were given. God commanded the observance of the Sabbath and the Hebrew Passover, the offering of sacrifices only by the priests on the altar, and the curtain to be within the temple. These and many more that were given by God, you neither accept nor practice."

The Chiones next said: "In your Churches you have many images and venerate them, which is contrary to the commandment of God. Moses wrote that, 'You shall not make for yourself a graven image, or any likeness of anything that is in heaven above, or is in the earth beneath, or in the water under the earth' " (Ex 20:4; Deut 5:8). Palamas explained that friends reverence one another but that does not mean that they worship each other as gods. It is true that Moses learned this from God and instructed the people of his time. This is obvious. Yet, at the same time, Moses himself made numerous images, types of the heavenly things within the curtain. Though the Cherubim are in Heaven, Moses made icons of them and placed them within the sanctuary of the temple. The temple itself was constructed in the likeness of the heavenly temple. If someone at that time had questioned Moses, "Since God forbids icons and images of things above and beneath, why have you made them this way," he would have answered that the icons and images God commanded were not to be worshipped as gods (Ex 20:5-23:24; Deut 4:19; 5:9). But for one to be guided with these images to God, this is good. The ancient Greeks lauded the creation as gods; Christians laud the icons and, through them, are guided to the glory of God. The Turks agreed that, in truth, Moses had made such images.

At last, the Turks got up to leave. As they departed, first the leaders and then the others, greeted Palamas with reverence. But one of the Chiones remained behind, insulted Palamas and slapped him in the face. The other Turks who were there restrained him. It was reported that this incident was made known to the Emir who punished the offender. This was written by one Taronitis, a physician, who stated that he did not know exactly what was reported to the Emir, but that he had written about those things that he had seen with his own eyes and heard with his own ears.

The Third Dialogue

Palamas's final dialogue with the Muslims took place in Nicea. Through the influence of Dr. Taronitis, Palamas was transferred to Nicea where the climate was much better and where medicine was more accessible. He was taken to Nicea alone; his fellow prisoners were taken elsewhere.

Dr. Taronitis preceded Palamas to Nicea and made arrangements for him to stay at the Hyakinth Monastery. He also arranged for a guide to show the city to Palmas. While they were sightseeing, they came to the eastern gate where a Muslim funeral procession was taking place,[15] which Palamas observed with great interest.

Later, on the way back to the monastery, Palamas found an imam sitting with several people in the shade. He used his experience of the funeral he had just witnessed as an opening for a theological dialogue with the imam. He asked if there were anyone present who could speak both Greek and Turkish. Someone came forth and so began the dialogue.[16]

Palamas asked the interpreter to convey to the Turks the following: "I know that what was performed in the open air funeral was good because, with their cries and shouts, they addressed God for the benefit of the dead person. I would like to learn what they said to God." The imam answered, "We asked God's forgiveness for spiritual faults on behalf of the dead person."

Palamas congratulated the Muslims for such an act

of seeking God's forgiveness. He added, however, that God, as judge, has the power to forgive and according to the Christian faith God forgives the entire human race through Christ. Prayers should be addressed to Christ because He, as the Logos, is always united to the Father who is never without reason-Logos.

The imam admitted that Christ is the servant of God. Palamas again spoke, "Yes marvelous one, you ought to be cautious, as you also believe in the great judgment day when both living and dead will be judged. Abraham your forefather—as it is written in the sacred book and the Hebrews preserved—addressed God as follows: 'shall not the Judge of all the earth do right?'(Gen 18:25). God shall judge the entire earth. According to Daniel, God is the king of all forever (Dan 6:26). The Logos does not differ in His divinity from the Father, as the sun's splendor is not different from the sun itself."

The imam decided to expand the discussion. More Turks and Christians gathered to witness the dialogue. Muslims, said the imam, accept all the prophets and Christ, as well as the four books that descended from heaven, which included the gospels of Christ. He then turned to Palamas and questioned him, saying, "How come you do not accept our prophet and you do not believe in his book, which also descended from heaven?"

Palamas responded, "For both of us, confirmed from olden times, the Law does not accept anything to be true without witnesses." He interpreted this to mean that the act witnesses to itself, and is also witnessed to by trustworthy persons. "Moses," he said, "educated the Egyptians with signs and wonders (Ps 135:9), divided the sea with his rod, and again the sea returned to its former place (Ex 14:16, 22, 27), and rained bread from heaven (Ex 16:4). Moses is trustworthy for [Muslims] as well. He is a 'trusted servant' of God (Num 12:7), but not son or Logos of God. Later, he ascended the mountain by divine command and there he died (Deut 32:49-50), and was gathered to his forefathers."

"Christ, however, who performed many great miracles is witnessed to by Moses and the other prophets and through the centuries he is called the Logos of God. [Muslims] also accept this. He, who is from eternity, was born from the Virgin Mary and ascended into Heaven and remains there forever. We hope that He will come again at the resurrection to judge the living and the dead (2 Tim 4:1; 1 Pet 4:5). I mention all these things about Christ, which you accept. We believe in Christ and His Gospels. For Muhammad, however, we do not find such witnesses, neither in the prophets nor in anything miraculous and worthy of edifying and guiding faith. Because of this, we do not believe in the book that he brought."

It became obvious that the imam was indignant. He retorted, "It was written about Muhammad in the Gospels but you eliminated it (Sura 61:6).[17] But, as you all know, Muhammad started from the end of the risen sun and came victorious to the sunset."

Palamas emphasized that in the Christian Gospels nothing had been eliminated and nothing had been altered by anyone. In fact, there are great curses and condemnations against anyone who would either eliminate or modify anything in the Gospels. Indeed a person who does so is cut off from the tree of life and has no place in the kingdom of Christ (Rev 22:19). No Christian would dare to alter or modify the Gospel, which is the Word of God. There are, also, numerous witnesses found in the various dialects into which the Gospel was translated from the beginning. Even from the beginning, the Gospel was not written only in one language. How, then, could it escape the attention of the various witnesses if a modification of the Gospel had taken place? Various nations have preserved the same Gospel—even the heretics. Christ ascended into heaven and will return for the Final Judgment Day. We do not expect, and cannot accept anyone save Christ, Himself.

Palamas acknowledged that Muhammad started from the east and came victorious to the sunset—the west. He accomplished this with war, the dagger, plunder, enslavement, and murders. None of those things comes from the good God. Homicide has been the way of such conquerors since the beginning of time. Alexander began from the west and conquered the entire east. Many others throughout time have dominated the world with their powerful armies. However, no other nation has entrusted their souls to those conquerors, as Muslims have done with Muhammad. Further, Palamas asserted, even though Muhammad both used force and promised pleasures, he did not conquer the entire Christian empire. The teaching of Christ, on the other hand, even though it averred almost all the excessive pleasures of life, had won over the whole Roman Empire to Christ. Even among those who were its enemies, Christianity prevailed without the use of force. Christianity, instead, suffers from the force of others but, to Christians, this is a sign of victory over the world (1 Jn 5:4).

Understandably, by this time the Turks had become very angry. The local Christians who were present signaled to Palamas not to be so bold and to be more moderate in his words. Understanding, Palamas changed his speech, smiled, and said, "Certainly, if we were in complete agreement with all these, we would be one religion!"

One of the Turkish bystanders said, "A time will come when we will agree with each other."

Palamas agreed and prayed that this would be soon. This third dialogue thereby ended in a friendly atmosphere. Palamas later wrote that he spoke thus, remembering the words of the apostle who wrote, "At the name of Jesus every knee shall bow, in heaven and on earth and under the earth, and every tongue confess that Jesus Christ is Lord, to the glory of God the Father" (Phil 2:10-11; see also Rom 14:11).

CONCLUSION

These dialogues provide interesting insight into the interaction between Muslims and Christians in the middle Ages. The encounter with the Chiones is also an example of how Christians, Muslims, and Jews interacted at that time, even if not on an equal basis. Though a true dialogue of equal partners between the adherents of these three faiths would have to wait for

modern times, it is evident that in the time of the Byzantines, people were able to discuss issues of faith and
theology with sincerity, boldness, and civility.

NOTES

1 See P. Chrestou on the activities of Gregory Palamas during his tenure as archbishop (in Greek) *Kleronomia*, vol. 16b
(1984), pp.224-238; V. Phanourgakes, "The adventures and
activities of Gregory Palamas during his imprisonment in
Asia 1354-1355" (in Greek) *Kleronomia*, vol. 16b (1984), pp.
249-274; Elias D.Nikolakakes "Saint Gregory Palamas Encounter with the Teachings of Islam" (in Greek) *Gregorios
Palamas*, vol. 81, no. 773 (May-August 1998), pp. 353-368.
For a discussion on the historical importance of the letters
of Palamas to better understand the Ottomans of this period, see the valuable work by George Arnakis, *The First Ottomans* (in Greek) (Athens, 1947), pp. 17-18.
2 Gregory Palamas, *Syggrammata*, ed. P. Chrestou, vol. 4
(Thessalonike, 1988), introduction, pp. 56-57.
3 Gregory Palamas, "Letter sent to His Church," 13-16, in
Chrestou, *Syngrammata*, vol. 4, pp. 127-129. The original text
and Modern Greek translation, Gregory Palamas, *Apanta ta
Erga*, vol. 7, ed. P. Chrestou (Thessalonike: To Byzantion, Pa-
terikai Ekdoseis, *Gregorios Palamas*, 1994), pp. 172-175; *The
letter sent from prison in Asia Minor*" trans. Daniel J. Sahas,
"Captivity and Dialogue: Gregory Palamas (1296-1360) and
the Muslims," in *The Greek Orthodox Theological Review*, vol.
25 (1980), pp. 118-132.
4 G. Arnakis, *The First Ottomans* (in Greek) (Athens, 1949),
pp. 18; "Gregory Palamas," in *Speculum* 26 (1951), pp.113-
114; "Gregory Palamas," in *Byzantion* 22 (1952), pp. 305-339.
5 P. Wittek, "Chiones," in *Byzantion* 21 (1951), pp. 421-423.
6 J. Meyendorff, *A Study of Gregory Palamas*, trans. George
Lawrence (London: The Faith Press, 1964), pp. 105-107.
7 Reference is made by Professor Chrestou in "The Activities of Gregory Palamas During his tenure as Archbishop,"

in *Kleronomia, op. cit.*, pp. 231.

8 "La captivité de Palamas chez les Turks, Dossier et Commentaire," *Travaux et Mémoires* (Paris: Editions E. de Boccard, 1979), vol.7, pp. 214-218.

9 M.Jugie, *Dictionaire de Théologie Catholique*, vol.11 (1932), c.1747. See also Sp. Vryonis, *The Decline of Medieval Hellenism in Asia Minor and the process of Islamization* (1971), p. 427.

10 J.Meyendorff, *A Study of Gregory Palamas*, trans. George Lawrence (London: The Faith Press, 1964), pp. 105-107. See also Alexander Zanemonets, "The Chionios Case and Judeo-Christian Religious Groups In The Fourteenth Century," in *The Church and the Library: Studies in Honor of Rev. Dr. George C. Papademetriou*, ed. Dean Papademetriou and Andrew J. Sopko (Boston: Somerset Hall Press, 2005), pp. 123-135.

11 Dialexis with the Chiones, *Syggrammata*, vol. 4, pp. 151

12 Dialexis with the Chiones, *Syggrammata*, vol. 2, pp. 149

13 Philotheos, "Engomion," 7:10, 7:25. For a good discussion on the *Chiones*, see Chrestou, "The Activities," in *Kleronomia, op. cit.*, pp. 230-236.

14 The "Dialexis" used in this study is the critical text included in Professor P. Chrestou, *Syggrammata*, vol. 4, pp. 148-165.

15 "Letter to his Church," 20-21, in Chrestou, vol.4, pp. 132; "Letter to an Anonymous," 3-4, in Chrestou, vol. 4, pp. 142-143.

16 "Letter to his Church," 19-22, in Chrestou, vol. 4, pp. 131-133. The entire dialogue with the imam is included in the same letter 20-29, in Chrestou, vol. 4, pp. 132-138; and in "Letter to an Anonymous" 4-12, in Chrestou, vol. 4, pp. 143-147.

17 The *Qur'an* claims that the coming of Muhammad was prophesized by Christ Himself. It states that: "And of Jesus, who said to the Israelites: 'I am sent forth to you by Allah to confirm the Torah already revealed and give news of an apostle that will come after me whose name is Ahmed.' " "Ahmed" means "the praised one." (Battle Array, Sura 61.6) *The Koran*, translation with notes by N. J. Dawood (New

York: Penguin Books, 1974), p. 106. Muslim interpreters and commentators refer to the Gospel of John 16:7 stating that, "If I do not go away, the Comforter (Παράκλητος) will not come to you." The Muslim commentators claim that the original Greek term used was (Περίκλυτος) which means "the praised one," a synonym of Ahmed. This has the same root as "Muhammad the praised one," which is the name of the prophet. The Muslims claim that the Christians corrupted the text and changed it from Περίκλυτος to Παράκλητος. The Muslim commentators further insist that even if the term Παράκλητος meaning Advocate was in the original text, it still refers to Muhammad who is the mercy of the whole world. See *The Holy Qur'an: Text, Translation, and Commentary,* by Abdullah Yusuf Ali (Doha-Qatar: Qatar National Printing Press, 1946; Washington, D.C.: The Islamic Center, 1946), p. 144, note 416 and p. 1540, note 5438. See also Archbishop Anastasios Yannoulatos, *Islam: A General Survey* (In Greek) (Athens, Greece: Editions Ethne kai Laoi, 1983), p. 140, note 17. Palamas as a Christian theologian categorically rejects this claim as completely unfounded. He argues for the integrity of the Gospel as received by the Church from the beginning.

ISLAMIC ARISTOTELIAN PHILOSOPHY

Gregorios D. Ziakas

Translated by George C. Papademetriou

ARISTOTLE AND THE ORIGIN
OF ISLAMIC "PHILOSOPHY"

Aristotelian thought, which was transmitted in the Islamic world through the great number of translations into Arabic, has become the object of study, great commentaries, and creative cultivation by the representatives of Islamic "philosophy." In particular, the form of Aristotelianism that was developed in the Islamic *falsafa* (philosophy) tradition is of great interest. In order to understand this, we must first say a brief word about the origin and content of Islamic *falsafa*.

The origin of Islamic philosophy is the result of a

Editor's Note: This study was included in the present volume on dialogue between Orthodoxy and Islam because it describes the bond between the two traditions created by Greek philosophy. As described in this study, Greek philosophy, and especially that of Aristotle, influenced the development and formulation of Islamic theology and dogmas. This interchange – in other words, dialogue – began as early as the eighth century with the translation into Arabic of practically all the existing works of the ancient Greek philosophers and Hellenistic intellectuals. Later, Greek philosophy and Islamic scholarship related to it also became a bridge between East and West, as the works of Aristotle and other Greek philosophers were transmitted to the Scholastic West through Arabic translations.

"great translation movement" that took place in the Islamic world between the ninth and the first part of the
eleventh centuries. The work of this translation movement set the basis for philosophy and sciences. With
the assimilation of the Greek spiritual legacy, Islamic
philosophy took its name from the transcription of the
Greek term "philosophy" into Arabic as "*al-falsafa*."
Failasūf (pl. *falāsifa*) was the name given to one who is
occupied with *falsafa*, that is, the "philosopher." Philosophy is also frequently characterized with the broader
term *al-hikmah* (wisdom), and the philosopher is then
al-hakim (pl. *hukamā*). These broader terms, however,
usually refer to ancient philosophy and its representatives, that is, the great Greek philosophers, as witnessed by the honorific name *par excellence*, "*al-hakim*,"
which referred specifically to Aristotle.[1]

Concerning "Islamic philosophy," R. Walzer asserts
that, at first, this could appear as a contradiction of
terms. The true philosophical thought is characteristic
of the Greek spirit: "Philosophy was native to ancient
Greece and bonded closely with the Greek way of life
and the Greek religion." Islam, on the other hand, has
a Biblical foundation. It developed as a religion from
inherited, basic teachings of Christianity and Judaism.
Islam does not have its basis in human reason, but in a
book of "revelation," that is, the *Qur'an*, which was en-
veloped with divine authority. This book did not come
from ancient Greek tradition but it owed its existence
to "divine revelation." Precisely for this reason, "the
convictions of a Muslim are the convictions of faith,
whereas the philosophy of Greece, with few exceptions,

maintained consequentially the primacy of reason."[2]

It is true that Islam never developed a recognized philosophical science in the same sense that philosophy was developed in the Western world as an independent science with trends and systems. Islamic philosophy remained within the borders of the Muslim community (*umma*) and never completely opposed Muslim religious life.[3]

In Islam, there is neither a duality between spirit and matter, nor a distinction between religion and state, or sacred and profane. The Muslim community is "undivided." Religion and state are one. The source of the unique "community of the faithful" is the "revealed book," the law of God. Whatever is irreconcilable with God's law has no place in the Muslim community. Consequently, Islam also knows no distinction between philosophy and theology such as occurs in Christianity. In the latter, each of these has its own objective and means of knowledge although they nevertheless touch and interpenetrate each other, since the autonomy of the territory of philosophy becomes that of knowledge of faith, which is the "handmaiden of theology." Because of this, the term *falsafa* cannot be rendered simply by the Greek term *philosophia*. Similarly, the characteristic term for Islamic theology, '*ilm al-Kalām*, can only be rendered with reservations by the term, *theologia*.

In spite of all this, there is no doubt that a distinct philosophical school, the *al-falsafa*, exists in Islam. Even though it remains on the margins of the Muslim community, *al-falsafa* represents one of the brightest manifestations of theoretical thought in Muslim history. Its development was served by the Muslim intellectual flowering, and it fostered a remarkable level of spiritual attainment.

Islamic philosophy, of course, was eclectic in that it applied the achievements of Greek thought in its own unique way. The distinct characteristic, moreover, of Muslim philosophers was an unusual acumen and a rare skill for synthesis. The preference for scientific classification that we encounter constantly in Muslim philosophy has its source in Greek logic and, especially, in Aristotelian logic and the introductory writings of commentators who intensely influenced the research methods of Muslim philosophers. Certainly, in some sense, this method had a restraining effect on knowledge because of a pronounced devotion to an old error that held that what was once classified could not change: this should have been understood in the essence of knowledge and not in the method. From another perspective, however, this method is absolutely necessary for the true scientific thought that so fruitfully influenced the history of Islamic philosophy. Especially, we must stress how Muslim intellectuals struggled for creative, scientific thought and a philosophical writing method that was finally sealed by Aristotelian thought, particularly by the commentaries on the works of Aristotle and the methodology used in them.

Islamic philosophy is divided along general lines into two great, geographically differentiated periods. From the beginning of the ninth century to the first half of the eleventh century, the eastern branch of philosophy flourished. In the twelfth century, a branch of Islamic philosophy was developed in Spain (Andalusia), that is, the branch of the school of the West (*Maghrib*). Aristotelian philosophy was utilized by Muslim *falāsifa* in both these periods of development of Islamic philosophy.

Three great philosophical personalities of the Eastern *falsafa* represented Aristotelianism in Islam: Abū Ya 'qūb al-Kindī, Abū Naṣr al-Fārābī, and Ibn Sīnā (Avicenna). In the twelfth century, *Maghrib falsafa* was represented by Ibn Bājjah (Avenpace), Ibn Ṭufayl (Abubacer), and the Aristotelian thinker *par excellence* Ibn Rushd (Averroes). It is certainly obvious that it is not possible here to explore the depth and breadth of the philosophical thought of all these important representatives of Aristotelianism in Islam. We will, however, simply try to describe some basic trends of their philosophical thought in order to form an impression of the way Aristotelianism was shaped in the Arabic tradition.

MAJOR REPRESENTATIVES OF ARISTOTELIANISM IN ISLAM

Abū Ya 'qūb al-Kindī

The first great representative of Aristotelian and Neoplatonic contemporary thought in Islam was Abu Ya 'qub al-Kindī. He was an offspring of a prominent Arab family. He was born in the beginning of the ninth century in Basra and died c. 870. As a young student, the influence exercised on him by the school of Gunde-

shapur turned him toward Greek learning. Because he
was the first to introduce the synthesis of Aristotelian
and Neoplatonic philosophy into the Arab world, he
received the honorific title "The Philosopher of the Arabs."[4]

He served as a philosopher in the court of Bagh-
dad, in the time of al-Ma'mūm and his successor, al
Mu'tasim, and the latter engaged him as a tutor for his
son. In his time, there had not as yet arisen a conflict
between Islamic theology (*Kalām*) and philosophy (*falsafa*) and, because of this, al-Kindī was considered to
be, at one and the same time, a philosopher and a theologian. The important position he enjoyed is unique in
the annals of the Islamic philosophy. This can be explained from the fact that he shared the religious views
of the *Mu'tazila*, which the two caliphs mentioned
above had imposed as the official confession of the
Muslim faith on all their subjects. In spite of his theological tendencies, Aristotle's works and method exercised a strong influence on his thought and for that
reason he is now classified primarily as a philosopher,
rather than a theologian. Al-Kindī collected the flow-
ers of Aristotelian Neoplatonic thought and forcefully
introduced philosophy into the theological systems of
the *Mu'tazila mutakallimūn*. He exerted every effort, on
the one hand, to create a "leading" Islamic theology
based on logical interpretation of "revelation," and on
the other hand, a philosophy whose purpose was to
utilize the whole of human rational ability for understanding God, the universe, and the human being. To
attain his goal, he looked to the Greek philosophical

tradition. Even though he was the first to undertake this, he succeeded, to a significant degree, in assimilating the attainments of Greek philosophy. It would be especially interesting, says Walzer,[5] to make every effort to discover his immediate predecessors in Syrian Christianity and, possibly, even in Greece, because this would give hope that someone would contribute to a work in the future on the history of the influence of Hellenism on Syrian Christianity and Medieval Islam.

There are three treatises that R. Walzer describes and analyzes, and that are very helpful for understanding al-Kindī.[6] The first one is a *Brief Introduction to Aristotle,* which gives an overview of the contents of his writings or, rather more likely, his summaries.[7] The second treatise, which is al-Kindī's main work, is addressed to the Caliph al-Mu'tasim under the title *Prime Philosophy* or *Metaphysics (Fi 'l-falsafa 'l-ūlā).*[8] This treatise begins with a significant introduction in which the basic Aristotelian principles are stated and, later, proceeds to the examination of theological problems. In it, al-Kindī makes every effort to prove the existence of God with Neoplatonic arguments. Only the first half of this work has been preserved, whereas the remaining section, in which the author appears to come to the same conclusions as the *al-Mu'tazila* in their interpretations of the *Qur'an,* has been lost.[9] The loss, however, of this section is compensated by the discovery of another work, that of an epistle that the philosopher sent to the son of the Caliph al-Mu'tasim, to whom he was a teacher. In this epistle, al-Kindī indicates to his pupil that a verse of the *Qur'an* (sura 16, 50 (48)-52 (50): cq. 23, 39-45 (46), which indicates that the stars worship God, is found to be in complete agreement with the Neoplatonic form of Greek astral theology. He states that the Greek metaphysicians had already, from the time of Plato and Aristotle, turned their attention toward the starry sky, to the rotary movement of the heavenly bodies and the divine nature manifested in them.[10]

In these treatises, however, as well as in numerous small ones (*Rasā 'il*) that are preserved,[11] al-Kindī was engaged in a struggle to introduce philosophy into the field of theology. Apparently, at this point he was influenced by the canonical Aristotelian tradition, the Neoplatonic type of the School of Athens, which entered into Syrian Christianity in the middle of the fifth century and was used by Syrian philosophers and theologians. He follows this tradition in his first treatise; but in an appendix he gives the differences that exist between human and divine knowledge and between human reason and the immediate knowledge from the revelation (*wahy*) of the prophet. He states that, "the common people are important by nature to receive such knowledge." There are, however, circumstances where revelation and philosophical knowledge guide to the same results; some fundamental principles of faith, however, cannot be proven by reason. There are truths from revelation that are guaranteed by the Scriptures, prophecy, and revealed religion.

Subsequently, al-Kindī deals with the problem of the world and primary "matter." In his *First Philosophy* and in the above-mentioned verse of the *Qur'an*, the form of the universe appears similar to that which Aristotle had constructed. On the other hand, however, his theological perspective is that of the emanation from the "One" of Neoplatonic teaching, which completes that of Aristotle. Certainly, in reality, neither one of these philosophical thoughts is related to the Islamic tradition, but al-Kindī makes an effort to find points of similarities.

First, let us see the problem of primary matter. In his discussion, al-Kindī follows the Aristotelian teaching on "form" and "matter," "movement" and "composites." According to Aristotle and the Neo-Platonists, the world is eternal and uncreated. Al-Kindī, in order to harmonize Greek philosophy with the Islamic religion, accepts the world as a creation of God and therefore temporal. He believes that the primary "matter" is a creation of God and therefore is not "eternal" as Aristotle believed. In order to render the Aristotelian terms "matter" and "form" he uses the Quranic words *tina* (clay) and *surah* (form). He therefore rejects the eternity of matter in Aristotle's teaching and accepts that the composition of matter, form, and accidents cannot be eternal. The eternal (*azali*) does not have relationship to "non-being," and does not have "prior" or "posterior." Consequently, its existence does not depend on another cause, as it neither has a subject, nor a predicate, it neither "produces" nor "causes." The *azali* (eternal) does not belong to a gender, nor is it corruptible. Regarding its existence, the *'ain*, that is, the primordial atom, the self of God, there cannot be a secondary self besides Him, and He is not transformed because He does not have an opposite. The eternal is necessarily perfect.

Beginning from these ideas, al-Kindī transformed

– with a small, but significant detail – the Aristotelian
form of the universe. For Neoplatonic-Aristotelian
thought, the heavenly sphere above, which is, after God,
the prime "unmoved mover" and inexhaustible source
of emanations, is the cause of life in the world under the
moon, that is, the world of the earth. According to al-
Kindī, this highest sphere is not eternal but was at some
time created by God. Consequently, if it has a beginning,
it will also have an end. It will last as long as God wills
it. It is subject to the divine ordinance on which all the
cosmic spaces depend. At some time it will be lost, as
the remaining places of the world will be lost, because
divine energy according to the will of God is not transmitted "infinitely" to the lower material stratum.[12]

From these examples, we are able to understand
that the abilities of analysis and especially of composition are absent from the philosophical thought of
al-Kindī. For him, philosophy remains, as in Christianity, the "handmaiden of theology." His analysis of
the meaning of creation is an effort to harmonize philosophy with religious law. R. Walzer testifies that, in
this point, some Christian commentator influenced al-
Kindī, possibly John Philoponos.

Abū Naṣr al-Fārābī

A philosophical viewpoint diametrically opposed
to that of al-Kindī is represented by Abū Nasr al-Fārābī,
or, Alfarabius, as he was known in the Medieval West.
He was born in 870, and died in Damascus in 950. In
him, Islamic philosophy attains its real dimensions as
the relation between philosophy and Islamic religion

is considered with a purer philosophical mind. "In his work there is no revelation to be kept in reverence."[13] Greek thought keeps, as much as possible, its own integrity and is examined in a new way through the lens of Islamic values.

Al-Fārābī was one who, as we saw above, contributed significantly to the Neoplatonic transformation of Aristotelianism in Arabic philosophy. Because of this innovation in interpreting Aristotelian philosophy – thus exercising a great influence on many Muslim intellectuals and especially on Avicenna – al-Fārābī was given the honorific title, "the second teacher (*al-mu'allim ath-thāni*)," the "first" and indisputable teacher of all philosophers having been, as we already mentioned, Aristotle.

From al-Fārābī we have commentaries on works of Aristotle[14] as well as personal treatises, among which the first place is occupied by *Maqāla fi ma āni 'l-'aql* (*Treatise on the Meaning of the Term "Mind"*). He was inspired by Plato's *The Republic* to write his treatise, *On the Ideal State* (*al-Madina al-fādila*). In addition to those already mentioned, there is the treatise, *On Harmony of the Divine Plato and Aristotle* (*Kitāb al-jam 'bain rai' yai al hakimain Aflatūm al-ilāhi wa Aristātālis*), published in 1890 and 1892 in Leiden by Dieterici.[15] Many of his works were corrected and republished by Bouyges in Beirut. One of the significant works that had been attributed to al-Fārābī, entitled *Fusūs al-hikam* (*Precious Store of Wisdom*),[16] was proven recently, through the research of M.S. Pines, to be the work of Ibn Sīnā (Avicenna).

In his work, when he attempts to harmonize Plato and Aristotle, al-Fārābī's pioneering metaphysical perceptions are clearly evident in his interpretation of Aristotle's thought. He accepts that, in reality, there is harmony between Plato and Aristotle with regard to the great metaphysical problems concerning the origin of the world, the mind, and the soul, as well as those relative to the reward for good and evil acts. In addition, there is harmony on ethics, politics, and logical problems in their teachings. Here, naturally, al-Fārābī sees Aristotle through the lens of Neoplatonism and bases his arguments for the harmony between the two philosophers on what is known to us as the "pseudo-Theology of Aristotle." Thus, whoever reads Aristotle's sayings on divine authority (*rububiya*) in his *Theologia*, cannot doubt that Aristotle accepted a creator who called forth this world from nothing. This is inferred so clearly from his expressions that it is impossible for it to remain a secret. There (in the *Theologia*), it becomes clear that the glorious God called matter forth from nothing (*abda'ha...la 'an shai'*) and that by the will of the Creator it received form and order.[17]

The broader interpretation of the thought of Aristotle by al-Fārābī is evident in his work on *Philosophy of Aristotle* (*Falsaf at Aristātālis*), published in 1961 by Muhshin Mahdi.[18] He followed Aristotle in his logic, physical science, psychology, metaphysics, and ethics. Even though he combined Aristotelian thought with Neoplatonic teachings, his knowledge of the thought of Aristotle (known as the *Stagirite*) is deeper and more refined than that of al-Kindī. The original philosophical spirit of al-Fārābī opened new horizons and prepared the way for more fertile Aristotelianism by subsequent intellectuals.

Ibn Sīnā (Avicenna)

The most important representative of Aristotelianism within Islam is Ibn Sīnā (Avicenna). He had such a great ability for analysis and composition, and was so influential for Muslim thinking, that he received the honorific title, *"al-shaykh ar-ra 'ls"* (the teacher *par excellence*).[19]

Doubtless, Ibn Sīnā is the most famous of all Muslim philosophers. He was the type of universal Muslim intellectual whose interests extended beyond philosophy into medicine, chemistry (alchemy), and politics – in which he actively, personally participated. He was born circa 980, in Bukhara, and died in 1037, in Hamadan. He wrote in Arabic and Persian, and the cultural importance of his work is shared between the Arabs and Persians. He left a rich, scholarly body of work consisting of upwards of 100 books. Among these, of greatest interest is the work, *Kitab as-Shifa*[20] (*The Book of Convalescence*). This work is a universal exposition of philosophy in eighteen books, divided into four sections: Logic, Physics (here psychology is included), Mathematics and, Metaphysics.[21]

Also important are the following works: *Kitab al-ishārāt*;[22] a number of smaller treatises;[23] *Kitāb al-Isāf*,[24] a commentary on the pseudo-Theology of Aristotle that was preserved only in outline and examines the "Eastern commentators" on Aristotle; and his famous medical encyclopedia, *Qānūn fi t-tibb* (*Canon on Medicine*).[25] This work is the famous *Canon* or *Liber Canonis* of *Cantica* of the Medieval Latin West. Finally, his work, *Eastern Wisdom* (or *philosophy*) (*al hikma al-mashriqiya*) merits mention here. The original of this latter work is lost, but we know its contents from references made by Averroes and from fragments and outlines that are preserved under various titles.

Even though Ibn Sīnā was introduced to the metaphysical thought of Aristotle on account of the commentary of al-Fārābī, he was very much influenced by Aristotle, even more than al-Fārābī. This is evident in *Kitāb as-Shifā'*. In the two first parts of his work, entitled "Logic" and "Physics," he follows Aristotle. Even though he does not depend immediately upon Aristotelian texts, in the first part of the book he follows the structure of the *Organ*; in the second part, however, he entitles his books according to the titles that the works of Aristotle bear, as for example, "On the Heaven and the World," "On the Soul," "On the Planets," and "On Animals." This work comprises the first philosophical encyclopedia of Islam and it very much influenced the philosophical world of the Islamic East and represented the teaching of Avicenna to the West.

Nevertheless, the Aristotelianism of Avicenna is strongly colored by Neoplatonism. As did al-Fārābī, Avicenna also undertook to synthesize the system of Aristotle with Neoplatonic teaching. In this attempt, he used a work now known to be falsely attributed to Aristotle, *Theology of Aristotle*, which Avicenna believed to be the genuine work of the *Stagirite*. The influence that this work exercised on his thought is evident from the fact that the only Commentary on Aristotle that we have under the name of Avicenna is that which he dedicated to the pseudo-Theology.[26]

Avicenna's philosophical system is characterized as "a successful synthesis of Aristotelianism and Neoplatonism."[27] This synthesis presents a creative conception, which could only be constructed by such an important, integrated, philosophical personality. His great contribution is that he created high philosophical and scientific terminology that was not only used in logic, but also in mathematics, psychology, and, in general, in all the sciences of his time.

Avicenna's teaching on the emanation from the One is central to his system. The starting point of his metaphysics is "being as being," as true and necessary existence (*al-maujud bima huwa maujūd*). Being is differentiated between "the necessary," which exists by necessity as absolute, transcendent existence, and "the conventional or accidental." The necessary and real being is self-sufficient and self-existent (*tamm al wujud*). All things emanate from the transcendent being (God). Conventional or accidental being emanates by necessity from the necessary being: it has only momentary existence and depends upon its accidents, which are in continual movement and change. In reality, it is also eternal because it constitutes the apparent manner of existence of the One. Everything has an inner truth, with which it is what it is (*haqiqa huwa bihā mā huwa*). The being that is perceived through the senses has three meanings: (1) "being" (*maujud*), (2) "thing" (*shai'*), and (3) the "necessary" (*daruri* or *lāzim*). These three meanings of being are primordial in the soul and, in some way, categorically conscious and *a priori* engraved in the soul.[28] This is a mode of knowledge that cannot proceed from something more knowable, as happens with that of consent (*tasdiq*), which results from principles of prior data. The more primordial, however, and primary concepts of self-characterized being are the three principles: "being" (*ον-maujūd*); "thing" (*πράγμα-shai'*); and, "one" (*εν-wāhid*), which are common to all being. These are known only within the cycle of the flux of being; in fact, within this cycle of the existence of being, nothing else exists that could be more known than these three primary principles. For this reason, it is difficult to define and express an opinion about the true condition of being. Certainly being includes in its cycle of existence the various conditions, but that being that is in "operation" is "posterior" and does not precede the primary condition which is "being *qua* being" (*al-maujūd bimà huwa maujūd*), primordially known. Human beings have some knowledge of the truth of being (*haquigat al-maujūd*), but do not have clear perception of the inner substance (*hypostasis*); they do not know if being is active or passive. Only analogically and with the study of signs are we led to the "relative" knowledge of being.[29] The whole is a kind of "individualism": the cosmos and its events lead to the movement of individuals, thus, in this way, the foundations of "individualism" were laid from the beginning of Muslim philosophy. The intermediary time is also individualized and owes its entire flux to its primary source. The true "Εv" (One, *Wāhid*) is a transcendent monad from which primary rational beings, the universal soul, and all life emanate. In the knowledge of the One, every-thing pre-exists in a primordial pre-existence and from there, afterwards, enters into the multiplicity of the perceptible world. The universal soul, the third in the triad of the divine emanation, is the Principle of all the souls, from the intermediary spherical rational beings as the revelation of the soul in the plants, the animals and in the human being.

Creation is a necessary emanation of the absolute goodness of the One and is, consequently, eternal. It proceeds from the necessary being by emanation and in splendor (*tajalli, fayd*) and is eternal because it is based on the mode of existence of the One necessary being. The mode of existence of the One is based on the mind and knowledge with which the One sees and knows Itself. Since the One is mind and knowledge, the One necessarily becomes creative because the di-vine essence is constantly thinking and acting. Conse-quently, creation is an inevitable and necessary conse-quence of its (the One's) thought. In fact, however, the One as absolute thinking being conceives the essence and order that exists within it. This order emanates au-tomatically from it (the One).[30] All these, however, do not have any relation with the will and desire, which are directed towards some object outside of the emana-tion. This is simply generosity and disinterested gift of Being.[31] The relation of all these toward the necessary being is found in that the One, by knowing its essence, knows at the same time whatever the essence by neces-sity causes. Therefore, God, by knowing His essence, knows also whatever is good in all those that emanate from it. This knowledge, however, is not natural: it is the order of the good within being that proceeds from the One (God). But here the question arises: Is this simple knowledge adequate for existence to emanate from the One, and for particular beings and things to begin to exist? Avicenna attempts to solve this difficulty by admitting intermediary spiritual beings, the primary heavenly rational beings that we mentioned above, which, as spiritual creatures, are found between Creation and its prime cause and the realized mind of the One. Here, in the thought of Avicenna, is found the relation with that of the heavenly "other" of Aristotle, from which result the souls of the planets, which are divine rational beings (an older perception, more in line with that of Plato). Even though according to Aristotle the eternity of the world is derived from the same natural existence of being, for Avicenna the eternity of the world proceeds from a gradation of the highest and necessary being in its creative fullness. The saying of Avicenna was, "from the One only one is possible to proceed." Later Thomas Aquinas and other Latin philosophers used the distinction that he made between intention *prima* and *secunda*. With his idea, however, that God by necessary inner nature is creator of the world, he came into conflict with the authorities of the Muslim religion, which teaches that God is absolutely free; likewise, also, with his teaching that the human soul is an eternal, intellectual nature (*mujarrad*) that is redeemed and arrives in the intelligent world. His belief that the soul is delivered from every materiality was dangerous from the Muslim religious point of view, as it denied the resurrection of the body – a belief that Avicenna considered simply a symbol for uneducated people. In his teaching on the eternity of the world, he also goes contrary to the principles of the religious teachings of Islam, which accepts the creation of the world from nothing.

These elements of his teaching brought on him the anger of teachers of the religious laws of Islam, although not only Avicenna but also almost all of the other Muslim philosophers were faithful and devoted adherents of the Islamic religion. These thinkers made every effort to reconcile Greek philosophy with the religious law of Islam, in the conviction that they would contribute a great service to their faith. Because of this, they provoked a reaction from teachers of the law who saw new teachings being introduced into their religion. The problem that arose in Islam is almost the same as that which arose in Christianity, relative to the relation between faith and reason. It differs, however, in the following detail: In Christianity, the problem was the reconciliation of religious faith with philosophical reason. In Islam, even though this question arose, it was not set forth explicitly. The conflict between the law teachers and the philosophers did not arise from the relation between reason (*'age*) and faith (*imam*), but from the relation between *falsafa* and *Shar'*, that is, between philosophy and the revealed law.

Al-Ghazali, representative of official Islam in opposing "philosophy"

From the time of Avicenna and afterwards, there

has been an open conflict between philosophy and Islamic religion. The famous Muslim theologian, al-Ghazali (d. 1111), battled philosophy by turning its own arguments against it. He writes against philosophy in the name of the religious law, having in mind chiefly the ideas of Avicenna. He specifically combats the teachings on the eternity of the world, the idea that God is by necessity – not by free will – Creator of the world, the limitation of the divine omniscience of the universal concepts of the secondary being, and the denial of the resurrection of the body. His polemical work entitled, *Tahāfut al-falāsifa* (*The Incoherence of the Philosophers*),[32] which was translated in the West during the thirteenth century, placed him among the "philosophers" because he enumerated and refuted the arguments of Islamic philosophers up to his time. The great Ibn Rushd (Averroes) refuted this work in his corresponding work entitled *Tahāfut at-Tahāfut* (*Incoherence of the Incoherent*).[33]

Ibn Rushd (Averroes), the Aristotelian par excellence

Ibn Rushd (1126-1198) was the most clear-sighted Aristotelian.[34] He was distinguished by his philological precision and his knowledge of the variations of the Aristotelian texts and their proper interpretation. He was born and lived in Muslim Spain in a cultural atmosphere completely different from that of the Eastern *falsafa*.

Averroes was intensely preoccupied with Aristotle and wrote commentaries on the entire series of the Aristotelian corpus: *The Posterior Analytics, The Topics, Physics, On Generation, On Heaven, The Meteorological,*

On Sensation, On Sleep, On Animal Stories, On Animal Movement, and the *Metaphysics.*

He worked on three forms of commentaries on Aristotle's writings: the *Great Commentary,* the *Middle Commentary,* and the *Small Commentary* that belongs to the philological category of paraphrases. The most important is the *Great Commentary,* which covers all the above-mentioned works of the Aristotelian corpus. The great service that Averroes offered in this philological study and in the criticism of the text is that he was the first to apply the method of separating the text from the interpretation and the commentary. This method, apparently, Averroes picked up from commentators on the *Qur'an.*[35] In his *Great Commentary,* he separates with great care the Aristotelian text from the commentary and the explanations of the commentators, and then interprets it critically. Each Aristotelian text is systematically separated into chapters and paragraphs, and he continues to interpret sentence-by-sentence, and chapter-by-chapter, with great care, diligence, and patience.[36]

In the *Middle Commentary,* Averroes records only the words at the beginning of every paragraph with which the Aristotelian text begins, and then he proceeds into the interpretation, commenting and presenting together the ideas both of Aristotle and of the commentators.[37]

The *Small Commentary* belongs to the philological category of paraphrases, commonly used by all the commentators up to Averroes's own time. In this commentary, Averroes develops the teaching of the philosopher, drawing evidence from the work of other authors.

Contrary to Avicenna, who was influenced by Neoplatonic/Aristotelian thought and wrote independent works on philosophy, only a few small treatises by Averroes were completely devoted to the treatment of philosophical issues.[38] His commentaries on Aristotle are both his main work and also the most important part of his philosophical studies. Even though the West knew Avicenna as the philosopher of the Arabs, Averroes became known as the "Commentator" *par excellence* and usually is addressed by this name.

Averroes, therefore, is a significant philologist as well as a philosopher. His system is different from that of the Eastern *falsafa* colored with Neoplatonism. Averroes relied more on the authentic Aristotelian works than on Neoplatonizing interpretation of them. For this reason his system is clearer and more philosophical. He placed himself against the views of the Eastern *falsafa*. Even though he refutes the twisted polemical work of al-Ghazali against it, he severely criticizes its conclusions, especially the philosophical thought of Avicenna and al-Fārābī, which wrote under the fascination and influence of the Neoplatonic teachings. Avicenna's complex metaphysical world does not bear a strong relation to the metaphysical system of Averroes, even though the differences between the two systems are not radical. Averroes's thought starts, as does that of Aristotle, with the fact of the empirical being, which he endeavors to interpret on the basis of the same natural principles, and not on principles that have an absolute metaphysical source. For this reason, he is more

Aristotelian than his predecessors who represent the Eastern *falsafa*.

According to Averroes, being is governed by the principle of causality, the coherence of the cause to the effect. In the same way as Aristotle, he also distinguishes two classes of causes. The first is that according to which the relation between the cause and effect could be reversed (for example, water and air). This does not arrive at the first cause. The second, in which it is not possible for the relation between cause and effect to be reversed, is limited to a first cause. For this second series of causes Averroes gives, as does Aristotle, the example of the relation of the father toward the son. The relations here cannot be reversed. There exists, therefore, one causal coherence, which governs being. In this coherence of things, the beings are distinguished as to higher and lower causes. If we begin from the higher to the lower, we will see that the highest cause is space; immediately following are the heavenly causes that are higher than the earthly ones, etc.

The highest and the first cause of all causes, however, is God, who is in the circumference of the world. From this first cause begins the chain of coherence of all causes that, through the heavenly spheres, descend to the earth. God, however, is not only the first cause, but also the highest concept of the universal being: within this a pure form consists and, in the concrete particular beings, expands a chain of ontologically rational concepts. Thus, all the causes having one source –the highest cause – we see introduced into the system of Averroes a monistic tendency of receiving being. According to him, the "prime mover" is simultaneously the highest form as well as the highest goal. He followed Aristotle in accepting that in the ultimate truth of divinity, pure form and ultimate goal are coincidental. Consequently, he poses the question of the existence of a separate essence (of divinity), which is the cause of the perceptible world. He introduced the Aristotelian idea of the "prime mover," but affirmed an antinomy in the Aristotelian thought. If, he says, we accept that the bodies are moved from outside, then we have difficulty interpreting the natural inclinations that are inherent in things, which push them to turn to their natural place. He expresses his opinion, therefore, that things certainly accept their movement from the prime cause, which however, simultaneously provides to nature an inner spontaneity through which everything inclines toward its natural place. Although Avicenna supports that only natural objects have such an inner spontaneous movement, and not the heavenly bodies (which for him are intellectual rational beings), Averroes expands this movement to the heavenly bodies. He notes, however, that the inner spontaneous tendency toward their natural place must not be perceived as the cause of their movement. The heavenly bodies are animated and are moved on the basis of the movement of their soul.

Therefore, the highest "mover" is the absolute One, God. Averroes, however, appears on this point to deviate from the Aristotelian thought. Aristotle accepts that God himself moves the world as "prime mover." Averroes introduces, after God – the highest of all causes, another prime moving cause that moves the universe. Also, contrary to Aristotle who accepts that the elements mutually create each other, Averroes believes that the cause of origin is the highest movement. He adopts, nevertheless, the Aristotelian concept that there exists in things a "material reason," which is the cause of origin and is higher than they are, that is, the rational forms. The distinction that he here makes between "form" in general and the "material form" is similar to that which is made by Albinos between "idea" and "form." Originating from the higher and purer forms of the heavenly bodies is a chain of causes and effects that reaches to the lowest form of matter.[39]

Averroes certainly tends to accept the creation of the world from nothing without, however, stating with clarity his views relating to the topic. On the one hand, he teaches that God is the first creative cause of the world, even though the world is rationally posterior to His creation; however, on the other hand, he accepts that the creative act of God is eternal and does not fall into the void and into nothingness. In this way, he tends to connect the world with God and considers Him coeternal with it. Nevertheless, he elucidates that the world is connected with God to the measure that it is the result of the divine creative act and energy. If God, who acts, is eternal, His energy must also be eternal. The world, however, is connected with God in an act that forms in creation and which, in its consequences, is distanced ontologically from the transcendent Creator. On the other hand, he rejects the idea that God creates the world from preexistent matter. In reference to time, he accepts that space and time are two concepts, which coexist. Time and creation coincide. In this way, the reasonable question arises, "What, precisely, is the world?" The question remains unanswerable. Here we have a philosophical thought that attempts to clarify what the world is *not*, without, however, telling us with clarity what it *is*.[40]

Averroes, therefore, attempts to follow his great prototype, Aristotle. The deviations that are observed in his system are the result of the influence of the later works of subsequent Greek philosophers, who influenced him through the commentators on Aristotle. Thus, in addition to the obvious presence of Neoplatonic teachings, we find in his system Stoic, Pythagorean, and other Greek philosophical views. His confession, however, is almost Aristotelian with a few deviations and contradictory concepts, which we observe here and there. There are also some significant divergences from Aristotelian thought that witness to the influence of Neoplatonizing Eastern *falsafa*. In this way, the Aristotelian theories on divinities and heavenly spheres are interpreted in accordance with Neoplatonic views, even though the conclusions for such an interpretation are found in the same Aristotelian teaching. Also, his tendency toward the monistic view of being and the belief that all causes have their source in the highest cause, are not very far from the views on relations with the system of Avicenna. Basing himself on the teaching of Aristotle, he formulated the theory of monopsychism according to which, for all human beings, there is one common rational soul.

Averroes was not against religion. On the contrary, he wrote, as we have seen above, some small treatises about the relation between religion and philosophy.[41] His life's great work, however, was the study, elaboration, and commentary of the Aristotelian texts and, even more, the exposition of Aristotelian ideas. His work, essentially, was ignored by the Muslim world. However, he exercised great influence on the intellectual history of the Latin world and motivated the scholars of the West to occupy themselves with the study of Aristotle.

NOTES

1 For an older bibliography on Islamic philosophy, see extensive list in the work of P.J. de Menasce, "Arabische Philosophie. Bibliographische Einfuhrungen," in *das Studium der Philosophie* No. 6 (Bern, 1948). T.J. de Boer. *Geschichte der Philosophie im Islam* (Stuttgart, 1901). See also by the same author, *De Wijsbegeerte in den Islam* (Haarlem, 1921). L. Gauthier, *La philosophie musulmane* (Paris, 1900). For a newer bibliography, see A.F. Ahwany, *Islamic Philosophy* (Cairo, 1957). Badawi, *La Transmission* (1968). Badawi, *Histoire de la philosophie islamique* (Paris, 1964). Montgomery Watt, *Islamic Philosophy* (1964). R. Walzer, *Greek into Arabic* (Oxford, 1962). R.Walzer, "Early Islamic Philosophy," *The Cambridge History of Later Greek and Early Medieval Philosophy* (Cambridge, 1967).
2 R. Walzer, "The Rise of Islamic Philosophy," *Oriens* 3 (1950), p. 2.
3 Anastasios Yannoulatos, *Islam* (in Greek)(Athens: Ethnoi kai Laoi editions, 1975), p. 170.
4 On al-Kindī, see Guidi-Walzer, *Studi su al-Kindī I* (1940). For a bibliography, see also H. Corbin, *Histoire de la philosophie islamique*, 355, v. 1 and p. 217 f. For an extensive bibliography, see the recent Dissertation by Faten Abntlel Azim Abntlele Bari, "The First Philosophy of al-Kindī," *Aristote-*

lian and Neoplatonic Elements (in Greek) (Thessalonike: Philosophical School, University of Thessalonike, 1979).

5 R. Walzer, "The Rise of Islamic Philosophy," pp. 5-6.

6 R. Walzer, "The Rise of Islamic Philosophy," p. 6 f.

7 Here Walzer makes reference to Guidi-Walzer, *Studi su al Kindi I* (1940).

8 This was published by al-Ahwani, Ahmad Fu'ād, *Kitāb al-Kindī fi 'l-falsafa 'l-lūlā* (Cairo, 1948).

9 Ibn an-Nadim informs us that the evidence for this work is in Fihrist, ed. Flugel No. 1-2.

10 R. Walzer, "The Rise of Islamic Philosophy," p. 6.

11 The most significant treatises preserved were published by Dr. Abu Rida, M.A.H., *Rasā 'il al-Kindī al-falsafiya*, 1-2 (Cairo, 1950-53).

12 R. Walzer, "The Rise of Islamic Philosophy," p. 8.

13 R. Walzer, "The Rise of Islamic Philosophy," p. 11. See also in the same work pp. 11-19 for the relative bibliography on al-Fārābī. For extensive research see H. Corbin, *Histoire de la Philosophie Islamique,* v. 2, p.356.

14 Significant is the following on "On Interpretation: Al-Fārābī's Commentary on Aristotle's 'On Interpretation'" (*De Interpretatione*). Edited with an Introduction by Wilchelm Kutsch, S.J. and Stanley Marrow, S.J. (2nd edition revue et corrigée). Dār el-Machreq (Beyrouth, 1971).

15 *Al-Fārābī's Philosophische Abhandlungen aus Londoner.* Leidener und Berliner Handschriften, hrsg. Von Freiedrich Dieterici (Leiden, 1890). German translation: *Al-Fārābī's Philosophische Abhandlungen. Aus dem Arabischen ubersetzt von F. Dieterici* (Leiden, 1892). For his ideal state see, *al-Fārābī', al-madina al-fadila*. F. Dieterici (Leiden, 1964).

16 A resourceful research in the work of al-Fārābī would give a new significant material to the history of philosophy. Significant preliminary work toward this direction are the studies of Ibrāhim Madkour, *La place d'al-Fārābī dans l'école philosophique_musulmane* (Paris, 1934) and Richard Walzer, "Al-Farabi's Theory of Prophecy and Divination," in *J H S* (1957). Prof. Mushin Mahdi at the University of Chicago today is continuing this research.

17 See al-Fārābī's *Philosophisöhe Abhandlungen* (German trans. 37, Arabic text 23).

18 al-Fārābī's *Philosophy of Aristotle*. Arabic text with an Introduction and Notes by Mushin Mahdi (Beirut, 1961).

19 Other historical witnesses confirm this title. For the most important bibliography on Avicenna, see Henry Corbin, *Histoire de la philosophie Islamique* v. 4, p. 357.

20 This is not in reference to a book on medicine where he deals with bodily illness, but rather a philosophical book engaged with the "health" of the mind and soul. For the influence of this work on the West, see A. Goichon, *La Philosophie d'Avicenne et son Influence en Europe Médiévale* (Paris, 1951), p. 15.

21 The "Metaphysics" of Avicenna exists in two Latin editions: *Metaphysica Avicenne sive eius prima philosophia optime Castigata per Reverendum sacre theologie bachalarium fratrem Franciscum de macerata ordinis minorum et per excellentissimum artium doctorem dominum Antonium frachantianum vicentinum philosophiam legentem in gymnasio patavino Impressa* ...Venetiis per Bernardinum Veneturn ... 1495 (photocopy edition, Louvain, 1961). *Avicenne perhvpatetici philosophi ac medicorum facile primi opera in lucern redacta ac nuper quantum ars niti potuit per Canonicos emendata: Logyca. Sufficientia. De celo et mundo* (ex translatione Dominici Gundisalvi). *De anima* (ex trans. Joannis Hispalensis et Dominici Gundisalvi). *De animalibus* (ex transl. Michaelis Scoti). *De intelligentiis. Alfarabius, de Intelligentiis.Philosophia prima* (ex transl. Dominici Gundisalvi) ... Venetiis 1508. The text, *Philosophia prima*, is the same as *Metaphysica Avicenne*. New critical edition, see Ibn Sīnā, al-Shifa: al-Ilahiyat (*La Metaphysique*) vol. I (texte établi et édité par G. C. Anawati et Said Zayed), Vol. II (texte établi et édité par Muhammad Youssef Moussa, Solayman Dunya et Said Zayed), revu et précédé d'une introduction par Ibrahim Madkour (Le Caire (Cairo), 1960). German translation, M. Horten, *Die Metaphysik Avicennas, enthaltend die Netaphysik, Theologie, Kosmologie und Ethik* (New York: Halle, 1907).

22 This book has been commented upon many times (Diet-

erici, Leiden 1892): *Kitab al-'isharat wa-t-tanbihat* (Das Buch der Lahrsatze und Bemerkungen): cf. the French edition by A.M. Goichon, *Ibn Sīnā (Avicenna), Livre de Directives et Remarques* (Beyrouth-Paris, 1951).

23 These treatises have been published many times. Among them are those by A.F. Mehren. These have been characterized as "mystical treatises" (*Mystische Abhandlungen*) (Leiden, 1889 and 1894).

24 This was published by Abd ar-Rahman and was translated into French by Georges Vajdam "Les Notes d'Avicenne sur la Théologie d'Aristote," in *Revue Thomiste*, II (1951).

25 See Ibn Sīnā, *Qānūn, fi t-tibb li-Abi 'Ali ash-Shaikh ar-Ra'is Ibn Sīnā ma'a ba'd ta'lifihi wa huwa l-mantiq wa 'ilm at-tabi'a wa 'ilm al-kalām* (Rome, 1593).

26 Cf. Louis Gardet. "En l'honneur de millenaire d'Avicenne," *Revue Thomiste* II (1951). On p. 345 Gardet observes: "*Ces gloses soulignent...les tendances néoplatoniciennes d'Ibn Sīnā. Tendances qui s'appuient sans doute sur le contresens historique de la pseudo-théologie attribuée à Aristote, mais qui n'en font pas moins intimement corps avec l'élan le plus personnel de la pensée avicennienne.*"

27 Etienne Gilson. *La philosophie au moyen-āge*, 2nd ed. (Paris, 1952), p. 356.

28 For the distinction between "being" (*maujūd*) and "is" (*wujūd*) according to Avicenna see A.M. Goichon, *Lexique*, p. 421, No. 754 (*maujūd* ="being") and p. 418, No. 748 (*wujūd* = "is"). *Maujūd* is the Aristotelian "potential" being, whereas *wujūd* is the particular "active" being.

29 See Avicenna perhypatetici...Opera... (Philosophia prima I, 6) f. 72r-72v. *Metaphysica Avicenne* II, 1. al-Ilahiyāt I, 5, p. 30 in the 1508 Venetian edition.

30 See also *Philosophia prima* VIII, 7 (f.101r): "Metaphysics of Avicenna" VIII, 7 al-Ilāhiyāt VIII, 7, p. 366.

31 See above *Philosophia Prima* VIII, 7 (f. 101r): al-Ilāhiyāt, VIII, 7, p. 367.

32 M. Bouyges in the series *Bibl. Arab. Scholast*, II (Beirut, 1927); 2nd ed.: al-Ma'āref (Cairo, 1955). T.J. de Boer gives an overview and summary in German in *Die Widespruche der*

philosophie nach al-Ghazali und ihr Ausgleich durch Ibn Roshd, (or, "Die Ewigkeit der Wellt bei al-Ghazali und Ibn Roshd," Dissertation (Strasburg, 1894).

33 M. Nouyges in the series *Bibl. Arab. Scholast*, III (Beirut, 1930). See M. Horton, *Die Hauptlehre des Averroes nach seiner Schrift "Die Widerlegung des Ghazal"* (Bonn, 1913). English trans S. van de Bergh, *Averroes' Tahāfut* (*The Incoherence of the Incoherent*), trans. from the Arabic with an Introduction and Notes (*Unesco Coll. Of Great Works, Arabic Series*), 1-2 (Oxford, 1954).

34 For the life and cultural center where Averroes lived and numerous related historical information, see the careful work of Ernest Renan, *Averroes et l'averroisme* (Paris, 1852); 8th ed. (Paris, 1925). The biographical and historical events that are included in this work of Renan later were re-evaluated and completed by new critical findings by Leon Gauthier, *Ibn Rochd (Averroes)* (Paris, 1948). Cf. *La theorie d'Ibn Rochd sur les rapports de la religion et de la philosophie* (Paris, 1909).

35 See E. Renan. *Averroes et l'averroisme*. 3rd ed. (Paris, 1869), pp. 59 f.

36 M. Bouyges published the Great Commentary: *Averroes, Tafsir ma ba'd al-Tabī'at (Grand Commentaire de la Métaphysique d'Aristote). Texte arabe inédit établi par M. Bouyges* (Bibl. Arab. Scholast.) (Beirut, 1938-1948).

37 For the Middle Commentary, *On Poetics*, see Ibn Rushd, Talkhis.

38 From these small treatises we mention here the two most important: *Fasi al magāl fima baina ash-shari 'a wa-l-hikma min al-ittisāl* M. Muller (Munich, 1859). This treatise treats the reconciliation of religious law with philosophy. The second treatise, *Kashf 'an ma', āhij al-adilla*, was published and translated into German by M. Muller, *Philosophie und Theologie von Averroes*, The first treatise was also published in 1959 by G.F. Hourani, *Ibn Rushd (Averroes) kitāb Fasl al-Magāl".* (Arabic) (Leiden, 1959) and trans. by the same author: *Averroes on the Harmony of Religion and Philosophy, a Translation with Introduction and Notes of K. fasl al-Magāl* (London, 1961).

39 The few ideas presented here were drawn from the work:

Die Epitome der Metphysik des Averroes. Ubersetzt und mit einer Einleitung und Erlauterungen versehen von Dr. S. van den Bergh (photocopy reproduction of the 1924 edition) (Leiden: Brill, 1970).

40 Cf. Roger Arnaldesz, "La pensée religieuse d'Averroes I. La doctrine de la création dans le Tahāfut," in *Studia Islamica* (Paris, 1957), no. 8, p. 110 f.

41 See note 38.

Speaking His Mind in a Multi-Cultural and Multi-Religious Society: John of Damascus and His Knowledge of Islam in Chapter 101 ("The Heresy of the Ishmaelites") of His Work Concerning Heresy

Radko Popov

Introduction

John of Damascus lived and worked in a multi-cultural and multi-religious society encompassing seventh century Damascus and Jerusalem. In this society, Judaism, Christianity, and Islam co-existed fairly peacefully. People of these faiths worked together in the civil administration of their society, though political and military power was exercised solely by the Muslims. Many of the theological writings of John of Damascus are marked by this multi-religious environment. He left us the first known Christian writing about Islam. Nevertheless, perhaps what is most striking about his writing is how firmly and strongly John of Damascus critiqued Islam while he was living under tolerant Muslim rulers.

Living under non-Christian rulers in a setting of

religious tolerance, Christians in this society themselves needed to treat theological disagreements in a
new way. The Byzantine emperor could no longer step
in and enforce the orthodoxy proclaimed by the Ecumenical Councils. It also meant that the emperor could
not harass orthodox theologians when their teachings
clashed with his own convictions.

We have no evidence that Muslim rulers ever punished John of Damascus for his very public polemics
against Islam and its Prophet. On the contrary, it is
widely believed that John of Damascus was protected
by the Caliph he served. It seems most remarkable that
a Muslim leader, whose own faith clearly forbade any
form of "graven images," would have offered protection to a Christian who was writing in defense of icons.
Although John of Damascus was not only a Christian
theologian but also one of the Caliph's highest civil
officials, the Caliph took a detached position in the
theological dispute between John of Damascus and the
Christian church authorities in Constantinople. The
Caliph's neutrality clearly amounted to protection of
John of Damascus given the widespread and serious
persecution the icon-venerators (*iconodules*) experienced in the Byzantine Empire.

Even if it is not extraordinary that John of Damascus had the freedom to write against the Byzantine
iconoclastic heresy, which at the time was the official
policy of the patriarchate in Constantinople, it is significant that he apparently had the freedom to write
against Islam.

The claim by Muhammad (570-622 CE) to be a prophet and a messenger from God to his fellow Arabs has been criticized and attacked almost from the day it was first put forward in the early seventh century CE. From the *Qur'an* itself we learn that the pagan Meccans called the messages "tales of the men of old!" (*Qur'an* 68:15),[1] while the Jews of Medina mocked Muhammad's claims saying: "Tales of the ancients, which he has caused to be written, and they are dictated before him morning and evening." (*Qur'an* 25:5.) These criticisms were taken up less than a century later by Christian scholars.

One of the first Christian critics of Islam was John of Damascus. As will be described below, although John of Damascus's critique of Islam was negative, it reflected extensive interaction between Christians and Muslims and an intimate knowledge of the *Qur'an* and other Islamic sources.

THE LIFE AND TIMES OF JOHN OF DAMASCUS

John of Damascus was born around 680 CE, and was raised in Damascus, about a half century after the Muslims conquered Syria. But before this time, important major developments in religion and empire had already taken place, developments that would be formative to his life. Between 608 and 629 CE, the eastern provinces of the Byzantine Empire had been occupied by the Persians. During that period, the pre-Chalcedonian Christians, regarded as heretics by the Orthodox Church,[2] had found themselves treated with a greater degree of tolerance and respect by the Persians than had been the case under the Byzantines. It is not surprising, therefore, that when the Muslim armies first appeared in Transjordan, Syria, and Palestine around 634 CE, many of the non-Orthodox Christians welcomed them, and saw them, as they saw the Persians, as liberators from the rule of Byzantine imperial administration and from suppression by the Orthodox ecclesiastical authorities. "What the Persian era showed was that a foreign overlord was not necessarily a persecutor, but a Chalcedonian nearly always was."[3] There were also other reasons why some Syrians welcomed the change: under the Byzantines (who ruled the area before and after the Persians), taxes were high, landowners exerted overbearing power over the peasants, and the Byzantines were involved in long, exhaustive, and mostly fruitless wars with the Persians.[4]

A group of Christians, who lived in the lands conquered by Islam, retained their loyalty to the Council of Chalcedon. Later they were known as Melkites[5] because of their adherence to the Orthodox dogmas and the suspicion that their political loyalty was to the Byzantine Emperor. It is understandable that among them emerged a different interpretation of the arrival of Islam in Syria. A prominent figure who was representative of this point of view was John of Damascus.[6]

John's family consisted of Greek-speaking Christians of Syrian descent. However, he was given the Arabic name Yahya ibn Mansur (which translates as "victorious"). Daniel Sahas observes that this name is not Greek in form, being closer to the name patterns of Syrian Christians of Arab descent.[7]

Despite his Christian Melkite background, John's family held an important hereditary public office in the court of the Muslim rulers of Damascus, the Umayy-ads. It is said that his father Sergius held the impor-tant position of *logothetes*, the chief financial officer for the caliph Abd al-Maliks. It is believed that it was his grandfather, Mansur ibn Sargun, who surrendered Da-mascus to the Arab invaders in 635 CE.[8]

Little is known of the early years of John of Damas-cus. Most details (but not all) concerning his life have come from the passionals written by John, Patriarch of Jerusalem (probably John VII, 964–969 CE), but based on an earlier biography in Arabic.[9] These notes have served as the main source of biographical information, although dating back to the tenth century, they have been noted by scholars as lacking historical detail. Nevertheless, they contain a number of valuable indi-cations that cannot be ignored.[10]

John's father Sergius looked for a Christian tutor who could provide the best possible education for John and his brother. The passionals regarding John of Damascus say that, while passing through the Damas-cus marketplace, his father came across several cap-tives, enslaved as a result of raids on the Italian coasts. One of these captives was a monk by the name of Cos-mas, purportedly from Sicily. As Sicily was a Byzantine province until 652 CE, when it was conquered by the Caliph Uthman, and Sergius found the monk in the 690s, chronological questions arise about the Sicilian background of Cosmas. In any event, Cosmas turned out to be extremely wise and well-educated. Sergius arranged for the release of this man, and appointed him tutor to his two sons. Under the instruction of Cosmas, John received a first-class Hellenistic education, including mathematics, geometry, music, astronomy, rhetoric, logic, philosophy (Plato and Aristotle), and theology. According to the enthusiastic language of his biographer, John soon equaled Diophantus in algebra and Euclid in geometry.

Following the death of his father, John assumed the administrative position of *protosymbulos* or Chief Councilor of Damascus in the government of Caliph Walid I (r. 705-715 CE).[11] It was during his term in office in Damascus that iconoclasm (image-breaking), a movement trying to eliminate the veneration of the icons, first appeared and gained support in the Byzantine court. In 726 CE, Emperor Leo III, the Isaurian, issued his first edict against the veneration of images and their exhibition in public places, because he felt they were close to idolatry. John of Damascus became one of the most active defenders of icons against the iconoclasm of the Emperor Leo III. From his position of relative security in Muslim territory, John wrote and spoke freely against the iconoclasts.

Then, at some point during the last 25 years of his life (probably in the second decade of the eighth century, when the administration of the Umayyad Empire was put in the hands of Muslim officials), John left his position at the court of the Umayyads and became a monk in Palestine. It was at this time that he changed his name from Yahya, taking the monastic name "John." According to a late tradition, he retired to the monastery of Saint Sava near Jerusalem, where his teacher Cosmas had earlier retired, though it is likely that he was associated with the Church of the Resurrection (The Holy Sepulchre) in Jerusalem itself.

It is believed that John of Damascus died around 750 CE, because at the iconoclast council of Hiereia (754 CE) he was anathematized under his name Mansur, which indicates that he was already dead.[12] Soon after that, at the Seventh Ecumenical Council at Nicaea in 787 CE, he was exonerated.

THE THEOLOGY OF JOHN OF DAMASCUS

While at St. Sava monastery, John of Damascus devoted his time to anti-heretical writing. Many of the theological works of John of Damascus are polemical. He wrote treatises against the Christological heresies of monophysitism, monothelitism, and Nestorianism. He also wrote tracts from an Eastern Orthodox perspective about other religious traditions, such as Judaism, Manichaeism, and Islam.

After growing up and working in the Caliph's court and knowing Islam, it is not surprising that he turned his attention to defending the Christian faith against Muslim teaching, which he considered to be a Christian heresy. One of his principal anti-Islamic writings is in his well-known treatise, *The Fountain of Knowledge*.[13] The treatise is divided into three parts, namely: *Philosophical Chapters* (*Kephalaia philosophika*), *Concerning Heresy* (*peri haireseon*), and *An Exact Exposition of the Orthodox Faith* (*Ekdosis akribes tes orthodoxou pisteos*). The second part of this treatise, *Concerning Heresy*, is to a large extent a copy of a similar work by Epiphanius, brought up to date by John of Damascus. The author indeed expressly disclaims originality, except in the chapters devoted to Islam, iconoclasm, and aposchitae.[14] To the list of 80 heresies that constitute the *Panarion* of Epiphanius, John of Damascus added 21 heresies that had sprung up since the time of Epiphanius.

It is in the last chapter (chapter 101), or what he called "The Heresy of the Ishmaelites," of *Concerning Heresy* that John of Damascus deals with Islam. This chapter was intentionally derogatory in tone – a sort of "anti-creed" that explained, "This is what we do not believe, and here's why ..." In contrast to the previous chapters on other heresies, which are usually only a few lines long, this chapter fills a few pages. It is one of the first explicit Christian polemical writings against Islam, and the first one written by an Eastern Orthodox theologian.[15]

THE HERESY OF THE ISHMAELITES

In "The Heresy of the Ishmaelites," John of Damascus introduces the beliefs of the Muslims as "the superstition of the Ishmaelites" and the "forerunner of the Antichrist": "There is also the superstition of the Ishmaelites which to this day prevails and keeps people in error, being a forerunner of the Antichrist."[16]

This grave accusation, "forerunner of the Antichrist," was directed against those who were believed to lead people astray from the Orthodox faith, by "deceiving" the believers. The expression, however, was not employed solely or for the first time against Islam and Muhammad. It was used before and after Muhammad against Emperor Leo III, his son Constantine V, later against Patriarch of Constantinople John VII Grammaticos (836-842 CE), and possibly for some other prominent political and religious leaders. It was a strong but common accusation in vogue at this time. John of Damascus also used this label for Nestorius, whom he called "Antichrist" as well as "son of Satan."[17]

He continues writing about the Muslims:

> They are descended from Ishmael, [who] was born to Abraham of Agar, and for this reason they are called both Agarenes and Ishmaelites. They are also called Saracens, which is derived from *Sarras kenoi*, or destitute of Sara, because of what Agar said to the angel: "Sara hath sent me away destitute."

John of Damascus calls the Muslims "Hagarenes," a name derived from Hagar, Abraham's concubine and the mother of Ishmael. The expression "the sons of Hagar," referring to the Muslims, was widely used by later Byzantine authors.[18] For the etymology of the name "Saracen," Chapter 101 refers to the incident in Genesis, chapter 16 and in particular to the dialogue of Hagar with the angel: "I'm running away from my mistress Sarai," (Gen 16:8),[19] which in a restatement can read "Sarah has sent me away, destitute" (*Sarras kenoi*.)

However, the Book of Genesis actually describes how Abraham, and not Sarah, sends Hagar away into the wilderness: "Abraham took some food and a skin of water and gave them to Hagar. He set them on her shoulders and then sent her off with the boy." (Gen 21:14.) Abraham gave them the bare necessities, but he knew the promise of God that Hagar and Ishmael would be fine: "I will make the son of the servant into a nation also." (Gen 21:11.) The small size of the provisions given to Hagar could be interpreted to mean that she was sent away destitute. Neither Hagar nor Sarah is mentioned by name in the *Qur'an*. John of Damascus, perhaps being aware of the arbitrariness of this explanation, states that this name is not his own invention, but that the Muslims "are called so."[20]

He continues to look at the Muslims' background:

> These used to be idolaters and worshiped the morning star and Aphrodite, whom in their own language they called Khabár, which means great. And so down to the time of Heraclius they were very great idolaters. From that time to the present a false prophet named Mohammed has appeared in their midst.

John of Damascus speaks of a change in the religion of the Ishmaelites, from the original religion of Ishmael (from Abraham) to idolatry, which is in accord with the testimony of the *Qur'an* and Muslim writers. According to Islam the pure religion of Abraham and Ishmael deteriorated with the introduction of images and alien practices in the worship. In antiquity Strabo describes the idol worshipping of the Arabs.[21] Another testimony is of Herodotus.[22] (Both authors mention other gods but not Aphrodite, who is called Venus in Latin. As the early Arabs may have worshipped a local version of Venus, and the day of Venus is associated with Friday, maybe it is not by chance that the first Arab Muslims chose Friday as a day of collective worship.) In a way, John of Damascus's awareness of the idolatrous character of the pre-Islamic religion in Arabia leads him to a positive recognition of Muhammad as the person who brought his people back to monotheism.[23] Also, John of Damascus is well informed about the time of Muhammad (570–632 CE). He accurately says that Muhammad lived during the reign of the Byzantine emperor

Heraclius (c. 575–February 11, 641 CE).

John of Damascus claims that Muhammad used Jewish, Christian, and heretical sources to devise his heresy:

> This man, after having chanced upon the Old and New Testaments and likewise, it seems, having conversed with an Arian monk, devised his own heresy.

John of Damascus is believed to have been the first to narrate in a polemical writing that Muhammad had been instructed by an Arian Monk, who, according to Muslim tradition, was called Bahira. At the time, the Nestorians were saying that Sergius, a Nestorian monk, had instructed Muhammad. Probably, John chose the Arians rather than the Nestorians because, to him, Islam looked to have more of an Arian influence.

Ibn Ishaq (704–768 CE), author of *The Life of Muhammad (Sirat Rasul Allah)*, who was a younger contemporary of John of Damascus, described the journey of the young Muhammad with his uncle Abu Talib and the encounter with the monk Bahira: "When the caravan reached Busra in Syria, there was a monk there in his cell by the name of Bahira, who was well versed in the knowledge of Christians."[24] According to Muslim sources, from which John of Damascus probably knew about the role of a monk, Bahira did not teach the young boy Christian dogmas, but warned his uncle to guard him against the Jews. It is obvious from the text of John of Damascus that the story of Bahira circulated in the first century of Islam in the Middle East, but the Muslim sources do not indicate the religious affiliation of the monk.

Looking further, it is clear from the text that John

of Damascus is well informed that Muhammad was a pious man:

> Then, having insinuated himself into the good graces of the people by a show of seeming piety, he gave out that a certain book had been sent down to him from heaven. He had set down some ridiculous compositions in this book of his and he gave it to them as an object of veneration.

The citizens of Mecca called Muhammad "al-Amin" (the trustworthy). In contrast to John of Damascus, later Byzantine polemics claim that Muhammad was an epileptic, and that under this condition he thought that he received revelations from God.

John of Damascus continues by moving to dogmatic issues:

> He says that there is one God, creator of all things, who has neither been begotten nor has begotten.

Here again, John of Damascus knew directly or indirectly the content of the short Sura (or chapter) Al-Ikhlas, as he quotes very precisely from it: "He begetteth not, nor is He begotten." (*Qur'an* 112:3.) In this regard Sahas notes that it seems that John of Damascus has detected the core of the *Qur'anic* message.[25]

With respect to the *Qur'an's* view of Jesus, John of Damascus wrote:

> He says that the Christ is the Word of God and His Spirit, but a creature and a servant, and that He was begotten, without seed, of Mary the sister of Moses and Aaron. For, he says, the Word and God and the Spirit entered into Mary and she brought forth Jesus, who was a prophet and servant of God.

The above paragraph shows that John of Damascus was well informed about the place Jesus has in the *Qur'an*. Muslims believe that Jesus (Isa al-Masih) is a word from God. This is confirmed in several places in the *Qur'an*. The angels speak to Zakariya that "Allah doth give thee glad tidings of Yahya, witnessing the truth of a Word from Allah." (*Qur'an* 3:39.) So John the Baptist will witness the Word of God (Jesus). Then the angels bring the same message to Mary: "O Mary! Allah giveth thee glad tidings of a Word from Him: his name will be Christ Jesus, the son of Mary." (*Qur'an* 3:45.) Again, through Muhammad, God is speaking directly to the Christians in the *Qur'an*: "Christ Jesus the son of Mary was (no more than) a messenger of Allah, and His Word, which He bestowed on Mary." (*Qur'an* 4:171.) Ibn Ishaq, the contemporary of John of Damascus, in his book *The Life of Muhammad*, also describes how the Muslim immigrants to Abyssinia declared to the Negus that they believed that Jesus is a word and spirit from God: "We say about him that which our prophet brought, saying, he is the slave of God, and his apostle, and his spirit, and his word, which he cast into Mary the blessed virgin."[26]

John of Damascus carries on with a further description of Muhammad's alleged claims and Muslim belief about Christ:

> And he says that the Jews wanted to crucify Him in violation of the law, and that they seized His shadow and crucified this. But the Christ Himself was not crucified, he says, nor did He die, for God out of His love for Him took Him to Himself into heaven.

Here we see another example showing that John of Damascus is well informed about the text of the *Qur'an* regarding the life of Jesus and how God elevated Him to heaven. The *Qur'an* speaks about the death of Jesus Christ and the related eschatological events, quoting His own words in the Meccan Sura Maryam: "So peace is on me the day I was born, the day that I die, and the day that I shall be raised up to life (again)." (*Qur'an* 19:33.)

Further, in the Sura An-Nisa we read exactly what John of Damascus describes as the intention of the Jews: "That they said (in boast), 'We killed Christ Jesus the son of Mary, the Messenger of Allah'; but they killed him not, nor crucified him, but so it was made to appear to them." (*Qur'an* 4:157.) In the next verse the *Qur'an* confirms, "Nay, Allah raised him up unto Himself." (*Qur'an* 4:158.) The elevation of Jesus to the heavens is also mentioned in the Medinan Sura Aal-E-Imran, in which God speaks to Jesus: "O Jesus! I will take thee and raise thee to Myself and clear thee (of the falsehoods) of those who blaspheme." (*Qur'an* 3:55.)

John of Damascus continues the story of Jesus's death and ascent into heaven, which is central to Christians, as he sees it presented by the *Qur'an*:

> And he says this, that when the Christ had ascended into heaven God asked Him: "O Jesus, didst thou say: 'I am the Son of God and God?' " And Jesus, he says, answered: "Be merciful to me, Lord. Thou knowest that I did not say this and that I did not scorn to be thy servant. But sinful men have written that I made this statement, and they have lied about me and have fallen into error." And God answered and said to Him: "I know that thou didst not say this word."

Again we see that John of Damascus quite precisely quotes from the Sura Al-Maeda: "And behold! Allah will say: 'O Jesus the son of Mary! Didst thou say unto men, worship me and my mother as gods in derogation of Allah?' He will say: 'Glory to Thee! never could I say what I had no right (to say). Had I said such a thing, thou wouldst indeed have known it. Thou knowest what is in my heart, Thou I know not what is in Thine. For Thou knowest in full all that is hidden.' " (*Qur'an* 5:116.)

From the teachings of Muhammad, John of Damascus transfers his critical attention to Muhammad's claim to prophethood:

> There are many other extraordinary and quite ridiculous things in this book that he boasts was sent down to him from God. But when we ask: "And who is there to testify that God gave him the book? And which of the prophets foretold that such a prophet would rise up?" — they are at a loss. And we remark that Moses received the Law on Mount Sinai, with God appearing in the sight of all the people in cloud, and fire, and darkness, and storm. And we say that all the prophets from Moses on down foretold the coming of Christ and how Christ God (and incarnate Son of God) was to come and to be crucified and die and rise again, and how He was to be the judge of the living and dead. Then, when we say: "How is it that this prophet of yours did not come in the same way, with others bearing witness to him? And how is it that God did not in your presence present this man with the book to which you refer, even as He gave the Law to Moses, with the people looking on and the mountain smoking, so that you, too, might have certainty?" — they answer that God does as He pleases. "This," we say, "We know, but we are asking how the book came down to your prophet." Then they reply that the book came down to him while he was asleep. Then we jokingly say to them that, as long as he received the book in his sleep and did not actually sense the operation, then the popular proverb applies to him (which runs: "You're spinning me dreams.")

The issue raised here by John of Damascus is the way the *Qur'anic* verses were revealed to Muhammad. Muslims believe that the *Qur'an* was revealed to Muhammad by God through the angel Gabriel. While this is not described in the *Qur'an*, there are many *hadiths* (oral traditions relating to the words and deeds of the

Prophet Muhammad) that speak on the issue. Although the *hadiths* were not yet collected, Ibn Ishaq, the contemporary of John of Damascus, describes in his biography of Muhammad how the revelations came to him in his sleep, or when praying or in a trance-like state.[27]

It is likely that John of Damascus knew about the way the *Qur'anic* text was revealed from conversations and disputes with Muslims not well acquainted with the oral traditions relating to the words and deeds of the prophet Muhammad, which were later collected as *hadiths*, or that he deliberately simplified the information he possessed on that issue:

> When we ask again: "How is it that when he enjoined us in this book of yours not to do anything or receive anything without witnesses, you did not ask him: 'First do you show us by witnesses that you are a prophet and that you have come from God, and show us just what Scriptures there are that testify about you'" — they are ashamed and remain silent. [Then we continue:] "Although you may not marry a wife without witnesses, or buy, or acquire property; although you neither receive an ass nor possess a beast of burden unwitnessed; and although you do possess both wives and property and asses and so on through witnesses, yet it is only your faith and your scriptures that you hold unsubstantiated by witnesses. For he who handed this down to you has no warranty from any source, nor is there anyone known who testified about him before he came. On the contrary, he received it while he was asleep."

Not only Christians, but also other contemporaries of Muhammad, demanded miracles or signs (*aya*, singular or *ayat*, plural) from him to show that he was a prophet of God. The holy book of the Muslims speaks of how idolaters, Jews, and Christians demanded proof from Muhammad. Several *ayat* point to this issue. In the Sura chosen for criticism by John of Damascus, Al-Baqara ("The Heifer"), we read about the pointlessness of bringing miracles to the Jews and the Christians: "And if you brought to those who were given the Scripture every sign, they would not follow your *qiblah* (direction). Nor will you be a follower of their *qiblah*. Nor would they be followers of one another's *qiblah*." (*Qur'an* 2:145.) Again, another Sura, Ar-Rad, states: "The unbelievers say, 'Why has a sign (*ayatun*) not been sent down upon him from his Lord?' Say: 'God leads astray whomsoever He will, and He guides to Him all who are penitent.' " (*Qur'an* 13:27.) Normally, Muslims consider that the greatest miracle performed by Muhammad is the *Qur'an* itself, and also that it is not Muhammad's miracle but God's.

John of Damascus pays attention to Muslim criticism of Christian dogma, particularly the "association" of Christ with God:

> Moreover, they call us Hetaeriasts, or Associators, because, they say, we introduce an association with God by declaring Christ to be the Son of God and God. We say to them in rejoinder: "The Prophets and the Scriptures have delivered this to us, and you, as you persistently maintain, accept the Prophets. So, if we wrongly declare Christ to be the Son of God, it is they who taught this and handed it on to us." But some of them say that it is by misinterpretation that we have represented the Prophets as saying such things, while others say that the Hebrews hated us and deceived us by writing in the name of the Prophets so that we might be lost.

It is clear from the above that to be able to give to the Christians these answers, Muslims knew about what kind of Old Testament quotations Christians cited as proof that Jesus is the promised Messiah. Muslims also accused Christians of attaching different meanings to those passages. The second answer Muslims give is that the Jews hated the Christians so much that they deliberately changed the scripture to deceive them.

Further, we read about the issues dividing Christians and Muslims concerning Jesus Christ:

> And again we say to them: "As long as you say that Christ is the Word of God and Spirit, why do you accuse us of being Hetaeriasts?" For the word, and the spirit, is inseparable from that in which it naturally has existence. Therefore, if the Word of God is in God, then it is obvious that He is God. If, however, He is outside of God, then, according to you, God is without word and without spirit. Consequently, by avoiding the introduction of an associate with God you have mutilated Him. It would be far better for you to say that He has an associate than to mutilate Him, as if you were dealing with a stone or a piece of wood or some other inanimate object. Thus, you speak untruly when you call us Hetaeriasts; we retort by calling you Mutilators of God.

The *Qur'an* often accuses Christians of associating others with God: "To set up partners with Allah is to devise a sin most heinous indeed." (*Qur'an* 4:48), also "Whoever joins other gods with Allah, - Allah will forbid him the garden, and the Fire will be his abode." (*Qur'an* 5:72) and again "Thy Lord does create and choose as He pleases: no choice have they [in the matter]: Glory to Allah! and far is He above the partners they ascribe [to Him]!" (*Qur'an* 28:68) The verb for "associate" or "join" used in the Arabic text of the *Qur'an* is "*shirk*." This word epitomizes the Islamic concept of the sin of polytheism, but in a more general way refers to worshipping other than Allah, associating partners with him, giving his characteristics to others beside him, or not believing in oneness of God. Within Islam, major *shirk* is a forgivable sin if one repents of it while one is alive; but, according to Islamic texts, anyone who dies with this sin unrepentant will never enter paradise. It is the vice that is opposed to the virtue of *tawhid*, literally "declaring [that which is] one," often translated into the English term monotheism.

John of Damascus presents as self-evident the postulate that God has Word and Spirit, and that they are inseparable from Him. If the Muslims in this dispute agree that Jesus is the Word of God, as the *Qur'an* suggests, and that the Word is part of God, then they have to agree that Jesus is God. If they do not agree with the above dogmatic arguments, then John of Damascus changes from a defense of the Trinity to counterattack. He says that if Muslims maintain that God is without Word and without Spirit, they are mutilating God and he calls them "mutilators."

John of Damascus looks at other issues of faith involved in Christian-Muslim controversy:

They furthermore accuse us of being idolaters, because we venerate the cross, which they abominate. And we answer them: "How is it, then, that you rub yourselves against a stone in your Ka'ba and kiss and embrace it?" Then some of them say that Abraham had relations with Agar upon it, but others say that he tied the camel to it, when he was going to sacrifice Isaac. And we answer them: "Since Scripture says that the mountain was wooded and had trees from which Abraham cut wood for the holocaust and laid it upon Isaac, and then he left the asses behind with the two young men, why talk nonsense? For in that place neither is it thick with trees nor is there passage for asses." And they are embarrassed, but they still assert that the stone is Abraham's. Then we say: "Let it be Abraham's, as you so foolishly say. Then, just because Abraham had relations with a

woman on it or tied a camel to it, you are not ashamed to
kiss it, yet you blame us for venerating the cross of Christ
by which the power of the demons and the deceit of the
Devil was destroyed." This stone that they talk about is a
head of that Aphrodite whom they used to worship and
whom they called Khabár. Even to the present day, traces of
the carving are visible on it to careful observers.

The *Qur'an* denies that Jesus died on the cross and
accordingly Muslims detest the cross as a symbol. One
hadith (Sahih al-Bukhari) says that when Jesus Christ
returns before the last judgment He will, among other
things, destroy crosses: "Narrated Abu Huraira: Allah's Apostle said, 'By Him in Whose Hands my soul
is, son of Mary (Jesus) will shortly descend amongst
you people (Muslims) as a just ruler and will break the
Cross and kill the pig and abolish the *Jizya* (a tax taken
from the non-Muslims, who are in the protection of the
Muslim government). Then there will be abundance of
money and nobody will accept charitable gifts.' "[28]

John of Damascus is also well informed that Mecca
lies in an infertile and inhospitable place without vegetation and that asses do not thrive in this desert environment. Abraham himself is quoted in the *Qur'an*
saying about Mecca: "O our Lord! I have made some of
my offspring to dwell in a valley without cultivation."
(*Qur'an* 14:37.)

When John of Damascus questions the Muslims as
to why they venerate the stone[29] of the Ka'ba, he says
that some of them reply that it is "because Abraham
had sexual intercourse with Hagar on it." However, no
hadiths or other sources connect the black stone with
sex and Abraham. Others supposedly answer that they
venerate the stone "because Abraham tied there his

camel when he was about to sacrifice Isaac."

Although the stone is not mentioned in the *Qur'an*, John of Damascus seems to use a particular Muslim popular belief, or perhaps a form of defamation propagated by Christians; either way, he is rebutting Muslim accusations against Christianity. One of the modern Muslim interpretations comes from Y. Michot, who stresses that "The Black Stone" is a mineral aspect or relic of the faith. It is important in popular religion and it is kissed because it was kissed by the Prophet.[30] Probably that answer was also current at the time of John of Damascus.

It is possible that when asked about the Ka'ba and the venerated stone, Muslims gave John of Damascus stories about different stones, and he was confused. Another stone connected with Abraham and venerated by Muslims is the Maqam Ibrahim (the Station of Ibrahim) located in front of the only door of the Ka'ba. It is a boulder about two x three feet in size. In order to complete the upper part of the walls of the Ka'ba, Abraham stood upon a large stone block, which he moved along when each section was completed. When the Ka'ba was finished, the large stone block was left outside, close to the eastern wall of the sanctuary. Today it marks the spot where Abraham used to perform prayers near the Ka'ba.

Then John of Damascus shows that he knows that the *Qur'an* is divided into chapters, Suras, and that each one has a title.

> As has been related, this Mohammed wrote many ridiculous books, to each one of which he set a title. For example, there is the book "On Woman," in which he plainly makes

legal provision for taking four wives and, if it be possible, a thousand concubines—as many as one can maintain, besides the four wives.

In this paragraph, John of Damascus obviously refers to the following *aya* from Sura An-Nisa, which translates as "Women" and not "Woman": "If ye fear that ye shall not be able to deal justly with the orphans, marry women of your choice, Two or three or four; but if ye fear that ye shall not be able to deal justly (with them), then only one, or (a captive) that your right hands possess, that will be more suitable, to prevent you from doing injustice." (*Qur'an* 4:3) Sahas notes that although these two texts show a striking similarity in their content, they differ considerably in their emphasis and intentions. John of Damascus's text seems to ignore the original emphasis and purpose of this legislation – namely to secure protection and justice for the orphans and widows of the battle of Uhud (23rd of March, 625 CE) – and to underline one-sidedly polygamy, which the author is interested in condemning and representing as a general practice among the Muslims in his time.[31]

After discussing marriage, John of Damascus logically considers divorce practices in Islam:

He also made it legal to put away whichever wife one might wish, and, should one so wish, to take to oneself another in the same way. Muhammad had a friend named Zaid. This man had a beautiful wife with whom Muhammad fell in love. Once, when they were sitting together, Muhammad said: "Oh, by the way, God has commanded me to take your wife." The other answered: "You are an apostle. Do as God has told you and take my wife." Rather—to tell the story over from the beginning—he said to him: "God has given me the command that you put away your wife." And he put her away. Then several days later: "Now," he said, "God has commanded me to take her."

Here John of Damascus refers to the Sura Al-Ahzab: "Then when Zaid had dissolved [his marriage] with her, with the necessary [formality], we joined her in marriage to thee: in order that [in future] there may be no difficulty to the believers in [the matter of] marriage with the wives of their adopted sons, when the latter have dissolved with the necessary [formality] [their marriage] with them." (*Qur'an* 33:37.) He knew the name of the adopted son of Muhammad – Zaid – but calls him a friend. If John of Damascus had known that Zaid was the adopted son of Muhammad, he would have included this fact to raise further accusations. He, and other later Christian writers criticizing Islam, look at this incident as a premeditated act and as evidence that Muhammad was not a prophet.

Muslims see this issue differently. First, God annulled adoptions with the following *aya*: "nor has He (Allah) made your adopted sons your sons." (*Qur'an* 33:4.) Then, as stated above in Sura 33, verse 37, Muhammad was commanded to marry the wife of Zaid, his former adoptive son, to confirm the revelation and to give an example to the Muslims.

John of Damascus goes on with his criticism of Islamic matrimonial (marital) customs by linking the incident with the regulations of divorce set down in the *Qur'an*: "Then, after he had taken her and committed adultery with her, he made this law: Let him who will put away his wife. And if, after having put her away, he should return to her, let another marry her. For it is not lawful to take her unless she have been married by another. Furthermore, if a brother puts away his wife, let his brother marry her, should he so wish."

Here John of Damascus gives a very basic view on divorce in Islam to serve his thesis that Islam does not have proper marital arrangements. He continues with the issues of sexual relations between a man and a woman:

> In the same book he gives such precepts as this: "Work the land which God hath given thee and beautify it." And do this, and do it in such a manner—not to repeat all the obscene things that he did.

Obviously, John of Damascus is not very clear on this issue and probably he has in mind the following *aya* from the Sura Al-Baqara: "Your wives are as a tilth unto you; so approach your tilth when or how ye will; but do some good act for your souls beforehand; and fear Allah." (*Qur'an* 2:223.) By vaguely suggesting but not clearly mentioning "the obscene things," John of Damascus possibly created a critical opinion about Islam by knowing and using the Christian readers' Pauline ideas of sexual sins.

He continues his criticism by writing about a Sura that does not exist in the *Qur'an*:

> Then there is the book of "The She-Camel of God." About this camel he says that there was a camel from God and that she drank the whole river and could not pass through two mountains, because there was not room enough. There were people in that place, he says, and they used to drink the water on one day, while the camel would drink it on the next. Moreover, by drinking the water she furnished them with nourishment, because she supplied them with milk instead of water. Then, because these men were evil, they rose up, he says, and killed the camel. However, she had an offspring, a little camel, which, he says, when the mother

had been done away with, called upon God and God took it to Himself.

There is no such Sura as "The She-Camel of God," but the *Qur'an* speaks in several Suras (7, 11, 17, 26, 54, 91) about the prophet Saleh and the female camel he asked God to create as a sign of his prophethood and the omnipotence of the One God. This story was clearly popular with Muslims at the time of John of Damascus, to warrant its inclusion in his critique of Islam. It is not surprising that the story was popular: similar stories circulated about other prophets and in particular about the Prophet Muhammad, because their teachings at the beginning were rejected by the people to whom they were sent.

According to the *Qur'an*, Saleh lived with the Thamud people in an area of the Arabian Peninsula. (There are several suggested places, including Petra.) They, like the people of Mecca, ware idolaters worshiping stone idols. Saleh, like the Prophet Muhammad, preached the One God: "O my people! Worship Allah: ye have no other god but Him." (*Qur'an* 11:61.) But the people of Thamud did not believe him, so they demanded that he should ask a miracle from God as proof of his prophethood. Allah responded to Saleh's prayers, as He responded to the prayers of Jesus to send a table laden with food, and created a pregnant female camel. (The *Qur'an* does not mention that the she-camel of God was pregnant, but the Muslim exegete ibn Kathir, in his *Stories of the Prophets*, says that the Thamud people asked for a miracle, specifically that a pregnant she-camel would issue from a rock.) Although the camel drank a huge amount of water, the people of Thamud benefitted greatly from the animal as she gave them a lot of milk in return. One of the conditions set by God was that the people should not harm the camel: "[I]nflict no harm on her, or a swift penalty will seize you!" (*Qur'an* 11:64.) Despite this commandment, the people slaughtered the camel, and as a punishment God destroyed their houses so that the people of Thamud perished in the ruins: "Blast overtook the wrong-doers, and they lay prostrate in their homes before the morning." (*Qur'an* 11:67.) The story recalls the situation of the Prophet Muhammad in Mecca, his preaching, and his conflict with the majority of his own tribe, Quraish.

John of Damascus somehow knows the story, but most probably from oral traditions as he mentions that the she-camel has offspring, which is not in the *Qur'an*. His arguments relating to it, as we see further, are weak:

> Then we say to them: "Where did that camel come from?" And they say that it was from God. Then we say: "Was there another camel coupled with this one?" And they say: "No." "Then how," we say, "was it begotten?" For we see that your camel is without father and without mother and without genealogy, and that the one that begot it suffered evil. Neither is it evident who bred her. And also, this little camel was taken up. So why did not your prophet, with whom, according to what you say, God spoke, find out about the camel—where it grazed, and who got milk by milking it? Or did she possibly, like her mother, meet with evil people and get destroyed?

The *Qur'an* gives answers to all these questions, and any knowledgeable Muslim should have answered that the camel is another miracle of God: like the creation of Adam without a mother and father from a cloth of blood, like other miracles such as the creation of Jesus without a father: "Such is Allah; He does what He wills." (*Qur'an* 3:40.) Obviously the story of "The She-Camel of God" is presented by John of Damascus in a way to satisfy and entertain a Christian audience.

Then comes more sarcasm only remotely connected to the actual text of the *Qur'an* or the beliefs of Muslims. Just for the sake of argument, John of Damascus ridicules Muhammad's representation of paradise:

> Or did she enter into paradise before you, so that you might have the river of milk that you so foolishly talk about? For you say that you have three rivers flowing in paradise—one of water, one of wine, and one of milk. If your forerunner the camel is outside of paradise, it is obvious that she has dried up from hunger and thirst, or that others have the benefit of her milk—and so your prophet is boasting idly of having conversed with God, because God did not reveal to him the mystery of the camel. But if she is in paradise, she is drinking water still, and you for lack of water will dry up in the midst of the paradise of delight. And if, there being no water, because the camel will have drunk it all up, you thirst for wine from the river of wine that is flowing by, you will become intoxicated from drinking pure wine and collapse under the influence of the strong drink and fall asleep. Then, suffering from a heavy head after sleeping and being sick from the wine, you will miss the pleasures of paradise. How, then, did it not enter into the mind of your prophet that this might happen to you in the paradise of delight? He never had any idea of what the camel is leading to now, yet you did not even ask him, when he held forth to you with his dreams on the subject of the three rivers. We plainly assure you that this wonderful camel of yours has preceded you into the souls of asses, where you, too, like beasts are destined to go. And there is the exterior darkness and everlasting punishment, roaring fire, sleepless worms, and hellish demons.

John of Damascus is right that the *Qur'an* speaks

of rivers in paradise; however, there are not three, but four: "in it are rivers of water incorruptible; rivers of milk of which the taste never changes; rivers of wine, a joy to those who drink; and rivers of honey pure and clear." (*Qur'an* 47:15.) The rest of the section above just pretends to be a scholastic argument. After a fairly coherent beginning it looks like the arguments are becoming more unimportant.

But the next section has more substance:

> Again, in the book of "The Table," Muhammad says that the Christ asked God for a table and that it was given Him. For God, he says, said to Him: "I have given to thee and thine an incorruptible table."

> Here, John of Damascus is certainly right. In the Sura "The Table" (Al-Maeda), Jesus is challenged by the Jews, to whom he was sent as a prophet, to perform a miracle, like the prophet Saleh, as a proof of his prophethood: "Said Jesus the son of Mary: 'O Allah, our Lord, send down to us a table [spread with food] from the heaven to be for us a festival for the first of us and the last of us and a sign from You.' " (*Qur'an* 5:114.) God answers the prayer of Jesus by sending a table laden with food as proof of His omnipotence, and at the same time warns the people to whom He sent Jesus as a prophet: "Allah said: 'I will send it down unto you: But if any of you after that resisteth faith, I will punish him with a penalty such as I have not inflicted on any one among all the peoples.' " (*Qur'an* 5:115.)

Suddenly John of Damascus goes back to the Sura "The Heifer (Al-Baqara): "And again, in the book of The Heifer, he says some other stupid and ridiculous things, which, because of their great number, I think must be passed over."

Again, we do not know what John of Damascus means by "stupid and ridiculous things" in Sura 2, Al-Baqara. Maybe, he is again feeding the negative attitude and prejudices of his audience.

As the end of John of Damascus's chapter "The Heresy of the Ishmaelites" approaches, we continue to read more unconnected statements about Muhammad. For example, he writes: "He made it a law that they be circumcised and the women, too."

There is nothing said directly about male circumcision in the *Qur'an*. However, there is indirect advice to Muslims, as they are followers of the religion of Abraham, that they must adhere to the instruction given by God to Abraham. "It is the religion of your father, Abraham." (*Qur'an* 22:78.) The Arabs as Semites practiced circumcision as part of cleanliness rituals, or as a tribal mark before accepting Islam. John of Damascus is critical of circumcision because, in his time, the view against circumcision had gained acceptance as a Christian norm. However, in the New Testament both views can be found, against and in favor of circumcision.[32]

Then, in this short sentence we come to a controversial issue: John of Damascus accuses Muhammad of making a law that women should be circumcised, too. While it is remarkable that John of Damascus would have such wide and intimate knowledge of Muslim customs, he is not very accurate on the issue.

Female circumcision is not a teaching of the *Qur'an* and predates Islam. It is practiced by a minority of Muslims today and surely that was also the case at the time of John of Damascus. During the time of the Prophet Muhammad it was practiced in the area of Hijaz, the mountain ridge along the Arabian Peninsula west coast where Mecca and Medina are located.

One *hadith* from the collection of Abu Dawood, quoting Umm Atiyyah al-Ansariyyah, narrates: "A woman used to perform circumcision in Medina. The Prophet (peace_be_upon_him) said to her: Do not cut severely as that is better for a woman and more desirable for a husband."[33] The author of the collection and many other classical Muslim commentators observed that this *hadith* is poor in authenticity and has a broken chain of transmitters. Accordingly there is a wide range of opinion among Sunni *ulema* (lawyers) about female circumcision – ranging from obligatory to forbidden.

A study about the range of the practice today found that female circumcision is also practiced among Coptic Christians in Egypt, Orthodox Christians and Falasha Jews in Ethiopia, and Protestant groups and Catholics in Sudan and Kenya.[34]

Finally, John of Damascus talks about issues important to Christians – the Sabbath and baptism. He mentions the Muslim position, but he leaves it without comment:

> And he ordered them not to keep the Sabbath and not to be baptized. And, while he ordered them to eat some of the things forbidden by the Law, he ordered them to abstain from others. He furthermore absolutely forbade the drinking of wine.

Here it is not clear whether John of Damascus means the Jewish Sabbath or the Christian Sunday, the day of the resurrection of Jesus Christ. The *Qur'an* prescribes the observance of the Friday in the Sura Al-Jumua: "O ye who believe! When the call is proclaimed to prayer on Friday (the Day of Assembly), hasten earnestly to the Remembrance of Allah, and leave off business." (*Qur'an* 62:9.) Islam chose Friday as a day of collective prayers in order to separate and distinguish itself from Judaism and Christianity.[35] Moreover, for Muslims there is no baptism. A ritual with similar meaning is the *shahāda*, or the profession of faith. John of Damascus is right that certain foods forbidden in the Old Testament are allowed by the *Qur'an* and that others are forbidden. He is totally correct about wine. Here the chapter finishes somewhat abruptly.

CONCLUSION

In his Chapter 101, "The Heresy of the Ishmaelites," John of Damascus reviews the origin of Islam, the Prophet, the Scriptures, the doctrines, and the religious and social practices of Muslims. Although well-informed about the content of the *Qur'an*, John of Damascus does not quote precisely from the holy book of the Muslims. Some of his information sounds like hearsay from *hadith* literature and his work takes the form of an apologetic lecture to a Christian audience. From his writings one gets the impression that Muslims are not able to answer the accusations raised by Christians; but any educated Muslim who has read the *Qur'an* can answer many of these. Also, in the eighth century there were many Muslim scholars available for disputes with Christians. Moreover, John of Damascus speaks haughtily of ignorant people of low cultural standing below the Christians. J. E. Merrill concludes that one cannot but note the tendency to discredit everything Muslim. It is as though the author had formed an unfavorable opinion in advance, and now brings in exhibits as proof.[36]

John of Damascus's information about Islam and the accusations he makes were repeated and elaborated in the following centuries by Byzantine polemics and right up to the nineteenth century by Catholic and Protestant theologians criticizing Islam. He set the scene and the tone for misinterpretation and misunderstanding of Muslims and their beliefs in the Christian world. The difference is that John of Damascus viewed Islam as a Christian heresy, whereas later Byzantine and European theologians regarded Islam as a pagan belief. He also failed to see in Islam a new dynamic and moral force.

Nevertheless, it is quite possible that with his writing John of Damascus stimulated the development of Muslim theology. One century later, Muslims started to use biblical texts in defense of the prophethood of Muhammad. This development come shortly after John of Damascus's challenges to Islam, such as: "And who of the prophets foretold that such a prophet would arise?" So Muslim scholars began looking for texts from the Prophets of the Old Testament to use them in disputes with Christians.[37] John of Damascus could also have stimulated the Mu'tazilite theology, according to which the attributes of God are not entities in themselves but are of the nature of God and constitute His essence.[38]

John of Damascus was a product of his times. His words represent the first substantive Christian engagement with the Muslim community in writing. But his tone is not conciliatory and clearly not an approach that promotes constructive engagement with Muslims. Having the benefit of historical hindsight, it could be said that he set the not always pleasant tone for future Christian-Muslim interactions up to the end of nineteenth century. Many misunderstandings of both simple people and the educated alike in the religious, political, and even economic sectors have their origins dating as far back as John of Damascus.

John of Damascus is a revered Father of the Church, and is recognized as a saint. He is considered an authoritative voice for medieval and contemporary Orthodox theology. Tradition attributes to John of Damascus the epithet "Chrysorrhoas"[39] (Golden-flowing). His memory is commemorated by the Eastern Orthodox Church on December 4, the date of his death, and by the Roman Catholic Church on March 27. As late as 1890 CE, Pope Leo XIII declared him a doctor of the Roman Catholic Church, and he is sometimes called the last of the Church Fathers by the Roman Catholic Church.[40]

John of Damascus's writings and life could be a lesson for Christian-Muslim relations today. Even if we differ in some central matters of theology, we share much in common with regard to our faith in One God. And when we disagree, the story of John of Damascus gives us a historical example of how, despite having differences, we can honor and respect one another.

Notes

1 All quotations from the *Qur'an* are from Abdullah Yusuf Ali, *The Holy Qur'an, Text, Translation & Commentary* (Lahore, 1938).
2 Orthodox, Chalcedonian, and Melkite are used as synonyms.
3 William H C Frend, *The Rise of the Monophysites Movement* (Cambridge: Cambridge University Press, 1972), p. 351.
4 Daniel J.Sahas, *John of Damascus on Islam: The Heresy of the*

Ishmaelites (Leiden: Brill Academic Publishers, 1972), p. 23.

5 The word comes from the Syriac word *malkāyā*, meaning "imperial." In Arabic, the word *Malakī* also means "imperial."

6 Hugh Goddar, *A History of Christian-Muslim Relations* (Chicago: New Amsterdam Books, 2000), p. 38.

7 Sahas, p. 7.

8 Sahas, p. 17.

9 Sahas, p. 33.

10 Sahas, p. 35.

11 Richard Hooker writes that Walid I instituted Arabic as the only official language of the empire. He decreed that all administration was to be done only in Arabic. It was this move that would cement the primacy of Arabic language and culture in the Islamic world.

12 Andrew Louth, *St. John Damascene: Tradition and Originality in Byzantine Theology* (Oxford: Oxford University Press, 2002), p. 7.

13 John of Damascus, *Fount of Knowledge*, Migne, *Patrologia Graeca*, XCIV, p. 533.

14 Sahas, p. 58.

15 Louth, p. 77.

16 John of Damascus, *De Haeresibus*, Migne, *Patrologia Graeca*, XCIV, cols. 763-73, 1864. All quotations from "The Heresy of the Ishmaelites" are from Frederic H. Chase, Jr., trans., *Writings. Fathers of the Church*, vol. 37 (Washington, DC, 1958.)

17 Sahas, p. 69.

18 Sahas, p. 70.

19 All quotations from the Bible are from New International Version.

20 Sahas, p. 71.

21 Strabo, *The Geography of Strabo: Literally Translated, with Notes*, trans. by H. C. Hamilton & W. Falconer (London: H. G. Bohn, 1854-1857), pp. 185-215.

22 Herodotus, *The Histories of Herodotus* (New York: Harper & Brothers, 1898), p. 73.

23 Sahas, p. 72.

24 ibn Ishaq, *Sirat Rasul Allah. The Life of Muhammad*, trans. by A. Gullaume (London, New York, Toronto: Oxford Uni-

versity Press, 1955), p. 79.

25 Sahas, p. 75.

26 ibn Ishaq, p. 152.

27 ibn Ishaq, p. 106.

28 Muhammad Muhsin Khan, *The Translation of the Meanings of Sahih Al-Bukhari*, vol. 1, Book 34, Hadith 425 (Cairo, 1959).

29 The Black Stone is built into the eastern wall of the Ka'ba.

30 Yahya Michot, Lecture, Introduction to Islamic Theology course, Hartford Seminary, Hartford, Connecticut, December 3, 2008.

31 Sahas, p. 90.

32 Jesus was circumcised (Lk 1:59), as were his disciples. The Apostle Paul let Timothy be circumcised (Acts 16:3). Paul cautioned the Corinthians against uncircumcising themselves (1 Cor 7:18), but also said that circumcision is nothing, and uncircumcision is nothing; but obeying the commandments of God is everything (1 Cor 7:17-20).

33 Umm Atiyyah; Abu Dawud, al-Bayhaq, *Partial Translation of Sunan Abu-Dawud*, Book 41: General Behavior (Kitab Al-Adab), Hadith 5251, University of Southern California, http://www.usc.edu/schools/college/crcc/engagement/resources/texts/muslim/hadith/abudawud/041.sat.html (accessed on February 17, 2009).

34 Carla Makhlouf Obermeyer, *Female genital surgeries: the known, the unknown, and the unknowable*, Med Anthropol Q., 1999 Mar; 13(1):79-106. http://csde.washington.edu/fogarty/casestudies/shellduncanmaterials/day%202/Obermeyer,%20C.%20(1999)%20Female%20genital%20surgeries.pdf (accessed February 18, 2009).

35 W. Montgomery Watt, *Muhammad: prophet and statesman* (London: Oxford University Press, 1961), p. 93.

36 John E. Merrill, "John of Damascus on Islam," *Muslim World*, 41 no. 1 (Jan 1951): 93.

37 Sahas, p. 81.

38 Sahas, p. 83.

39 *Chrysorrhoas* is also the ancient Greek name of the main river of Damascus and it means "golden stream."

40 Sahas, pp. 38-48.

CONTEMPORARY DIALOGUE

Byzantine and Contemporary Greek Orthodox Approaches to Islam

Anastasios Yannoulatos

Translated by George C. Papademetriou

Introduction

Eastern Orthodoxy encountered Islam from its inception, since Islam emerged and spread where Orthodox Christianity flourished, that is, in the Middle East. The author offers an overview of Byzantine and Orthodox dialogues and relations with Islam. Eastern Christians had the *Qur'an* available in Greek and lived in dialogue with Muslims. Theologians such as John of Damascus, Abukarra, Gregory Palamas, and Gennadios Scholarios lived in Islamic societies and dialogued with and critiqued Islam. The meeting with Islam not only took the form of a polemical clash and confrontation but also evolved, after the fall of Constantinople in the fifteenth century, into many centuries of silent coexistence, often articulated on the intellectual level with a concrete form of theological dialogue that sought to define the differences and the positions of the two religious forms and experiences. The first patriarch under the Muslims, Gennadios Scholarios, presented a confession of faith that was translated into Arabic for the sultan, who was interested in learning about Christianity. In the modern move toward inter-religious dialogue, Orthodox Christians and Muslims, having co-existed for centuries, have had numerous conferences and dialogues, despite differences and past conflicts. This essay presents a historical overview of these dialogues and relationships.

HISTORICAL OVERVIEW

The Three Phases of Byzantine-Islamic Dialogue

Christian Byzantium, as a political and social entity, having experienced the aggressive impulse of the new religion, mobilized an entire defensive system. Within this defensive dynamic, a series of theological treatises appeared, having the external scheme of a dialogue, a *dialexis*, between representatives of Islam and Christianity. Some of these treatises summarize real discussions and dialogues between Christians and Muslims.

The Byzantines lived nearest the cradle of the Muslim world and had the potential for knowledge of Islam from the original sources, something that took place later for Western Christians who lived farther away geographically and sociologically. The analysis and criticism of the entire *Qur'an*, with the translation of many sections into Greek by Niketas of Byzantium, was completed a little before the time of Patriarch Photios, in the ninth century. The first Latin translation of the *Qur'an* was realized much later, in the middle of the twelfth century.

We can discern a dramatic evolution of the Byzantine theoretical stance in opposition to Islam. In the first phase, which lasted from the eighth century until the middle of the ninth century CE, its disposition was more of taunting and undervaluing Islam. Saint John of Damascus (d. 750 or 784) was one of the first Christians to occupy himself with the topic. He thought that the new Muslim religious teaching was not a serious issue. From the theological aspect, Islam for him was a religious fabrication appropriate only for a primitive people. John of Damascus conceptually presented some parts of Islamic teachings, which he characterized as "worthy of laughter."[1] It is usually thought that John of Damascus considered Islam a "Christian heresy." This is true, as he stated in the section "Against Heresies" of his main work, *On the Source of Knowledge,* in which he characterized the Ishmaelites or Hagarenes as the 101st heresy.[2] However, in the terminology of John of Damascus, the word "heresy" has a wider application that also includes the Greek schools of philosophy and other religious forms.

The Bishop of Charan, or Karron, of Mesopotamia (Iraq), Theodore, named Abukarra (d. 820 or 825), methodically considered the new religion in his work *Against the Jewish and Saracene Heresies.*[3] Written in dialogical form, it can be considered the first serious attempt to understand and encounter Islam. Theodore combated the Muslim criticism of Christianity and developed various well-thought-out arguments from Christian doctrine, emphasizing that the truth of Christianity is derived from fact and that it is compelling despite all external weaknesses.

This first period of comparative writing by Christians of the East on Islamic religion took place in Syria, then the center of the Caliphate. The works of the two theologians referred to above express a living experience based on immediate contact with Muslims in personal dialogue. Both writers knew the *Qur'an* in the original and lived within a Muslim society.

In the second phase (middle of the ninth to the middle of the fourteenth centuries) the center of writings about Islam moved to the capital of the Byzantine Empire. The impressive successes of Islam, especially its spread, began to become a nightmare for the Byzantines. They saw this new religion, in spite of – or possibly because of – its logical and moral weaknesses, become a serious threat to the Empire. For that reason, a more aggressive posture was adopted.

Many polemical texts were published during this period (such as those of Samona Gazes,[4] Euthymius Zigabenus,[5] Niketas Choniates,[6] Bartholomaios of Edessa,[7] etc.). The most representative of these is the work authored by Niketas Choniates, *Refutation of the Book Forged by the Arab Mohammed*.[8] This treatise is a typical polemic attempt to prove that Islam is an incoherent religion.[9]

The third phase in the Byzantine encounter with Islam (mid-fourteenth to mid-fifteenth centuries) can be characterized as mild criticism and objective evaluation of Islam. In the discussions and dialogic communications, the protagonists were exceptional Byzantine personalities such as Saint Gregory Palamas (d. 1359),[10] the monk Joseph Bryennios (d. 1425),[11] and emperors such as John VI Katakouzenos (d. 1383)[12] and Manuel II Paleologos (d. 1425).[13] In the last century of Byzantium, the Byzantines developed an interest and disposition to dialogue with Muslims. The Muslims, however, appeared to avoid dialogue. The Emperor John Katakouzenos characteristically noted the following:

> The Muslims hinder some of them to engage in dialogue with the Christians. Evidently, if they never dialogue between them, they will never come to the knowledge of the purity of truth. The Christians on the other hand, trusting the purity of their faith and that they hold correct and true dogmas without any reservations, do not prevent anyone from engaging in dialogue, but with permission and authority, each one of them engages in dialogue with all those who are willing and desire to be engaged in dialogue.[14]

The basic theoretical elements of Islamic-Christian Byzantine dialogue can now be summarized. In the beginning the Byzantines saw Islam as parallel to, and a renewal of, Arianism. The Muslim criticism of Christianity was focused mainly against the divinity of Christ and the dogma of the Holy Trinity and, secondarily, against certain forms of Christian worship and the inconsistency of Christians toward their faith.

The Christian criticism of Islam had as its primary goal the person of Muhammad, doubting his prophetic office. The main arguments were that Muhammad was not foretold by the prophets, that he did not present witnesses for the prophecies that he received, that he neither performed miracles nor foretold the future, and, generally, that his moral constitution was not sufficiently high-level. Most of the Byzantines considered that Muhammad served the work of the Antichrist and that he was the forerunner of the Christian "last age" (the end of the world). Moreover, some did not hesitate to characterize him as the Antichrist. These strict characterizations were abandoned later, at least from the official texts. Subsequently, the Byzantines preferred theoretical conflict with the Muslims through comparing the doctrines and lives of the founders of the two religions, that is, Jesus and Muhammad.

Also, the Christian writers turned against the *Qur'an*. They compared it to the Holy Scriptures, pointing out what they considered to be falsifications, misunderstandings, and inconsistencies, attacking especially the Muslim conviction that the *Qur'an* is the uncreated word of God. In a historical analysis of its information and doctrines, they concluded that the holy book of Islam consisted of underdeveloped theological and ethical teachings. Also, sharp criticism was exercised against the family laws of Islam (laws on marriage and sexual behavior), the views on "holy war" and slavery, and the materialistic understanding of the other life with images of gluttony and sexual satisfaction.

Both the attack on Islamic views and the defense against Muslim criticism were carried out on the basis of philosophical reflection and the witness of the Holy Scriptures. Whether or not the arguments used were convincing, the Byzantines in their treatises showed that there exists an area of common meaning in the two religions that makes "dialogue" possible.

Introduction of Serious Christian-Muslim Dialogue

The Byzantines introduced and are the forerunners of the Christian-Muslim dialogue that is promoted in our day on an international level. To make this clear, I will expand on three characteristic examples:

1. The atmosphere of Muslim-Christian dialogue takes on an excellence and elegance in a brief text of Saint Gregory Palamas (d. 1359), an Athonite monk who later became Archbishop of Thessaloniki.

These dialogues[15] are apparently a summary of real conversations. Gregory Palamas was clear and steadfast in his Christian positions but, simultaneously, remained calm and patient in his opposition to Muslim tenets. Since he was interested in convincing his partners in conversation, he supported his arguments on the existing common points of the two religions. For example, he began with the definition of God as accepted by the Muslims in the witnesses of the *Qur'an*, wherein Christ is portrayed as Logos of God.

> Only God is eternal being and remains forever, without beginning, unchangeable, without end, unaltered, unconfused, infinite [he avoids the title "Father"] ... This God who is the only being without beginning cannot be without reason [*alogos*]... cannot be without wisdom [*asophos*]; therefore, reason [*logos*] and wisdom [*sophia*] are of God.[16]
> But also the *logos* (reason) was never without spirit. You also as Turks confess this; you say that Christ is God's reason (*logos*), and the spirit is of God, because the Holy Spirit cannot be separated ... There was never nor ever will be a time when God was without spirit [*apnous*] or without reason [*alogos*].[17]

Palamas, in referring to the Triune God, used the following image: "At the same time as the sun's splendor is born from the sun, the sun's rays proceed from it."[18]

The arguments presented by Palamas are versatile

and dialectically selective. He does not avoid touching critical points in order to maintain a superficial impression of harmony. In reference to his view on Muhammad, Palamas answered, with courtesy but also clarity, as follows: "He who does not believe in the words of the Master, cannot love the Master; for that reason we do not love Muhammad."[19] He sees Muhammad in the same way that his Byzantine predecessors did: Muhammad is devoid of any prophetic witnesses and miracles and for that reason is unconvincing.[20] To the usual Muslim argument that the success and victories of Islam prove its supersession, Gregory Palamas responded that this might be true "in war and sword and killing and plunder ... These do not proceed from God who is good."[21]

During the entire dialogue, Palamas made every effort not to touch the religious sensitivity of the Muslims. Even though there was no agreement, there was a climate of respect and mutual esteem. "Following the dialogue the Turkish leaders rose and greeted the Archbishop of Thessalonike with reverence and departed."[22] Whenever Palamas realized that his dialogic partners found themselves in a difficult situation, he hastened by versatility and kindness to contribute calmness to the electrified atmosphere. He used discretionary humor: "I cheered them with a smile to the imam, saying: 'If we would agree in words, then we would be of one faith.'"[23] In this way friendship was retained, even though agreement was not. As one Muslim expressed, expectantly and full of hope: "There will be a time when we will agree with each other."[24]

2. Another distinguished Byzantine personality who engaged gracefully and gently the burning issues of the Christian-Muslim dialogue were the Emperor Manuel II Paleologos (d. 1425). The work that he left us refers with clarity to a "dialogue"[25] that took place (1390 and 1391) when Manuel was staying in the Turkish court in Proussa. There he had opportunity to have dialogues with Muslim intellectuals on theological issues. In the first of the twenty-six dialogues are criticisms of the various theological views of Islam. The subsequent dialogues deal with the theological proofs of basic Christian dogmas and moral doctrines. In the works of Manuel, the scornful expressions and insulting adjectives that were traditionally used by the Byzantines were avoided. The atmosphere was conducive of real and objective dialogue. The first dialogue begins as follows:

> I was seated at supper by the fire and an old man (Muslim) was doing his usual thing - one thing with our, and another with his own, children. Both being sons, mind and wisdom participate, and not a small mutual understanding of the word. And the old man told me: "It is my concern, I believe burdensome: I beg you to listen to me and transmit the word in our absence."[26]

The entire text demonstrates that Manuel was a well-educated and deep theologian, an articulate speaker with personal, penetrating thought and sincere interest for true dialogue with the Muslims.

3. This disposition toward creative dialogue was continued during the early years following the capture of Constantinople by the Turks. A little after the fall, the conqueror, Sultan Muhammad, accompanied by theologians of the court visited (1455 or early 1456)

the newly elected Patriarch Gennadios Scholarios and asked to be informed with precision about the religion of the Christians. The presentation of the Christian teachings by the Patriarch impressed the conqueror, but it was impossible for the military man to assimilate the philosophical distinctions of the theologian. Hence, he asked Scholarios to write a synopsis of all that he had presented orally. Gennadios therefore wrote *On the Only Way for the Salvation of Mankind.*[27] This text was translated into Turkish-Arabic by a competent Greek translator and was given to the Sultan, who asked for a shorter, more concise, and simplified exposition.

Gennadios composed a new text in summary, known as the *Confession of Faith,*[28] in which he left out numerous points, changed others for simplification, and added new clarifications. In this work every effort was made to adapt the Christian positions to the level of Turkish theological thought. A theologian and church leader who stood before an all-powerful Muslim ruler represented the Christian teaching here. Consequently, everything was set aside, including the polemical and taunting phrases of the writers of the Byzantine period, who by writing from their place of security let loose attacks against their adversaries far away, thereby gathering laurels from their fellow believers.

Gennadios attempted to articulate the known "dangerous" Trinitarian and Christological dogmas, using language easily accepted and understood by his conversational partner. He used the symbol of fire to clarify the dogma of the Holy Trinity: "I believe that from the nature of God springs the Logos and Spirit as from the fire spring light and heat."[29] Gennadios refrained from problematic allusion to Islam or to the prophet whose name was brought up by the listener. The conversation remained serious and objective. An austere defender of Orthodoxy, in his dialogue with the Muslims Gennadios Scholarios used accessible language, not strictly dogmatic, which would accommodate primary understanding and promote continued discussion. This principle, which was applied in a responsible manner at that critical historical moment and generally continues to be in force in contemporary inter-religious dialogue, is summarized beautifully in a position noted at the end of his confession:

> ... That to the uninitiated the principle of more admissible lessons of our prodigious faith must be given with greater precision, as was done here and stated clearly in order to make possible the translation into another language, just as these (lessons) were interpreted in Arabic well.[30]

Some fifteen years later, Gennadios had another opportunity for dialogue with Muslim leaders. In 1470 a Turkish soldier under orders from his superior summoned Scholarios from the Monastery of Prodromos and brought him to Pheres, where two Pashas wished to be informed with regard to the divinity of Jesus. The wise old patriarch, using his theological and philosophical armor, took as the starting points of the development of the Christian positions those that the pious Muslims already accepted, especially underlining the self-consciousness of Jesus Christ, whom the *Qur'an* acknowledges as Logos and Spirit of God. He also did not hesitate to use the Sibylline oracles and the pagan Greek "oracles" that he considered vehicles of divine messages. In relation to religions outside Christianity, Gennadios accepted that God does not find it difficult to see in the redemptive plan even the work of the demons. God educated human beings with infinite tolerance.[31]

With these texts the Orthodox theologian and patriarch, Gennadios Scholarios, who was apparently pressured by new historical circumstances, opened a new road of theological dialogue with Islam. He avoided sharp attacks, made use of Muslim convictions and, without betraying his faith, attempted in accordance with economy to adapt his language to the theological and spiritual level of his conversationalists, showing them his love and respect, regardless of their convictions.

The Phase of Silence and Monologue

The atmosphere that had begun to be shaped in the last century of the Byzantine Empire changed quickly during the Turkish occupation that followed (mid-fifteenth to the mid-eighteenth centuries). The dialogue that had begun was disrupted and entered a fourth phase. For the Orthodox Christians in the Balkans it was a period of long silence and resistance, while for the Muslims it was a period of dialogue from a position of power.[32]

During this fourth phase, the Eastern Orthodox Church underwent difficult experiences. In spite of the tolerance that some of the enlightened leaders of the Ottoman Empire had, Muslim triumphalism burst out often, and various politico-social pressures created waves of Islamicization in Asia Minor, the Balkans, and Crete.[33] For the first time, the phenomenon of crypto-Christians appeared – that is, groups of Christian people under unimaginably great pressure that were forced to accept Islam externally, while secretly keeping Christian convictions within their family and personal lives.[34] Finally, after a few generations, the Islamic majority absorbed them. This phenomenon, however, lasted only a few centuries.

An answer to the monologue of coercion by the Ottomans was given by the vigorous liturgical life of the Orthodox, which had as its center the Holy Eucharist and the holy days of the Passion and the Resurrection, with an experiential participation in the mystery of the Cross of Christ. It presented a unique "mystical dialogue," in which Orthodox Christians responded to the pressure with an enduring silence, full of prayer and doxological attention to the paradoxical will of God and to the eschatological hope of liberation.

In our time we could say that we have already entered into a fifth phase – for the Orthodox – of the Muslim-Christian dialogue. For the last thirty years, meetings between Muslims and Christians have been concentrated in academic circles. At present, dialogue is promoted mainly in university circles representing both religious communities, in scholarly institutions or research centers, and in international church organizations.

There have been two very important watersheds in this dialogue in our time. The first is the Second Vatican Council, which deeply changed the attitude and the stance of the Roman Catholic world in regard to this problem, especially the declaration on the relationship of the Catholic Church with non-Christian communities (*Nostra aetate*).[35] The second is the inter-religious dialogue initiated by the World Council of Churches and implemented in the 1970s, which led to the establishment of the Department of Dialogue with Men of Other Faiths and Ideologies, later called Dialogues with People of Living Faiths.

The Orthodox cooperated from the beginning, with great interest, in this W.C.C. department. The present author had the opportunity to be a member of this first group of cooperation for many years. Also, in the inter-church agency of European churches, the Conference of European Churches, a special interest has developed for Christian-Muslim dialogue.[36] From my personal experience, I can discern the sincere desire for a thoughtful Christian-Muslim dialogue and for active participation by the Orthodox.

The Framework and
Problematic of the Contemporary Phase

New Situations and Horizons

The contemporary phase of the Christian-Muslim dialogue is developing in new situations and perspectives. First, following the last 150 years of research, a more exact scholarly knowledge of Islam has set aside serious misunderstandings and, for that reason, an exact positioning of the topics for discussion and correct evaluation. Second, at least from the Christian side, the attitude and disposition have changed. Many Christians today, along with self-criticism, show understanding and respect for the spiritual treasures that the Muslims have preserved. Also, the role of spiritual power within history is acknowledged. In ages past, it was mainly the negative points and differences that were emphasized. Today, the positives are underlined as well as are the common spiritual ground and common spiritual experience.

Third, we now see Islam as a system of ideas and values influencing millions of people with whom we are called to live and work together on our small planet, on this unique megalopolis, with the intensity of mutual dependence of human beings. Often we are obligated to encounter the new challenges of our age, no longer speaking to one another, or one against the other, but sharing in common the new signs of the times and the new, thorny problems set forth by the coming world.

Fourth, in the contemporary age, inter-religious dialogue from the Christian side represents Christians of various churches. The immediate participation of the Orthodox in this dialogue of Christians with Muslims, as will be pointed out later, has something special to offer.

Impasse and Hope (Expectations)

A dialogue that has as its purpose the objective and sober understanding of religious perspectives and experiences of other human beings exhibits broad, common, fundamental convictions that support both Islam and Christianity. Christians can rediscover forgotten points of emphasis – for example, intense experience of the transcendence of God, obedience to God's will, awe in communication with God, mobilization of the whole of the psychosomatic participation in prayer, etc.

However, we should not look at things romantically. Dialogue presupposes that both sides desire such relation and quest. To date, this desire has been cultivated more in the Christian world. In the Muslim world, a similar desire does not appear. In contrast, we have several examples of new outbreaks of fanaticism and enmity (for example, Persia, Lebanon, Libya). For that reason it is best to speak of a dialogue between *some* Christians and *some* Muslims.

A dialogue certainly can contribute to overcoming the long period of misunderstandings, but ultimately it is natural to arrive at the boundaries where the two religious experiences are radically distinct. Such clear structural difference culminates in the faith of Christians in the mystery of the Holy Trinity and in the mystery of the incarnation of the Logos – the divinity of Jesus Christ. Muslims respect Jesus as a great prophet but reject the Cross and especially its significance for the salvation of humanity. The Cross remains a "scandal" and "foolishness" for classical Muslim thought. In addition, there is opposition to the basic worship experience of Christians, that is, the Holy Eucharist – personal, experiential communion with Christ. When the Muslims converted Christian churches to Muslim places of worship, they first destroyed three elements: the symbol of the Cross; the Holy Altar table; and the iconostasis (icon screen) with the figures of the saints who lived "in Christ."

Thus, even though we agree about what constitutes

the first stage of religious experience, the Muslims remain at this first stage and refuse to proceed and to accept that which constitutes the deeper Christian experience: the experience of the communion of God and humankind in Christ through the Holy Spirit. Here the dialogue can do nothing more than correct the misunderstandings created by fanatics. The dialogue can contribute to expressing greater accuracy in descriptions of religious experiences, thereby making it possible to arrive at clear distinctions and freedom of choice.

Muslim-Christian dialogue appears more hopeful when Christians and Muslims, with respect to their differences, sit together to face new topics such as the challenges of our technocratic age and the emergence of the new world community. If each party, after delving into its deeper religious convictions and experiences, could interpret them in order to face specific critical issues, this would contribute not only to mutual awareness but also to spiritual communication and contact. Such issues are, for example, secularism, impersonalization of society, destruction of the physical environment, human rights, world justice, and world peace.

Also helpful to the rapprochement of Christians and Muslims is their participation in a broader conversation on the dynamic of religious ideas. The writer is obligated to confess that he felt this polite approach in three instances:

(1) In the first inter-religious meeting at Colombo, Sri Lanka (1974), organized by the W.C.C., "Toward a World Community"; (2) In the second inter-religious conference, organized by UNESCO (Bangkok, 1980),

for the study on the attitude of the various religions toward protection of human rights; and (3) At the convo-
cation of the World Conference on Religion and Peace
(Nairobi, 1984), on how each religious person in the
world can struggle for world peace and disarmament.
Such common-life events and the mutual seeking by
representatives of various religious convictions simultaneously broaden the bilateral dialogue and reveal a
common ground for monotheistic, prophetic, religious
experiences.

The Special Contribution of the Orthodox

It is obvious that the cultural tradition and heritage
of the Christians of the East bring them much closer to
the Muslim world, with whom they have coexisted for
many centuries. In spite of deep theological differences
and dramatic conflicts in the past, there is a move from
many sides toward one common cultural ground.

A significant affirmation that resulted from scholarly research is the close relationship of Eastern Christianity to Islam from the outset. Orthodox Christians
followed various expressions and aspects of Islam, recognizing enough connecting signs, even in an altered
form. I would venture to risk the proposal that the
creation of the Islamic faith, to a great extent, was the
result of a deficiency created by an unfortunate "dialogue" between Muhammad and corrupted Christian
views that were widespread in his time. It is indisputable that the *Qur'an* has absorbed, adopted, and transformed numerous Christian views that Muhammad
absorbed from direct communication with Eastern

Christianity. Muhammad met and had relationships with numerous witnesses, such as a Christian monk or monks from the East. In studying the basic theological trends in the *Qur'an* one can confirm its continuous underlying dialogue with Christian views, which at times derive from following the "positive way" (faith in God, angels, prophets, written revelation, respect for the person of Jesus, the ever-virginity of Mary) and at other times from following the persistent "negative way" (the fatherhood of Allah and the rejection of the divinity of Jesus Christ, the crucifixion, the resurrection, and teachings on the Holy Trinity).

Many Muslims encountered Christianity as an altered version or variation of Islam, and the Orthodox saw the latter as a corrupted Christianity, which was not understood in its depth. Many points in the teachings of Islam were the result of a "hasty dialogue," in which Christian positions were described and interpreted superficially, even though they were not understood. In the typical life of worship – the daily rhythm of Islamic prayer – one clearly receives the impression that it is similar to the prayer form of the Eastern monks. Abba Kassianos (d. 435), in describing the manner of monastic prayer in the East, wrote the following:

> All the Eastern monasteries, and especially those in Egypt, have the following canon (practice) of prayer and psalmody: The brothers gather together during the time of the synaxis. When the psalm is finished, they do not kneel immediately, but before bending the knees for a while remain standing with their hands extended. After that they fall to the ground and for a while again, in a kneeling position, pray. Then all rise together and again raise their hands upwards to heaven, this lasting a longer time with greater

intensity, and they complete their supplications. No one bends his knee or rises from his kneeling until the one who makes prayer for them bends first and rises first.[37]

This description fits the basic stages of the Muslim *Rak'ah*.

As the evolution of Islam continued, its basic conversation was always with the Christians of the East. The *Sufi* trend is greatly indebted to the same dialogic coexistence of Muslims with monks of the Eastern Church. The Christians of the East also contributed substantially to the development of Muslim philosophy and science. For example, the Persian Christians during the period of the Abbasids translated into Arabic numerous Greek philosophical and medical works that had a great impact on medieval Muslim philosophy.[38]

The Islamic world, in its first eight centuries, never ceased to be in a creative cultural dialogue with its great, respected neighbor, Orthodox Byzantium. Many elements of Muslim literature witness to the ability of Islam to assimilate from the already developed technology of Byzantium. These include even the method of the hermeneutic of the *Qur'an* as it appeared in the commentaries of the *Tafsir*, the technique of copying manuscripts, the art of making miniatures, and music and melodic reading. After the conquest of the Byzantine Empire, the Muslims not only were inspired by, but also literally copied, the architectural expression of the Orthodox temple, especially the most typical masterpiece, *Hagia Sophia* (Holy Wisdom). Essentially, they adopted this great accomplishment of the Christian East as a source of inspiration that defines the architectural line of Muslim sacred places up till the present (for example, contemporary creations of Muslim architecture from the Middle East to Malaysia).

In addition, Orthodoxy, from its long coexistence – which I call the "dialogue of life" – with the Muslim world, offers something important to the balance in contemporary Christian-Muslim dialogue: a witness to the Passion and the honor of persecutions, making up for a series of failures of the West. Many Muslims in Asia and Africa express strong criticism for all that they claim to have suffered from Christendom. They refer to the pressures of colonialism by the Christian nations in the nineteenth and twentieth centuries. To this Muslim criticism the Orthodox offers the Christian side – an exceptional counterweight experience – reminding Muslims that it is not Christianity in its entirety that is responsible, but only a limited number of "Christian" European nations. The Christians of the Eastern Churches have only to state a long history of trials in which they were oppressed and harassed by Muslim nations (Turkey, Syria, Egypt, etc.).

At the same time, the Orthodox are obligated to remind those in the West that their actions in the past deeply wounded the relationships of Christians with Muslims, the prime victim being the churches of the East. Even though belonging to history, it should not be forgotten that the Crusades weakened the Christian Byzantine Empire, incited Muslim expansionism, and broke down the coexistence and harmony that had been cultivated during the period of the Abbasids. Further, they so embittered Eastern Christians that the miserable Orthodox Christians of the fifteenth century preferred the "Crescent" to the "protection of Rome."

In the twentieth century, after World War I, many "Christian" powers abandoned and betrayed the Christian populations of Asia Minor and stood aloof with relative apathy toward the new uprooting of the Orthodox Christians from Constantinople and Northern Cyprus. Finally, numerous missions of Western churches, instead of bringing Christ to the Muslim populations of the Middle East, wounded and divided the Orthodox Churches. The pain in question is not only for the past. Numerous Orthodox local churches live even today under Muslim authority, hardly tolerated. These Orthodox usually have to make every effort to survive, avoiding rather than seeking dialogue, which presupposes freedom: equality of the persons involved in theoretical considerations and freed from fear of the powerful. Certainly, these possibilities are not offered where Muslims make up the great majority and have national authority in their hands.

I should add, when alluding to the mistakes of the West already mentioned, that greater care should be taken in the future to avoid a new mistake: that in the name of cultivating a good climate for the Muslim-Christian dialogue, the poor and miserable Orthodox minorities who live in Muslim majorities are forgotten or even sacrificed. Parallel to the polite stance and respect for Muslims who live in the West, similar support is needed for Christians who are oppressed in intolerant Islamic environments in Africa and Asia. The contemporary Muslim-Christian dialogue should take into consideration these international situations that require coexistence and mutual dependence.

The Dialogue: Rejection or Trust in the Orthodox Christian Experience

Much opposition has been raised in the Christian world to the danger that inter-religious dialogue may hold for Christians. What if the final result would be a compromise and an expression of losing the faith? This issue is related to the more general problem of understanding non-Christian religious experience and the true stance of human beings of other religions or those without religious convictions.

In the Protestant world, one observes views that preclude each other, that is, from the most positive and syncretistic to the most negative and fanatic.

In the Roman Catholic world, the cohesive position of the church throughout the centuries gives a balanced orientation and, especially after Vatican II, an openness and broadness.

The Orthodox world does not make decisions by an official church agency. The East has always allowed greater margins of personal freedom and expression, but within a continuous living Tradition. Drawing from the theological and spiritual experience of Orthodoxy, one could outline certain defining elements:

1. In Eastern Christianity, which for the greater part of its life was developed within cultural, linguistic, and religious pluralism, one observes a basic stance of respect for the religious experiences of other human beings, that is, toleration and understanding. In its basic theological convictions, there exist characteristics be-

longing to all human beings, which Saint Gregory the Theologian, Patriarch of Constantinople, called "god-like and divine": prime knowledge of God; inclination toward God; and desire to seek God. This religious experience – I boldly use the term – is biologically rooted in the living relationship of God to the primitive human being. The image of God was not lost with the fall and always remains the recipient of messages of the divine will and presence.

2. Independent of all other human beings who believe or do not believe, for Christians only one God exists: "God who made the world and everything in it" (Acts 17:24),[39] "one God and Father of all, who is above all and through all and in all" (Eph 4:6). God acts in the world and in history, revealing God's glory. Human beings may have a variety of perceptions of God, but other gods do not exist. "The earth is the Lord's and all that is in it, the world and those who live in it" (Ps 24:1). Throughout human vicissitudes, God's presence and concern for the human being and God's interest in the salvation of the entire world have always existed. Religious experience, therefore, expresses not only one persistent course of the human being toward the highest reality, but even an absorption of rays of the divine reflection of the glory of God in the world.

3. In addition to the definitive "New Covenant" – the new treaty contracted by God with human beings in the Christ – other "covenants" with broader and special content also existed, maintaining their significance and validity. The first covenant was with Adam and Eve, that is, the representatives of the entire hu-

man race. The second covenant was with Noah and the new humanity who were saved from the deluge (Gen 9:8; 13:6). The third covenant (Gen 15:18) was contracted with Abraham, the originator of a people, who was destined to play a basic role in the salvific plan of God. Muslims emphasize faithfulness to Abraham, and we could say that they participate in this covenant, having made a unique historical movement *in retro*. God's final and definitive covenant with Jesus Christ is potentially with the entire human race, for Jesus as the "new Adam" is representative of all humanity. For us, Christ, "the true light, which enlightens everyone, was coming into the world" (Jn 1:9). The all-radiant, shining figure of Christ, even if reflected by the hollow mirror of a fragmented Christology or hidden by the fog of the various heretical interpretations, faintly sheds light on the Muslim experience, as well.

4. Orthodox theological thought leaves broad margins in the activity of the Holy Spirit beyond any definition, description, or limitation. The Orthodox East's "economy of the Word," with hope and humble expectation, is parallel to the "economy of the Spirit." The basic prayer with which almost every Orthodox prayer service begins underlines the consciousness of the Christians of the East that the Holy Spirit is "everywhere and fills all things" and continues to act for the fulfillment and complete salvation of the entire world. "The wind [Spirit] blows where it chooses" (Jn 3:8), as the acting and binding power of the love of God. "The Holy Spirit holds everything, the visible and the invisible,"[40] we persistently chant. In the theology of

the Eastern Church, one meets an effusive certainty that the Holy Spirit works in a manner that surpasses human thought and imagination and, consequently, cannot be enclosed in any theological schema, description, or foresight. Every high and substantial good is the result of the Holy Spirit. The elements *par excellence* of a harmonious coexistence are the fruits of the Holy Spirit: "love, joy, peace, patience, kindness, generosity, faithfulness, gentleness, and self-control" (Gal 5:22b-23a). In this assurance of the Apostle Paul, we can discern traces of the action of the Holy Spirit wherever these fruits exist. It appears that numerous such elements exist in the life of many Muslims.

5. Finally, relationship and dialogue with every human being requires the obligation of a universal love, which constitutes the nucleus of Christianity: "God is love, and those who abide in love abide in God, and God abides in them" (1 Jn 4:16b). The Hebrew Scriptures' concept of the neighbor was unimaginably broadened in the Second Testament, when Jesus, speaking of love without boundaries, protected a heretic, the Samaritan. With this parable Jesus Christ not only demolished every racial and religious concept of neighbor but also reversed the longstanding question, "Who is my neighbor?" (Lk 10:29), with the new, dynamic one, "Which of these ... do you think was a neighbor?" (Lk 10:36). Our obligation is to become "neighbor" to every human being regardless of race, religion, or language, whether virtuous or sinful. A human being, although having a different creed, never loses the basic attribute of the spiritual native land. Even if one ignores it, one

does not cease to be a child of God, made in the image of God, and, therefore, a brother or sister.

A dialogue in the above framework, which respects the principles and understanding of others, does not occasion syncretism or discoloration of the Christian faith. On the contrary, a dialogue that is genuine and fertile demands substantial Christian knowledge, consistency, and repentance – that is, a continuous living of our Christian faith in humility and genuine love. This is precisely the "perfect love [that] casts out fear" (1 Jn 4:18), every kind of fear, and fills us with hope. The power of the truth of God creates unexpected openings through the impasse. Our obligation is to share with other human beings the certainties and deeper spiritual experiences that God has freely given us. We should proceed not in a bombastic manner, but in simplicity and peace, with gratitude and knowledge, with respect for the person and freedom for our dialogic partner.

NOTES

1 John of Damascus, *Source of Knowledge,* in J. P. Migne, ed., *Patrologia Graeca* (Paris, 1857-1866) (hereafter, *P.G.*), vol. 94, cols. 765 and 772d.

2 *P.G.*, vol. 94, cols. 764-773.

3 *P.G.*, vol. 97, cols. 1462-1609.

4 "Dialexis with Ahmed the Saracen," in *P.G.*, vol. 120, cols. 821-832.

5 "Dogmatic Panoply," para. 28, in *P.G.*, vol. 130, cols. 1332d-13.60d.

6 "Treasury of Orthodoxy," para. 20, in *P.G.*, vol. 140, cols. 105a-121c.

7 "Censure of the Hagarene," in *P.G.*, vol. 104, cols. 1384a-1448a.

8 *P.G.*, vol. 105, cols. 669-805.

9 For more on this period, see G. Giiterbock, *Dem Islam im Lichte der Byzantinischen Polcmik* (Berlin, 1912); W. Eichner, "Die Nachrichten iiber dem Islam bein den Byzantinern," *Der Islam*, vol. 23 (1936), pp. 133-162, 197-244; D. Sdrakas, The *Polemic of Byzantine Theologians against Islam* (in Greek) (Thessalonike, 1961); J. Meyendorff, "Byzantine Views of Islam," *Dumbarton Oaks Papers, vol.* 18 (1964), pp. 115-132; A. Th. Khoury, *Les théologiens byzantins et l'Islam, Textes et auteurs* (VIIIe-XIIIe s.) 2nd ed. (Paris: Beatrice-Nauwelaerts, 1969); Khoury, *Der theologische Streit der Byzantinen mit dem Islam* (Paderborn, 1969).

10 "To the Atheist Chiones: Dialexis Authored by the Physician Taronites Who Was Present and Witnessed the Event," *Soter,* vol. 15 (1892), pp. 240-246; Palamas, "Letter, from Asia While Being Held Hostage, Sent to His Church," *Neos Hellenomnemon,* vol. 16 (1922), pp. 7-21; Palamas, "Letter to Monk David the Disypaton," *Deltion of the Historical and Ethnological Society of Greece,* vol. 3 (1889), pp. 229-2.34.

11 "A Dialexis with an Ismaelite." See A. Argyriou, *Annual of the Society for Byzantine Studies* (in Greek), vol. 35 (1966), pp. 158-195.

12 The anti-Islamic work of John Katakouzenos is basically divided into two parts: the first, *Against the Mohammedans,* includes four apologies; the second, *Against Mohammed,* four discourses, in *P.G.,* vol. 154, cols. 372-692. The author here based his work on numerous points on *Confutio Alcorani* by the Florentine Dominican monk Ricoldo da Monte Croce (d. 1320), which was translated by Demetrios Kydones.

13 "Dialogue Which Took Place with Some Persian with the Rank of Mouterizes in Ancyra in Galatia," in *P.G.,* vol. 154, cols. 124-174.

14 In *P.G.,* vol. 154, c. 380bc.

15 See note 10, above.

16 "To the Atheist Chiones," pp. 241-242.

17 "To the Atheist Chiones," pp. 241-242.

18 "To the Atheist Chiones," p. 242.

19 "To the Atheist Chiones," p. 245.

20 "Mahomet, however, we do not find witnessed by the prophets, nor a foreign work giving worthy testimony to believe him. For that reason we neither believe him nor the book written by him ..." (Palamas, "Letter to Monk David," p. 232).

21 Palamas, "Letter to Monk David," p. 233.

22 "To the Atheist Chiones," p. 246.

23 Palamas, "Letter to Monk David," p. 233; Palamas, "Letter from Asia," p. 19.

24 Palamas, "Letter to Monk David," p. 233.

25 See note 13, above.

26 In *P.G.*, vol. 156, col. 133b.

27 The full title, revealing the history as well as the character of the text, is "Gennadios the Monk and Patriarch of Indigent Christians, known as Scholarios, On the Only Way to Human Salvation. Given at the Sultan's Request after Dialogues Taken Place in His Presence at the Patriarchate. After This, Another Shorter Text Was Given, Translated Both into Arabic and Given to Him," in L. Petit, X. Siderides, M. Jugie, eds. *Oeuvres complètes de Gennade Scholarios* (Paris: Maison de la Bonne Presse, 1930), vol. 3, pp. 4.M-452.

28 "A Confession of the wise and honorable Gennadios, Patriarch of Constantinople and New Rome, told to the Hagarenes on the true and blameless faith of the Christians. He was asked by the Emir Sultan Mahomet, 'What do we believe as Christians?' He answered as follows," in Petit, Siderides, Jugie, *Oeuvres complètes de Gennade Scholarios*, vol. 3, pp. 453-458. See also J. Karmiris, *Ta dogmatika kai symbolika mnemeia tes Orthodoxou Katholikes Ekklesias*, 2nd ed., vol. 1 (Athens, 1960), pp. 429-436.

29 Karmiris, *Ta dogmatika*, p. 433.

30 Karmiris, *Ta dogmatika*, p. 436.

31 "Questions and Answers on the Divinity of Our Lord Jesus Christ," in Petit, Siderides, Jugie, *Oeuvres complètes de Gennade Scholarios*, vol. 1, pp. 458-475.

32 The disposition for a critical confrontation with Islam during the long experience and attitudes of the Byzantines and the need for theological enlightenment were brought to

Russia by Maximos the Greek (1470-1556), who wrote three treatises in Russian on Islam. In doing this he contributed to the critical theological discourse in sensitizing the Russians and, more generally, the spiritual resistance of the Russian people to the pressures of Islam. See Gregory Papamichael, *Maximos the Greek. The First Enlightener of the Russians* (in Greek) (Athens, 1950), pp. 176-186.

33 See I. K. Vogiagides, "Historical Studies: Turkification and Islamization of the Greeks in the Middle Ages" (in Greek), *Epeteris Philosophikes Scholes Pan. Thessalonikes,* vol. 2 (1932), pp. 954-155; E. Petrovich, "Islamization" (in Greek), *Serraika Chronika,* vol. 2 (1957), pp. 160-174; Sp. Vryonis, The *Decline of Medieval Hellenism in Asia Minor and the Process of Islamisation from the Eleventh through the Fifteenth Century* (Berkeley, Los Angeles, and London: University of California Press, 1971); A. E. Vakalopoulos, *History of Modern Hellenism Tourkokratia, 1453-1669* (in Greek) (Thessalonike: S. N. Stakianakes, 1976), vol. 2, pp. 51-73; P. Chidiroglou, "Islamization of Crete" (in Greek), in *Pepragmena tou IV Dicthnous Kretologikou Syncdriou,* vol. 3 (Athens, 1981), pp. 336-350.

34 See G. K. Lameras, *On the Crypto Christians in Asia Minor* (in Greek) (Athens: G. E. Kalergy, 1921); A. A. Papadopoulos, "The Crypto Christians of Pontos" (in Greek), *Hemerologion Megales Ellados* (1922), pp. 169-180; N. P. Andriotes, *Crypto Christian Literature 36* (in Greek) (Thessalonike: Demosieumata tes Hetarias Makedonkon Spoudon, 1953); N. E. Melioris, The *Crypto Christians* (in Greek) (Athens: Editions Henoseos Smyrnaion, 1962); A. Ch. Terzopoulos, "The Kostoi or Crypto-Christians of the Sourmenon" (in Greek), *Archdon Pontou,* vol. 30 (1970-71), pp. 398-425.

35 See Walter M. Abbott, ed., *The Documents of Vatican II with Notes and Comments by Catholic, Protestant, and Orthodox Authorities* (New York: Herder & Herder and Association Press, 1966), pp. 660-668.

36 The relevant conferences were given hospitality twice in Austria; the first took place in February 1978, at Salzburg and the second in March 1984, at Saint Polten.

37 Abba Kassianos. See *Evergetinos,* 6th ed., vol. 2, Proposal

11 (Athens: *Hiera kai Sevaste Despotike Mone Metamorphoseos tou Soteros*, 1978), p. 166.

38 R. Walzer, *Greek into Arabic*, Oriental Studies 1 (Oxford, 1962); B. Spuler, "Hellenistisches Denken in Islam," *Spatula*, vol. 5 (1954), pp. 179-193; A. Yannoulatos, *Islam: Scientific Religious Overviews of Islam* (in Greek) (Athens: Editions Ethnoi kai Laoi, 1975), pp. 165-166.

39 All biblical quotations are from the *New Revised Standard Version*.

40 *Parakletike. Anavathmoi*, Sunday, Tone Plagal First.

THE JESUS PRAYER AND DHIKR: A POTENTIAL CONTRIBUTION TO CHRISTIAN-MUSLIM DIALOGUE

Samira Awad Melki

INTRODUCTION

The quest for holiness, or for being united with the holy, is not foreign to humankind. All the rituals, in the different religions, reflect the human need to achieve union with God. The most important among these rituals is prayer since it is a continuous series of spiritual exercises in order to get out of the self and be united with God. Prayer is the greatest revolution in history since it reverses all the laws of the universe in order to make the heart a dwelling for that Who cannot be contained in a place (Chariton, 1997, 21). [*Editor's Note: See references at the end of this chapter for full citations.*] Accordingly, prayer is that religious experience through which man hopes to achieve his holiness.

Religion approaches philosophy when it is confined to dogmas, opinions, and theories, and deprived of its ritual aspect. This opinion was voiced by the well-known Lebanese scholar Adib Saab in his "Introduction to the Philosophy of Religion." Dr. Saab sees that rituals are a religious experience for both the community and the individuals, and that religion is a practical issue or a way of life, and he concludes that the religious experience, in one of its meanings, is "the whole religion" (Saab, 1994, 144). The opinion of this professor becomes clearer when he articulates that the religious experience is one like any other moral, political, or artistic experience. But it is not the same for all individuals no matter how similar are their individual experiences. He concludes that the religious experience is a call to holiness (Saab, 1994, 158).

Meanwhile, holiness, according to Dr. Mahmoud Ayoub, is not an inner characteristic subsisting in a person or a thing, but is an acquired state or attribute. The attainment of this state in the lives of human beings was the most important thing that humanity sought in its long religious history (Ayoub, 2000, 213).

Among the different people with religious experiences, there is a group of men and women who devote their whole life to prayer. They are named differently in different religions: monastics, monks, ascetics, hesychasts, or Sufis. Actually, monasticism is one of the components that make up the religious and intellectual heritage of Christianity. The same applies to Sufism in Islam. Christian monks are called, in many writings, ascetics and Hesychasts.

Sufism, asceticism, and Hesychasm are spiritual tendencies that move humans away from the materialistic world and elevate them to the spiritual realm. Most of the Sufis or ascetics are attracted to this life where they become engaged in seeking holiness through the practices required by this experience. Prayer occupies the first place of these practices.

This article will present two forms of prayer: the Jesus Prayer in Orthodox Christianity, and Dhikr in Islamic Sufism.

CHRISTIAN-MUSLIM DIALOGUE

Christian-Muslim dialogue is not novel, rather it is believed by the scholars of both traditions to be as old as Islam itself. It started with the prophet Mohammad and has continued in different forms till the present. Sometimes, it took the form of a defense, and other times it was in the form of discourse. We find in history, especially in the biographies of a good number of Sufis, that the most peaceful encounters were those that joined Sufis to Christian Hesychasts, most specifically monks. Metropolitan Kallistos Ware observes that no one so far has presented any definite proof pointing to the time and place of these encounters. Accordingly, he raises the question: did Hesychasm influence Sufism or was it the opposite? Was that a mutual influence? And he concludes that these questions call for further investigation and research.

This article is an attempt to investigate the role these two rituals played in the piety of the two traditions, the similarities and differences between the practice of the Jesus Prayer in Orthodox Hesychasm and Dhikr in Islamic Sufism. It will also examine the role they can play in the ongoing Christian-Muslim dialogue. We start with Ware's question. Our methodology includes a portrayal of the Jesus Prayer in the Eastern Orthodox

Church and its practice, and Dhikr in the Sufi under-standing and teachings and its practice.

In the last two centuries, many scholars have dealt with the relations between these two groups and gave opinions on the similarities and differences between the two practices. These opinions and comments will be presented and categorized in this paper. Our aim is to investigate the influence of these relations and the positions taken by the scholars on Christian-Muslim dialogue. In fact, the study of the relationship between the Jesus Prayer and Dhikr, and between Hesychasm and Sufism, is not a new field of study, but it attained a more important dimension and acquired greater im-petus with the expansion of the volume of Christian-Islamic studies and the increase of interest in them.

The Jesus Prayer and Dhikr

The Jesus Prayer is a christological prayer since it is addressed to Jesus, centered around the person of the incarnate Lord. At the time of its composition, it was among the simplest Christian prayers, consisting of only one short sentence: "Lord Jesus Christ, Son of God, have mercy on me." Some use different ver-sions by adding or eliminating words to this formula. Due to its simplicity, a number of Orthodox believ-ers, through the ages built their spiritual life around these few words, and through this prayer entered to the depths of the secrets of Christian knowledge. This prayer also acquired some other names, such as the prayer of the intellect, unceasing prayer, and others. It is agreed among the instructors of the Jesus Prayer that in the beginning it is repeated by the lips. Then, after persistence and endurance, it enters the heart and takes control of the person whose heart acquires more harmony with its rule. At the end, it becomes unceasing prayer.

In contrast, Dhikr literally means remembrance. But, in religious terms, Dhikr means the praise of God using specific definite clauses, repeated according to certain rites, and it might be said loudly or in secret. These clauses might be simple words from among the names of God, like repeating: "Allah, Allah," or a composite, like saying: "There is no deity but Allah (*Lā ilaha illa Allāh*)" (Ajam, 1999, 363). Muslims believe that God enjoined Dhikr, in a way different from those through which He legislated the other Islamic duties, without delineation, due to the ease of practicing Dhikr by the believers. Some believe that any work done to please God is Dhikr (Alameddine, 1999, 143).

The majority of scholars agree that these two forms of worship are a proof of the similarity among the paths to reach the life of holiness in the two religions. The cause of this similarity is simply the resemblance of the experience or the inspiration of the successor by the precursor. Alameddine, a well known scholar who devoted many studies in Arabic to Sufism, quotes the English orientalist Raynold Nicholson, in speaking about the relationship between the Christian monks and Muslim Sufis, stating that Christian monks often appear in the position of instructors who advise and correct the Muslim ascetics. The garb of wool (*suf*), from which the name Sufi was derived, is of Christian origin. The vow of silence, Dhikr (remembrance), the ascetic exercises, might be all attributed to the same origin. The same can be said about the idea of divine love (Alameddine, 1999, 44). Alameddine cites the contemporary orientalist Julian Bultick, who said that Islamic Sufism emerged, most specifically, from the Christian spirit: the terms Sufi, contemplation (*fikr*), private prayers of recollection of God (*adhkar* and *awrad*), the principle of *walāyah* instead of holiness, and reliance (*tawakkūl*) are all borrowed by the Islamic Sufis from Christianity (Alameddine, 1999, 48).

A large number of studies compare Christianity to Islam and examine their relationship from different historical, pietistic, social, and political aspects. It is remarkable that many of these studies deal with different issues of the relations between Christian monasticism and Islamic Sufism, accepting or denying the influence of Christian asceticism on Sufism.

Sufism, in its intellectual notion, concrete practice, and the spiritual paths followed by the Sufis, is neither a philosophical attitude nor a scientific approach, neither a religious mania nor a run away from the social and economic responsibilities in life. It is a firm belief in divine love and annihilation (*fanā'*) in Him. The aim of this self-annihilation is to subdue the carnal soul (*nafs*), preventing it from wallowing in bodily pleasures, and making it pure and clean in order to reach the contemplation of the Creator or meeting with Him (Alameddine, 1999, 13). In other words, what characterizes Sufism is that it is built on living deeds, practice, and experience. For this reason, the instrument of knowledge for the Sufis is a special faculty different from the logical mind, called affection (*wijdān*), or discretion, temperament or taste (*dhawq*), or direct inner vision ('*ayān*), through which occurs the communication between the Lord and the slave (Badawi, 1975, 20).

Consequently, we see that the Sufis differentiate between the knowledge of the manifest (*zaher*) and inner or esoteric knowledge (*bāṭin*). By the knowledge of the manifest they mean the Shari'a since it deals with the manifest deeds. Inner or esoteric knowledge deals with the inner works of the heart. This is all connected to the meaning of the inner vision (*mushāhadah*). When the Sufis speak about God's contemplation, they do not mean seeing with bodily sight through the eyes, since it is impossible after the annihilation of their attributes in God's attributes, but they mean knowing God in their hearts and feeling His presence (Alameddine, 1999, 18). In order for the Sufis to contemplate God, they remember Him with different kinds of remembrances (*adhkar*), until their souls sense the meaning of their remembrance and get to that warming without sensations (Ajam, 1999, 365). To assure this, Badawi states: "In fact, Sufism in its essence is founded on two fundamental principles: 1) the esoteric direct experience of the communication between the master and the slave, 2) the possibility of union between the Sufi and God" (Alameddine, 1999, 15).

Thus, it is possible to question the potential contribution that these two prayers might offer to the Christian-Muslim dialogue, taking into consideration the concept of religious experience together with the narratives of the Sufis visiting Christian monasteries and building relationships with monks, in addition to what was demonstrated by modern studies and agreed upon by scholars, including the similarity between the Jesus Prayer and Dhikr.

As mentioned earlier, we will not present a comparison of the Jesus Prayer and Dhikr. In reality, the views differ in defining the scope of differences and similarities. Furthermore, opinions differ according to the background of the scholar and his or her principal attitude toward Christian-Muslim dialogue. The same applies to defining the impact of Eastern Christianity on Islamic Sufism in general, and on the evolution of Dhikr in specific. While some see this similarity as a mere coincidence, others see it differently, and their attitude toward dialogue plays a crucial role in defining their positions.

SUFISM AND HESYCHASM

The positions of contemporary scholars and orientalists of the two previous centuries, who dealt with the comparison of the Jesus Prayer with Dhikr, fall in form and content under five categories:

The first category states that the similarity between the Jesus Prayer and Dhikr is a result of the influence of monasticism on Sufism. Most of those who adopt this position are the orientalist and those influenced by them.

Massignon held that the Sufis imitated the Christian monks in wearing the wool (*suf*), but he considered Sufism to be an integral part of Islam. He, however, observed that certain aspects of Sufism are in apparent disagreement with the Sunnah or Prophetic tradition (Manoufi, 31). The orientalist Nicholson is also among those who agree with this view. He points to the origin of the term Sufism (Tassawuf) relating it to the *suf* that the Sufis wore in imitation of the Christian monks. He asserts that the vow of silence, Dhikr and other concepts, can be related to Christian origins. In addition, Nicholson believes that the ascetic and hesychastic tendencies in Islam are in harmony with Christian practices and are nurtured by them. Many hagiographical Christian texts can be found in the biographies of the old Sufis where some Christian monk assumes the role of the mentor who gives instructions to the Muslim ascetics (Nicholson, 1914).

The orientalist Margolioss says that the ideas of monasticism and asceticism came to the Arabs as a consequence of trade. He concludes: "Islamic Sufism is brought from the Syrian monasticism in Al Sham and it follows its rules" (Khafagi, 1938).

Sabyha Thuwaynī sees that "love" as practiced by Rābi`ah al-`Adawīyah is foreign to Islam. She considers more likely that in Rabi'a was incarnated or matured a local sense, which is a continuation of the Gnosticism that presented itself in the Christian monastic asceticism, whose spark made up the rational transformation caused by the light of Islam. Then, the matter had its time extent for assimilation and reincarnation, mimesis developed, and the inherited overflowed to the top after some time, in what is called by Thuwaynī "the fixed and the variable" in the lap of the same culture.

So, Thuwaynī finds in the biography of Rabi'a a reproduction of the phenomenon of Hind, the daughter of
Moundher, the king of Hīrah, who followed Christianity and became a nun (Thuwaynī, 2005).

E. G. Browne, in his study of Sufi asceticism asserts
that the Sufis were impressed by Christian monasticism and this appears in their quietude, asceticism, and
love for God (Browne, 1980, 175). With David Zeidan,
the issue moves further. Zeidan considers the Sufis as
Jesus followers who practiced their pietistic devotions
in their own context using Christian methods, among
which is Dhikr (Zeidan, 1998).

In the same context, Maria Jaoudi places the Christian ascetics in contrast with the Sufis and she compares Rābi'ah al-'Adawīyah [d. 801] with Theresa of
Avila [d. 1582], Jalālud-Dīn Rūmi [d. 1273] with Francis of Assisi [d. 1226], and some other Sufi poets to John
of the Cross [d. 1591]. Jaoudi considers that Christian
love has three stages and places, with each of them
contrasting a stage of Sufi teaching and forming a parallel to it (Jaoudi, 1993, 80-90).

The second category ascribes the similarity between
the Jesus Prayer and Dhikr to the fact that the religious
experience is the same one, and God is the same One.
Among the supporters of this view is Nasrollah S. Fatemi who compares the Jesus Prayer to the Sufi Dhikr.
He concludes with the assertion that a state of spiritual
perfection that leads to the knowledge of divine unity
ensues, where a bridge is built above the chasm that
separates God from man. This can be attained when
the human soul transcends the limits of personality by

losing the self, which is in the state of self conjecture. He states this opinion to verify that the unity of experience leads to the unity of knowledge, to God Himself (Fatemi, 1973, 51).

The third category insists that Sufism is purely Islamic. Among the adherents to this view are non-Muslim scholars like William Chittick, who considers that the impact of Christianity on Sufism is influenced by the opinions of the orientalists who did not admit the presence of any aspect of asceticism in the religion of the desert, Islam. For that reason, they tried in different ways to prove that Sufism was influenced by Christianity, Judaism, Zoroastrianism, or Buddhism. Chittick sees that the new Islamists agree with the orientalists, consequently with the West, in rejecting Sufism and considering it as a divergence from Islam. He places this rejection in the class of being influenced by the West, which, although the Islamists call for rejecting and criticizing it, they are also fond of it technological and weapon development. They, in pretending that the origin of Sufism is outside Islam, neglect the spiritual aspect of Islam and replace it with what serves their goal of building authoritative societies. Chittick prefers to use the term "Sufism" in talking about Islam, while he dislikes using the term "asceticism" because the latter is connected to Christian heritage, which preceded Islam, and consequently there exists no equivalent term in Islam. This is analogous to not using the term "theology" in speaking about Islam where it has no equivalent (Chittick, 2003).

Carl Ernst, in defending the Islamic origin of Sufism, argues that modern studies on Sufism show that many of the assumptions made by the orientalists are still active and adopted by some contemporary scholars, despite the increase in the volume of available data. Ernst insists on the Islamic origin of Sufism without denying the influence of others on it and its influence on them. In order to support his point, he presents the opinions of some English scholars, among them William Jones, who visited the East toward the end of the eighteenth century, and John Malcolm, who visited it in the first half of the nineteenth century. Both of them did not see in Sufism anything really common with Islam, but they saw that it shares many concepts with Christianity, Greek philosophy, Indian Vedanta, and it shows the impact they had on it. In relying on these two scholars, Ernst concludes that the term "Sufism (*tassawuf*)" was itself invented toward the end of the eighteenth century to describe those parts of the eastern civilization that attracted Europeans (Ernst, 2005, 8). Among the orientalists whose views are presented by Ernst is James Graham who considered that Sufism becomes an attractive system as it approaches Christianity, and rejects Mohammad's law (Ernst, 2005, 13).

In addition, Ernst refers to what Mount Stewart Elphinston, the British delegate to Afghanistan, wrote in 1808,: "the soofees... consider the peculiar tenets of every religion as superfluities, and discard all rites and religious worship, regarding it as a matter of little importance in what manner the thoughts are turned to God, provided they rest at last in contemplation on his goodness and greatness" (Ernst, 2005, 13).

At the end, Ernst criticizes the Muslims who believe that Sufism is foreign to Islam, and considers that what they adopt is due, to a large extent, to their adoption of the western view and their admiration of western technology that provides them with what they need to build power in their society, while Sufism hinders this with its values (Ernst, 2005, 14).

In his comparison between Sufism and Christianity, Ernst discusses what is attributed to the Prophet in *hadith* saying: "There is no monasticism (*rahbanniyya*) in Islam." Ernst believes that monasticism, as practiced by monks in celibacy and seclusion, is not among the constituents of Islamic religion (Ernst, 2005, 99). He adds that monasticism, in its western form, is equal to the Sufi method where there is a master or instructor and disciples (Ernst, 2005, 121). In fact, this does not apply to the Sufis of the early centuries when methods and regulations did not exist.

The fourth category sees that the similarity is in the techniques and not in the essence because the dogmatic difference cannot be separated from the practice (the difference between practice (*ṭarīqah*) and law (*sharī'ah*)). Some Christian and Muslim scholars present this conclusion, according to a polemic position they adopt, while others adopt these conclusions without any prejudice. Among those is Metropolitan Kalistos Ware, who starts from the fact that "enough has been said about the Hesychast understanding of the heart and about the practice of Jesus Prayer to suggest many parallels between Eastern Orthodoxy and Islamic Sufism. In particular there are striking similarities between the physical techniques of Byzantine Hesychasts, with the regulation of breathing, and the bodily exercises that accompany Dhikr among the Sufis. So close are the points of similarities as to render it highly probable that there has been some direct contact between the two traditions" (Ware, 2002, 15). But he sees that he, as a Christian, would not be honest in neglecting that the Jesus Prayer is an invocation of Jesus Christ, the second person in the Holy Trinity. This prayer does not invoke God alone as the Supreme Being, but God as incarnate "the Son of the eternal Father who is also Son of Mary." Ware affirms the universality of Christ the Logos, "the true light that enlightens everyone who come into the world" (Jn 1:9), and in emphasizing the historicity of the Jesus Prayer he underlines that the call in it is directed to Christ by His human name, "Jesus," given to him by Mary and Joseph, His foster father.

Ware utilizes an example, stating that in a frame we can place any picture we want. By analogy, he deduces that the Jesus Prayer and Dhikr are two pictures that can have the same frame. The name of Jesus is the picture, while the repetition of prayers and the techniques form the frame that resembles other frames in other religions. The main point in the Jesus Prayer is neither how to pray nor the external techniques, but to whom we address it. In the Jesus Prayer, words are clearly addressed to Jesus Christ the incarnate Savior, Son of God and Mary (Ware, 2002, 21-23).

Elliot Miller refuses the comparison of Sufism with asceticism because he believes that there is no similarity between Islam and Christianity. Accordingly, he considers Sufism as one of the wide roads that are mentioned in the Christian Bible as not leading to the Kingdom of Heaven, while Christians have to follow the narrow road that leads to it. He closes his discussion with the conclusion that, despite the merits of Sufism, it is a delusion and deceit to believe that it might lead to God (Miller, 1986).

The fifth category holds that there was a mutual influence between the followers of Sufism and Hesychasm. Those belonging to this category observe that the practice of the Jesus Prayer in Christianity was affected by the Islamic Dhikr. The Christian heritage, under Islamic rule, was changed and enriched from various eastern influences. For this reason, they see that the Jesus Prayer may be regarded as a framework of a number of methods. They cite in this regard the practice of Saints Niciphoros of Jerusalem, Gregory the Athonite, and Gregory Palamas, who show in their teachings an inspiration by the practice of Dhikr, in the reiteration of the prayer, breath control, and other practices. In addition, they note the similarity between the two practices through an analysis of the prayers in both Christianity and Islam. They also see that the definitions of the Jesus Prayer and Dhikr are similar, that the two exercises are based on similar presuppositions, they share the same origin and goal, and they have the same ritual countenances in order to keep the remembrance of God.

In this context, John Meyendorff states in his book *Saint Gregory Palamas and Orthodox Spirituality* that what is common between the Jesus Prayer, Dhikr, and

Yoga is the method that is built on the regulation of breathing with the repetition of the prayer. He mentions that Niciphoros of Jerusalem did not attribute an important role to this method in his theology. This method is not more than a means among a number of means to guard the heart. He also tells about meetings that took place in the thirteenth century between monks and Sufis, among which are the meetings of Philotheos and Gregory Palamas, according to their biographies. He also mentions that the prayer of the name was so popular in the Islamic circles that it becomes impossible to deny the encounter between the two spiritualities, monastic and Islamic. Although this prayer was propagated and became popular among both Christians and Moslems, Meyendorff asserts the distinction between the two groups in the practice of the same technique (Meyendorff, 1974, 62)

Prayer, the Heart, and Mystical Theology

After this presentation of the views of scholars organized in the aforesaid five categories, we cannot but conclude that the influence between Islamic Sufism and Orthodox Hesychasm represented by monasticism was mutual at different levels and spread in different periods. This conclusion opens the door for us to tackle the mystic (or Sufi, ascetic, or hesychastic) theology. This theology seems to be common in its components and motives despite the dogmatic differences behind it. This is because each of the two systems, Monasticism and Sufism, rests dogmatically on a different religion. The basic character of Hesychasm, like the basic identity of Sufism, points to the same way, is hindered by the same obstacles, and leads to the same intentions, regardless of the dogmatic differences.

Accordingly, it becomes clear that in Hesychasm, as in Sufism, the heart and remembrance of God occupy a high position. In principle, Hesychasm means the inner prayer in general, and it includes more than one style of prayer. But most of those who dealt with Hesychasm in the past restricted it in one specific spiritual road that is the invocation of the name of Jesus. Some used the term "Hesychasm" to point to the bodily exercises that accompany the prayer. But the invocation of the name of Jesus assists in concentration in a way to throw out thoughts and instill inner peace and stillness in the heart, which is kept busy with Jesus instead of being occupied by other thoughts and imaginations (Ware, 2000, 75).

On the other hand, William Chittick speaks about the cosmology of Dhikr and sees that the "first function of the prophets is to 'remind' people of their own divinely given reality." He concludes that the *Qur'an* employs this term, and some of its derivatives, to point to this reminder, and at the same time, to remembrance, which is the response of people to this reminder. At the same time, remembrance is the awareness of God and its expression, whether in words or in silence. He concludes that Dhikr, as remembrance, leads to the "presence with the One Remembered." This presence is knowledge in the heart that changes the world to a mere remembrance through which all that is in the world becomes blessed (Chittick, 2002, 48-63).

Vincent Rossi sees that, in the Christian-Muslim dialogue, there are obstacles of a serious nature that cannot be removed by mere words or emotional ecumenism. These obstacles are due to the natures of Christianity and Islam. Neither conferences nor words can change these natures. All that is hoped is to deepen our understanding, not only of the religion of the other, but primarily of our faith. This in itself is not an insignificant achievement. He sees in Dhikr and the Jesus Prayer a common issue between Christians and Muslims, based on the fact that God's remembrance is central in the practice of Sufism and Hesychasm. The invocation of the divine name or the remembrance of God is the essence of prayer in both of Dhikr and the Jesus Prayer. If the God we seek to remember is the Deity, "There is no deity but Allah" (*Lā ilaha illā Allah*), and if human nature is one according to both traditions, Sufism and Hesychasm, it is unlikely that the God of Muslims is a different God from the God of the Christians. Furthermore, Muslims and Christians should have the same kind of heart (Rossi, 2002, 74).

Seyyed Hossein Nasr argues that the dogma of the heart is universal. The prayer of the heart in Christianity occurs in the heart. Likewise, the *Qur'an* in Islam has much to say about the hearts "that find rest only in the remembrance of God." Sayyed Hussein Nasr relates peace and stillness to being and the heart. Based on the *Qur'an* verses, the Sunnah and Hadith, the wise Muslims developed the dogma of the heart on which they built various methods of prayer.

In speaking about Dhikr, he says that in it, men

and women unveil the cover that disguises the inner light of the heart that is illuminated by nature. Once this inner light appears, it shines upon the whole human being because the heart is the center of our being. Dhikr, in the absolute, is by itself the heart understood spiritually. Dhikr, as exercised in Sufism, is the highest stage of the prayer of the heart, uttered by the heart. The spiritual journey performed by the Sufi is in entering the heart, assisted by Dhikr, in order to attain, at the end, the identity of both the heart and Dhikr. The Sufi does not pray only to pray but to become prayer, to live at the center of the heart, to experience and know everything from that heart.

The similarity between the language of Sayyed Hossein Nasr, who expresses an Islamic experience, and the language of the Christian Hesychastic and monastic fathers is clearly revealed. In fact, returning to the writings of a number of great Sufis, like Ibn Qayyem Al-Jawziyya, Ibn Arabi, and Rumi, shows the same. This positive view leads us to see the root of this speech and language resemblance in the similarity in the religious experience, which is composed of prayer and worship.

Seyyed Hossein Nasr, among other scholars in the Christian-Muslim dialogue like Custinger, Chittick, Wares and others, refers to Frithjof Schuon who speaks about a transcendent unity among religions located in the heart. This unity was previously mentioned by the Sufis Ibn Arabi, Rumi, and Al Hallaj (Cutsinger, 2002, 240). A theological analysis can be carried on this point. Most probably, this analysis will attribute this transcendent unity to the image and likeness of God, implanted in all human beings.

The mentioned coincidence and harmony in the spiritual method, and specifically in the exercise consisting of the invocative prayer of the heart, the Jesus Prayer and the Sufi Dhikr, forms an interesting natural point of rapprochement between Orthodox Christianity and Islam. According to Seyyed Hossein Nasr, another point of encounter can be the "Sufi (mystical) theology," common to Hesychasm and Sufism. He sees that these two theologies, Hesychasm and Sufism, form the highest levels of self understanding for each tradition (Samsel, 2002, 205)

Conclusion

After presenting the Jesus Prayer in Christian Orthodox monasticism, Dhikr in Islamic Sufism, and the main opinions of orientalists and scholars in the field of religions and Christian-Muslim dialogue, as well as the relationship between Sufism and monasticism and the similarities and differences between the two systems, Jesus Prayer and Dhikr, we can conclude:

Sufism and Orthodox Hesychasm, as two methods of progress toward God, are similar. They give an opportunity for an ascetic theology to exist and embrace a large number of commonalities.

The practice of the Jesus Prayer in Orthodox Christianity and Dhikr in Islam, as two methods of prayer that bring people closer to God, are similar in the method and means and they developed in mutual influence.

Much of the language among the Hesychasts as

among the Sufis is similar due to the contact between the two groups, and because of the similarity in the religious experience lived by the Hesychasts and the Sufis.

The interest of the scholars in the inner dimension of religion, more than the outer, is increasing. In Islam there are two dimensions, the inner represented in the *ṭarīqah* and the outer represented in the *sharī'ah*. Similarly in Christianity, the outer dimension is the dogma, and the inner is Hesychasm. The *ṭarīqah* in Islam is the practice of *sharī'ah,* and Hesychasm in Christianity is the practice of dogma. Accordingly, the concentration on the inner dimension in both religions might contribute positively in developing a more meaningful Christian-Muslim dialogue.

In closing, we can summarize: it is important to examine the ability of the mystic theology to play the role of a point of intersection between Hesychasm and Sufism. Progress in this context should have a positive impact on the Christian-Muslim dialogue. Both Hesychasm in Christianity and Sufism in Islam are inner dimensions that assist in establishing this theology. This, in turn, contributes positively in the self development of the two sides of the dialogue, while at the same time advancing the dialogue itself toward its real goals.

References

Browne, E.G. "The Sufi Mysticism: Iran, Arabia and Central Asia," *The Suit Mystery,* ed. N.P. Archer (London: The Octagon Press, 1980).

Chariton, Igumen of Valamo, ed. *The Art of Prayer: An Orthodox Anthology.* translated by E. Kadloubovsky and E. Palmer (New York: Faber & Faber, July 1997), reprinted.

Chittick, William C. *Mysticism in Islam*. A lecture delivered at the David M. Kennedy Center for International Studies, Brigham Young University, May 2003. http://meti.byu.edu/mysticism_chittick.html. Checked May 10, 2006.

Chittick, William C. "On the Cosmology of Dhikr," *Paths to the Heart: Sufism and the Christian East*. ed. James S. Cutsinger (Bloomington, Indiana: World Wisdom Inc., 2002), pp, 48-63.

Cutsinger, James S. "Hesychia: An Orthodox Opening to Esoteric Ecumenism," *Paths to the Heart: Sufism and the Christian East*. ed. James S. Cutsinger (Bloomington, Indiana: World Wisdom Inc., 2002), pp. 225-251.

Elliot Miller. "Sufis: The Mystical Muslims," *Forward magazine*. 1986. http://www.equip.org/free/DI200-3. htm. Checked on May 10, 2006.

Fatemi, Nasrollah S., "A Message and Method of Love, Harmony, and Brotherhood," *Sufi Studies: East and West*, ed. L.F. Rushbrook Williams (New York: E.P. Dutton & Co., 1973), p. 51.

The Encyclopaedia of Islam, http://en.wikipedia.org/wiki/Encyclopaedia_of_Islam. Last modified February 2007. Checked on February 28, 2007.

Ernst, Carl W. *The Shambala Guide to Sufism* (Boston: Shambala Publications, 1997).

Jaoudi, Maria. *Christian and Islamic Spirituality* (New Jersey: Paulist Press, 1993).

Massignon, Louis. *Essai sur les Origines du Lexique Tech-*

nique de la Mystique Musulmane (Paris: Librairie Philosophique J. Vrin, 1954).

Meyendorff, John. *St. Gregory Palamas and Orthodox Spirituality*. Trans. Adele Fiske (Crestwood, New York: St. Vladimir's Seminary Press, 1974).

Nasr, Seyyed Hossein. "The Heart of the Faithful is the Throne of the All-Merciful," *Paths to the Heart: Sufism and the Christian East*. ed. James S. Custinger (Bloomington, Indiana: World Wisdom Inc., 2002), pp. 32-47.

Nicholson. Reynold A. *The Mystics of Islam* (London: Routledge; London: Kegan Paul, 1914). http://www.sacred-texts.com/isl/moi/moi.htm. Checked on May 10, 2006.

Papademetriou, George C. *Introduction to Saint Gregory Palamas* (Brookline, Massachusetts: Holy Cross Press).

Rossi, Vincent. "Presence, Participation, Performance: The Remembrance of God in the Early Hesychast Fathers," *Paths to the Heart: Sufism and the Christian East*. ed. James S. Custinger (Bloomington, Indiana: World Wisdom Inc., 2002), pp. 64-111.

Ware, Kallistos. "How Do We Enter the Heart?" *Paths to the Heart: Sufism and the Christian East*. ed. James S. Custinger (Bloomington, Indiana: World Wisdom Inc., 2002), pp. 2-23.

Ware, Kallistos. *The Inner Kingdom*. The Collected Works, Vol. 1 (Crestwood, New York: St. Vladimir's Seminary Press, August 2000).

Zeidan, David. *Church Planting in the Me and Identity of Muslim Converts* (1998). http://www.angelfire.

com/az/rescon/CHRPLTNG.html. Checked May 10, 2006.

References in Arabic

Ayoub, Mahmoud. *Studies in the Christian Islamic Relations*. Part I (Balamand, Lebanon: Center of Christian Islamic Studies, University of Balamand, 2000).

Badawi, Abdulrahman. *History of Islamic Sufism* (Kuwait: Wakalat Al Matbou'at, 1975).

Thuwaynī, Sabyha. "Rabi'a Al A'dawyia of Basra. An Iraqi Saint," *Mesopotamia*. Special issue (2 & 3), 2005. http://www.mesopotamia4374.com/adad2/rabaa.htm. Checked on May 10, 2006.

Al Khufagi, Mohammad Abdumini'm. *Literature in the Sufi heritage* (Cairo: Gharib Printing House, 1938).

Saab, Adib. *Living Religions* (Beirut: Dar An Nahar, 1993).

Saab, Adib. *The Introduction to the Philosophy of Religion* (Beirut: Dar An Nahar, 1994).

Saab, Adib. *Unity in Diversity* (Beirut: Dar An Nahar, 2003).

Al A'jam, Rafic. *Encyclopedia of Islamic Sufism Terms*. The encyclopedia of Arabic and Islamic Terms (Beirut: Librairie du Liban, 1999).

Alameddine, Suleiman Selim. *The Islamic Sufism* (Beirut: Dar Nawfal, 1999).

Al Manufi, Abulfeid. *The Introduction to Islamic Sufism* (Cairo: National house, N.D.).

وب، محمود. *دراسات في العلاقات المسيحية الإسلامية*. الجزء الأول. البلمند. لبنان، الكورة: مركز الدراسات المسيحية الإسلامية، جامعة البلمند، ٢٠٠٠.

وي، عبد الرحمن. *تاريخ التصوّف الإسلامي*. الكويت: وكالة المطبوعات، ١٩٧٥.

يني، صبيحة. "رابعة العدوية البصرية. قديسة عراقية". *ميزوبوتاميا*. العدد الممتاز المزدوج (٢و٣). ٢٠٠٥. ١٠ أيار ٢٠٠٦. http://www.mesopotamia4374.com/adad2/rabaa.htm

خفاجي، محمد عبد المنعم. *الأدب في التراث الصوفي*. القاهرة: دار غريب للطباعة، ١٩٣٨.

شعب، أديب. *الأديان الحيّة*. بيروت: دار النهار، ١٩٩٣.

شعب، أديب. *المقدمة في فلسفة الدين*. بيروت: دار النهار، ١٩٩٤.

شعب، أديب. *وحدة في التنوع*. بيروت: دار النهار، ٢٠٠٣.

عجم، الدكتور رفيق. *موسوعة مصطلحات التصوّف الإسلامي*. سلسلة موسوعات المصطلحات العربية والاسلامية. بيروت : مكتبة لبنان، ١٩٩٩.

لم الدين، سليمان سليم. *التصوّف الإسلامي*. بيروت: دار نوفل، ١٩٩٩.

منوفي، أبو الفيض. *المدخل إلى التصوف الإسلامي*. القاهرة. الدار القومية، د.ت.

GLOSSARY OF SELECTED TERMS

Ascesis: a person's effort as well as the method he or she uses to pass through the three stages of the spiritual life: purification of heart, illumination of the *nous*, and unity with God. It is a human struggle to keep the commandments of Christ.

Baqa': with literal meaning of permanency, this term describes a particular state of life with God, through God, in God, and for God. It is the summit of the mystical *manazil*, that is, the destination or the abode.

Baṭiniya': the term means those who seek the inner or spiritual meaning of the *Qur'an*, as against the esoteric or material meaning. The epithet Batini was also applied at times to certain Sufis.

Fana': important technical term of Sufism meaning "annihilation, dissolution." The Sufi who attains
perfection must be in a kind of a state of annihilation.
The Sufi is one that has nothing in one's possession nor
is possessed by anything. This denotes the essence of
fana'. When this feeling attains its perfection, it is called
fana'-ikulli or "absolute annihilation."

Hal: Sufi technical term, it is to become the actu-
alization of a divine encounter (*wadjd*) – the point of
equilibrium of the soul in a state of acceptance of this
encounter.

Heart (in the Orthodox tradition): the spiritual center of a person's being. It is the domain that is manifested through ascesis in grace and within which God
is manifested. It is also called the center of powers-en-
ergies of the soul.

Hesychia: quietude, stillness, or peace of the heart,
the undisturbed state of the *nous*, the liberation of the
heart from thoughts, passions, and the influence of the
environment; it is the dwelling in God. A hesychast is
one who struggles to achieve the returning of the *nous*
back into the heart, following a specific method.

'Išq: describes the irresistible desire to obtain possession of a loved object or being (*ma'shuk*). With the
Sufis, *Išq* becomes a part of the life of faith as a natural
development of the measured affection (*mahabba*) mentioned in the *Qur'an*.

'Āttihad: in the technical language of the Sufis, the
name *ittihad* is given to the mystical union by which
the creature is made one with the Creator or to the the-

ory that such a union is possible. The meaning of *ittihad* in the terminology of the Sufis is the "passing away of which is willed by the creature in that which is willed by God."

Nafs: is an Arabic word meaning *self*. In Sufi teachings, it means more of a false ego.

Nous: the word has various uses in the Patristic teaching. It indicates either the soul or the heart or even energy of the soul. Yet, the *nous* is mainly the eye of the soul, its purest part, the highest attention. It is also called noetic energy and not identified with reason.

Sufism: a mystic tradition that found a home in Islam encompassing a diverse range of beliefs and practices dedicated to Allah, divine love, and sometimes helping a fellow man or woman.

Tağalyiat (plural of *tajalli*): or theophanies in the realm of being are manifestations of the divine Truth with regard to infinite perfection and eternal glory. The divine theophanies are essentially the outpouring of His Beauty, His Perfection, and His Love, which are expressed in the immense theatre of the universe.

Tawakkūl: "to entrust [to someone], have confidence [in someone], a concept in Islamic religious terminology, and especially that of Sufism, with the sense of dependence upon God.

Wağd: "ecstasy, rapture," refers to a divine influx of inspiration that strikes the inner being of the Sufi, generating either sadness or joy. It may also change his or her condition in some way, making one absent from one's personal qualities by means of a vision of God.

Walāyah (alt. wilāyah): the spiritual authority and

charisma of a particularly spiritually-gifted person like a Sufi saint or ascetic.

Wird: the definite time of day or night that the pious believer devotes daily to God in private prayer. It also means the formula of prayer recited on this occasion, called properly *hizb*.

Contemporary Dialogue Between Orthodox Christians and Muslims

George C. Papademetriou

The Eastern Orthodox Church has encountered Islam from the first decades of Islam's appearance, and they have interacted in a variety of ways. Most frequently, their encounter took the form of polemical clash and confrontation. However in the many centuries of silent coexistence, they also expressed a concrete form of dialogue that sought to define the differences and the positions of the two religious forms and experiences.

The present study focuses on the contemporary academic dialogues between Orthodox Christianity and Islam that began in the spring of 1985 at Holy Cross Greek Orthodox School of Theology in Brookline, Massachusetts. The Ecumenical Patriarchate of Constantinople initiated these dialogues and further meetings were held under its auspices at the Orthodox Center in Chambésy, Istanbul (Constantinople), Athens, and Amman. This article presents the issues discussed, pointing to the fact that peaceful coexistence and justice may only prevail on a basis of mutual knowledge and understanding of the other.

Dialogue in the modern setting is a conversation between two persons who recognize each other as equal partners searching together for the truth. In the case of theological dialogue, the two partners are engaged in conversation concentrating on theological truth, that is, the highest reality, the Truth Itself or God.[1] Muslim and Orthodox Christian theologians have started to come together in the spirit of dialogue and reconciliation to discuss in depth the problems of spiritual life and common social issues. The present study describes some of the contemporary dialogues that have taken place between Orthodoxy and Islam.

For centuries the two religions have lived together and experienced the religious life in the same community settings. They have also shared in spiritual experiences and personal relationships as human beings.[2] Despite long ages living on the same territory, Orthodox Christians and Muslims have mostly been engaged in polemics, and seldom in friendly dialogue or *dialexis* (conversation). Prior to the twentieth century, the goal of dialogue was to persuade or convert the interlocutor to one's side. The Archbishop of Tirana and All Albania, His Beatitude Anastasios Yannoulatos, recently presented an excellent history of Orthodox Christian-Muslim relations and dialogue. He describes the coexistence of these two communities as follows:

> The Eastern Orthodox Church has met with Islam from the first decades of its appearance, in a variety of forms of dialogue. The meeting of Islam not only took the form of polemical clash and confrontation but also evolved into many centuries of silent coexistence, often articulated on the intellectual levels with a concrete form of dialogue that sought o define the differences and the positions of the two religious forms and experiences.[3]

In contemporary America and Europe, where freedom and democracy are a reality and dialogue takes place among people of various religions, it was inevitable that dialogue take place between Orthodox Christians and Muslims. I will attempt to describe recent attempts at dialogue in "... simplicity and peace, with gratitude and knowledge, with respect for the person and freedom of our dialogue partner."[4]

Academic dialogue and exchange between Orthodox Christians and Muslims took place for the first time in 1985 on the campus of Hellenic College/Holy Cross Greek Orthodox School of Theology, in Brookline, Massachusetts. In a word of welcome, His Eminence Archbishop Iakovos of blessed memory referred to the relations of these two religions in the past. He stated:

> These religious traditions (Orthodox Christian and Muslim), lived side by side for many centuries in what was once the Ottoman Empire, a dominion comprising the lands from Egypt and North Africa to the Bosporus and the Dardanelles. Their common denominator was the faith in one God, in one Supreme Being, in whom we exist, move, and have our being. This has enabled Christians and Muslims to develop mutual respect and tolerance for one another and to set an example of what we today call "coexistence."[5]

Orthodox and Muslim scholars of international reputation gathered in Brookline on March 17-19, 1985, and made scholarly presentations, from which ensued vigorous – and heated – friendly discussions. The keynote speaker was His Eminence Metropolitan Constantine of Derkon, of Constantinople/Istanbul, Turkey, a member of the Holy Synod of the Ecumenical Patriarchate and head of the commission for the dialogue with Islam. The speakers addressed the symposium on various topics, and discussed "a variety of issues having historical, ethical, theological, and philosophical interest."[6]

After this start, several academic consultations took place between Muslims and Christians (including Orthodox Christians, Roman Catholics, and representatives from other Christian confessions). They were co-organized by the Orthodox Center of the Ecumenical Patriarchate, under the direction of His Eminence Metropolitan Damaskinos Papandreou of Switzerland, and the Royal Academy for Islamic Civilization Research, under the supreme chairmanship of His Royal Highness Crown Prince El Hassan bin Talal of the Hashemite Kingdom of Jordan.

The first such consultation in Chambésy took place on November 17-19, 1986. The general topic of the conference was "The Meaning of Authority." The three main subjects discussed at the conference were: "Authority and the Family"; "Authority and Religion"; and "Authority and the State."

Metropolitan Damaskinos in his closing remarks stated, "The two religions began a conversation, and many issues will be clarified during our dialogues. There will definitely be progress in dissolving the clouds provoked by fanaticism."[7]

The second consultation on Muslim-Christian dialogue took place in Amman on 21-23 November 1987. The main topic was "Model of Historical Co-Existence between Muslims and Christians and its Future Prospects." In a parallel symposium organized for youth, the common humanitarian ideals for Muslims and Christians were discussed.[8]

On December 12-15, 1988, the third consultation of Muslims and Christians was held in Chambésy. The general topic was "Peace and Justice in the Tradition of Two Monotheistic Religions." There were five sections, each with one presentation and two respondents (or discussants). The co-chairmen were Metropolitan Damaskinos and Crown Prince Hassan. Approximately 65 academicians attended, including Islamicists, historians, and theologians such as His Eminence Joseph Cardinal Ratzinger, now Pope Benedict XVI, from the Vatican, the Minister of Education and president of the Royal Academy for Islamic Civilization Research (Al-Albait Foundation), Dr Nassir El-Din El-Assad, the Minister of Education of Islamic Affairs and Sacred Shrines, Dr Abdul Aziz El-Khayyat, all from Jordan, His Excellency Karolos Papoulias, Foreign Minister of Greece, later president of Greece, and many others.

The conference addressed the basic common fundamental presuppositions of the two religions on peace and justice. The most important foundational presuppositions were the projection of a common reference to the content of the divine and human law, and the analogous understanding of the sacredness of the human person. The objective was to seek cooperation in order to overcome the contemporary crisis of conflict, and to work to achieve peace, justice, and human rights.

From his perspective as Foreign Minister of Greece, Karolos Papoulias stressed the importance of the dialogue between Orthodoxy and Islam, especially in the effort to attain peace and harmony between peoples. He pointed out that religion is not and cannot be indifferent to the human existential struggle for peace and justice.

Metropolitan Damaskinos pointed out that the goal of these conferences was to overcome the historical problems of conflict and seek peaceful coexistence between the two religions. He pointed this out in awareness of the difficulties faced by inter-religious dialogue and especially the difficulty that exists on the level of political conflict. Dialogue seeks to bring out the shared values of both religions, which will facilitate peaceful coexistence and lead to the analogous expression of political goodwill. Then-Cardinal Ratzinger spoke on the contemporary obligation of the Christian Church, and religions in general, to contribute in their own way. He also spoke on the necessity for religious leaders to use their positions to influence their societies in order to overcome the present crisis.

Crown Prince Hassan stated that the goal was neither a missionary effort to proselytize the other, nor a dialogical exercise on the basis that there is a "thesis" with a contrary "antithesis" that leads to a "synthesis." The aim is not to produce a new religious type acceptable to all. Rather, the goals of the dialogue are: a) to undertake the education of all people in authentic knowledge and understanding in order to attain mutual understanding and tolerance, and to seek the spirit of cooperation and friendship among all peoples; and b) to be able to develop within this framework and to defuse potential problems of common interest that constitute a threat to our shared values and heritage.[9]

The fourth academic consultation of Muslims and Christians took place on September 10-14, 1989, at the

Ataturk Cultural Center in Constantinople-Istanbul. The co-chairs were Metropolitan Damaskinos, Crown Prince Hassan, and Professor Emel Dogramaci, Dean of the Philosophical School of the University of Ankara. This dialogue was held under the auspices of a committee organized in Turkey and the Royal Academy for Islamic Civilization Research (Al-Albait Foundation), together with the Orthodox Center in Chambésy. The general topic was "Religious Pluralism in the Bible and the *Qur'an*." Both Christian and Muslim academicians presented scholarly papers and responses on this significant topic.

The main issues raised by the discussion are summarized here. First, the topic of religious pluralism is important wherever there are people of different religious faiths living in the same area. In these situations, it is essential that these people may be influential in all areas of life, without fear. Second, pluralism and a variety of religions constitute a resource for a healthy society. Religious pluralism must not become an object of manipulation by political interests that create conflicts and encourage dissensions, or provoke the renewal of older divisions. It must, rather, become the means for religious tolerance and mutual respect, and must promote moderation and equal opportunity for all people in such a way that all doors are open for negotiation on particular objectives and harmonization of differences. Third, the spirit that prevailed in this conference of Muslims and Christians found expression in an atmosphere of mutual understanding and respect.

The participants at the conference declared their

conviction that it is undesirable to do away with their differences or to envision a super-religion that would aim to absorb the others. Rather, they hope for mutual understanding, recognition, and respect for their differences. One may declare without danger of falling into error that the conflicts and the state of war that we see today in the areas where we live, and generally in the world, are neither religious wars, nor conflicts between nations, nor struggles among enemy blocs, but conflicts that have their source in uncontrolled greed and political interests. Metropolitan Damaskinos pointed out that pluralism in the areas where Islam and Christianity coexist is essential because it is closely related to tolerance: "Indeed, the boundaries of religious tolerance are formed precisely where there is intolerance that usually leads to religious hatred and fanaticism." He also spoke of the basic criteria for religious pluralism, which are: a) respect for the particularity of the religious faith and harmonious living of the followers of the two religions, as is dictated in the biblical tradition; b) the security of the organic and governing identity of every religion in the wider politico-social framework; c) the recognition of freedom of worship and the particularity of the religious life of the followers of the two religions in the wider social reality; d) the security of the freedom to organize and the practice of government of the local religious communities in wider areas such as education, justice, economics, etc.; e) a favorable disposition toward fuller, dynamic interrelations between the followers of every religion for the most successful encounter of the needs of states and their

internal policies as well as their foreign relations; and
f) the institutional guarantee of constant efforts by central administrations, with the assistance of local governments, to control and prevent violent incidents.

These criteria are expressions of the spirit of the sacred scriptures of both religions. Their opposite would
be a religious hatred that provokes violence and a chain
reaction that leads to fanaticism among the followers
of all religions. Religious pluralism, to the contrary,
opens new horizons of inter-religious dialogue and cooperation in the direction of a shared encounter with
various problems in contemporary society. At the end
of the Conference, the participants had an audience
with His All Holiness Ecumenical Patriarch Demetrios
I of blessed memory.[10]

The fifth international consultation between Mus-
lims and Christians was held in Amman, Jordan, on
July 26-28, 1993, under the leadership of Crown Prince
Hassan and Metropolitan Damaskinos.

At this conference, 62 academicians participated
from 23 countries, including several prominent personalities, both Muslims and Christians. It began with
the reading of a message from His All Holiness Ecumenical Patriarch Bartholomew I, who wrote, "We enter the historical and crucial moment of transition." He
continued, "under the present circumstances, the responsibility and uninterrupted mission of religions, especially Christianity and Islam, is to witness the goodness and love of all persons and to search for peace,
freedom, and justice among all people."

The general topic was "Youth and the Values of

Moderation." Scholarly papers were presented from both traditions and discussions were held on the following three topics: 1) the values of moderation in Islam and Christianity; 2) great tensions and provocations in the contemporary world; and 3) the role of youth in the dissemination of moderation in a changing world. Reference was made to the Third Pre-Conciliar Pan-Orthodox Conference of the Orthodox Church that met in Chambésy in 1986 and emphasized that the Orthodox Church promotes the spirit of peace, justice, freedom, brotherhood, and love among all the peoples in the world as well as the eradication of racial and other discrimination. This conference emphasized that Orthodoxy condemns war as an evil that results from sin.

The consultation discussed a moderation that leads to respect for religious freedom among all people and faiths. Several statements were issued in a communiqué. First, moderation is the underpinning spirit of the message of the Sacred Scriptures of both religions that recognize the unity of the human race, as well as the value of the responsibility under God. Second, when moderation is a way of life, then freedom, justice and peace prevail, while the absence of moderation leads to confusion of the human spirit, violence, tyranny, oppression, and the abolition of social order. Third, youth as a present treasure and the hope of the future have a special responsibility for the creation of a harmonious society, which will be based on the values proclaimed by Christianity and Islam – through education the youth ought to be instructed to approach the rich spiritual and cultural heritage of their own religion, and to understand in a positive way the other religion in order to avoid repeating the misperceptions and errors of the past, while governments, leaders of communities, and educational institutions have a special responsibility to tread this path in order to embody these high ideals in their policies and programs. Fourth, the conferees agreed, during discussions on the provocations in their countries, that true civilization and culture could not flourish without the spiritual and moral values that exist in the teachings of both religions. Fifth, the consultation was held in an atmosphere of brotherhood, open-mindedness and sincerity, however, the participants proclaimed their sorrow for the clashes and tensions in some countries in the Middle East, Central Asia, and Eastern Europe, especially in Bosnia-Herzegovina.

The conferees, on the basis of their religious convictions, unanimously condemned: exploitation of religious feelings to attain political goals; violence and the commission of crimes; destruction of religious properties and sacred places of worship; killings and mutilations; and, the displacement of innocent citizens. For this reason, the participants directed an appeal to all sides embroiled in conflict to take every possible step toward an immediate end to all acts of war and violence and to take the necessary actions and measures to resolve conflicts through negotiations and peaceful means.

The conference concluded with closing remarks from both co-chairmen. Metropolitan Damaskinos pointed out that "giant" preparation is needed for the two religions to stand together against political systems, economic groups, and social interests to eliminate violence. The conference ended in the hope that all people of goodwill would make every effort to co-operate in order to attain peace, justice, and harmonious coexistence of persons of all faiths.[11]

The sixth Muslim-Christian consultation took place September 8-10, 1994, in Athens, Greece, in an environment of friendship and common vision for future peaceful coexistence in a just society. I was privileged to participate in this consultation. Again, the co-chairs were Metropolitan Damaskinos and Crown Prince Hassan. The general topic was "Education for Understanding and Cooperation." The three areas of discussion were: 1) educational difficulties; 2) educational practices; and 3) educational dynamics. The subtopics were: "Education Complexity"; "Education Reality"; and "Education Dynamism." The Metropolitan opened the conference with a message from Ecumenical Patriarch Bartholomew. In the absence of Crown Prince Hassan, Dr Nassir El-Din El-Assad, President of the Royal Academy of Jordan, presented greetings on behalf of Crown Prince Hassan.

His Excellency, George Papandreou, Minister of Education in Greece [now Prime Minister] was present and pointed out that the history of the Balkans should be re-written and that the social and cultural differences there must not be a source of conflict. He emphasized that, through dialogue and education, and through praising the richness of each religious heritage and people, a re-orientation toward mutual respect and understanding could be brought about. He emphasized that a new generation must not be nurtured on fanaticism and misinformation.

At the end of the conference a communiqué including the following points was issued and distributed to the press:

1. The participants stressed the relevance of Muslim-Christian dialogue in the context of religious plurality that characterizes today's world. They also emphasized the urgent need to address together problems, conflicts, and tensions that threaten harmonious and peaceful co-existence, to prevent the exploitation of religious sentiments in exacerbating division. The participants were aware of their common responsibilities in dealing with the materialistic culture that prevails in today's world, and offering a contribution by persons of faith toward the meaning of existence, life, the world, and history.

2. In this context, the participants chose to study the issue of education as a means of better and mutual understanding and cooperation, in view of its crucial role in shaping the consciousness and value systems of younger generations. As a future-oriented activity, education should be rooted in our respective faith traditions; it should also be concerned with enhancing objective information about each other, and underlining the common fundamental moral and spiritual values. As education is a continuous process, no effort should be spared in combating misconceptions, prejudices, and the distortion of each other's images.

3. The participants agreed that educational programs within one community should be attentive to the faith and traditions of the other. This should be

undertaken with a spirit of objectivity, openness, and tolerance, and should ensure that, while we refer to the realities of history and the authentic sources of our religions, we should learn to understand each other in the way we would each like to be known and understood.

4. The participants were well aware of the great influence of the mass media, and called for a critical approach to reductionist, stereotypical, essentialist, and sensationalist portrayals of religious communities. They believe in the necessity for active cooperation in correcting their mutual perceptions as conditioned by the media. This cooperation involves revising textbooks and developing new educational materials through the joint efforts of specialists from the two religious communities, as well as encouraging governments to take up inter-religious concerns in new educational curricula.

5. The participants underlined the need to clarify and sharpen concepts, definitions, and analyses as they examine the conflicts of our time in a way that will enable them to elaborate a common strategy for a just peace. Muslims and Christians were called upon to protect their respective communities from the divisive effects of aggressive policies, and those that display double standards, through the channels of education, dialogue, and mutual cooperation.[12]

On June 3-5, 1996, the seventh Christian-Muslim consultation took place in Amman, Jordan. There were 43 Christian and Muslim participants from 14 countries. The main theme was "The Educational System in Islam and Christianity," under which three main topics were discussed: 1) philosophy of education; 2) problems of education in the contemporary society; and, 3) necessary characteristics of our educational system. The subtopics were: "Philosophy of Education in Islam and Christianity"; "Problems of Education in Modern Society"; and "Features of An Educational System We Need."

Crown Prince Hassan made the important observation that the educational values of Islam and Christianity converge in their reference to God, humanity, and the universe. All of us are therefore responsible for eliminating the causes of the mutual antipathies that are developed in school manuals. We are obliged to transmit to future generations sincere faith, brotherhood, and philanthropy, as well as universal justice and freedom.

Metropolitan Damaskinos read a message sent by Patriarch Bartholomew and then offered his own keynote address. He emphasized the importance of implementing lofty Christian and Muslim educational values in the experiences of persons of both faiths.

Both the Crown Prince and the Metropolitan contextualized the ongoing academic consultations between Muslims and Christians as being objective discussions of the two faiths and representative of their genuine desire for peaceful coexistence of persons of all faiths.[13]

The eighth academic consultation between Muslims and Christians was held in Constantinople/Istanbul on June 3-5, 1997. Again, the principal sponsors were the Orthodox Center of the Ecumenical Patriarchate at

Chambésy and the Royal Academy for Islamic Civilization Research. The general theme was "Perspectives of Cooperation and Participation between Muslims and Christians on the Eve of the New Century." The subtopics were: "Principles and Historical Perspectives of Cooperation and Participation"; "Perspectives of Cooperation and Participation at Local and Regional Levels"; and "Perspectives of Cooperation and Participation at International Levels." The 40 representatives, twenty Muslims and twenty Christians, included political personalities of both faiths, as well as prominent scholars who presented papers and made responses on the topic.

Ecumenical Patriarch Bartholomew addressed the conference and emphasized the unity of human beings and the coexistence of all persons in peace, saying, "The book of history is open before us. The pages are blank and wait to be written by us. It depends on us if we will write with blood or with ink; with the pen or with the sword; with philanthropy or with inhumanity; with God or against His commandments." He emphasized the need to prepare the ground for love and tolerance to dominate society and uproot hatred from the hearts of all people.

Princess Rahmah bint El-Hassan, the daughter of Crown Prince Hasan, read a message from her father. The president of the Royal Academy of Jordan, Dr Nassim El-Din El-Assad, gave a welcoming address to the participants.

In his keynote address, Metropolitan Damaskinos emphasized that, in view of the fact that Muslims and

Orthodox had peacefully coexisted for many centuries in the East, they are ready today for a common endeavor to eliminate social oppression and address spiritual problems in the world. Cooperation between monotheistic religions is necessary in order to defend peace, social justice, and human rights. In his closing remarks, the Metropolitan pointed out that at this consultation special efforts were made to analyze the current international and regional realities. This perspective resulted from globalization and the formulation of a new world order. The participants felt the imperative to encounter with responsibility and courage the new challenges and the tremendous consequences to the lives of individuals, families, and communities. People of faith, both Muslims and Christians, are called upon to create a common moral basis and spiritual dimension for the confirmation of human dignity and the struggle for peace, justice, and human rights, including religious freedom.

The consultation ended with a reception hosted by Ecumenical Patriarch Bartholomew at the Ecumenical Patriarchate at the Phanar.[14]

The ninth academic consultation between Muslims and Christians was held in Amman, November 10-12, 1998, with a theme of "Muslims and Christians in Modern Society Images of the Other and the Meaning of Co-citizenship."

Princess Rahma bint El Hassan read a message from Crown Prince Hassan, which emphasized the development of a common code for co-existence whereby each will recognize the other on all levels and respect equal-

ity for all in order to attain lasting peace for all humanity. He proposed the following practical measures: a)
complete and unconditional constitutional and legal
security for full freedom of religious conscience as
well as other religious liberties for all the citizens of
Christian and Muslim states; b) legal protection of the
equality, civil rights, and all the internationally guaranteed human rights of the followers of other religions
in a constantly widening pluralistic synthesis of the societies of almost all modern states. The Crown Prince
invited all the participants for dinner at the Palace Bas-
man and was personally present at the consultation's
last session.[15]

Since the sudden illness of Metropolitan Dam-
askinos, the inter-religious dialogue activities of the
Ecumenical Patriarchate were entrusted to Bishop
Emmanuel Adamakis of Reghion, now His Eminence
Metropolitan Emmanuel of France, Director of the Li-
aison Office of the Orthodox Church to the European
Union. Continuing the work of earlier consultations,
the tenth session of the Muslim-Christian Dialogue
Conference was held in Manama, Kingdom of Bahrain,
28-30 October, 2002, following a proposal by His All
Holiness Ecumenical Patriarch Bartholomew I, which
was accepted by His Majesty Sheikh Hamad Bin Issa
Al-Khalifa, King of the Kingdom of Bahrain. The title
of this session was "The Role of Religion in Peaceful
Coexistence," under the patronage of His Excellency
Sheikh Abdullah Bin Khalifa Al-Khalifah, Minister of
Justice and Islamic Affairs in the Kingdom of Bahrain,
representing His Majesty the King of Bahrain.

Other important recent developments include the Brussels Declaration of December 20, 2001. This Declaration came out of an inter-religious meeting at the invitation of Ecumenical Patriarch Bartholomew and His Excellency Romano Prodi, President of the European Commission, in Brussels, Belgium, on 19-20 December 2001. The title of the meeting was "The Peace of God in the World, Towards Peaceful Coexistence and Collaboration Among the Three Monotheistic Religions: Judaism, Christianity, and Islam." In light of the year of this meeting, the participants were "mindful of the horrific terrorist attacks of September 11th in the United States of America."

The Ecumenical Patriarch has also given two other important speeches on this topic in the past few years. His lecture at the Islamic College in Libya, on 11 September, 2003, was entitled "The Necessity of Inter-Religious Dialogue – The Relationships between Christianity and Islam." His speech at the International Conference on "Islam in a Pluralistic World," held in Vienna, on 16 November, 2005, was entitled "Cultures in Conflict and Dialogue."

Besides these major international consultations and conferences, other important local and regional conferences took place with the co-sponsorship or representation of the Ecumenical Patriarchate. Their consistent objective has been to develop harmony between the two faiths and create an atmosphere of peace and friendship.[16]

In addition to the dialogues sponsored by the Ecumenical Patriarchate and the Crown Prince of Jordan, there also have been other academic dialogues. The faculties of the University of Athens, Greece, and the University of Teheran, Iran, sponsored three dialogues between Islam and Greek Orthodoxy. Both sides presented significant scholarly papers. The first two took place in Athens, in 1990 and 1992, and the third in Teheran on September 13-20, 1994. Many theologians and philosophers participated in these dialogues.[17]

Other dialogues have taken place since then, including Peace and Tolerance I: "The Bosphorus Declaration," Istanbul, Turkey (1994); "Religion, Peace and the Olympic Ideal," Athens, Greece (2004); and Peace and Tolerance II: "Dialogue and Understanding in Southeastern Europe, the Caucasus and Central Asia," Istanbul, Turkey (2006).

CONCLUSION

Past generations were divided by fear and mistrust of people of other faiths. Today, through genuine dialogue, people can overcome their fears and suspicions, and cooperate and live together in a civil society. Recent dialogues between Muslims and Christians held in Chambésy, Constantinople, Athens, and Amman were very fruitful in seeking greater understanding and mutual trust. These are a good beginning, but it is imperative to develop additional opportunities for dialogue.

In the spirit of hopefulness, Professor Anastasios Yannoulatos, Archbishop of Tirana and All Albania, offered the following statement on the relations between Orthodox Christianity and Islam:

Of all living religions, Islam is closest to Eastern Christianity both in spiritual and geographical terms. For all our profound theological differences and dramatic clashes in the past, we stand largely on common cultural and religious ground; a more thorough understanding of the spiritual wealth of our respective worlds is our mutual duty - and one full of promise.[18]

NOTES

1 Asterios Argyriou, *Qur'an and History* (in Greek) (Athens: Apostolike Diakonia, 1992), p. 166.
2 Argyriou, p. 197.
3 Anastasios Yannoulatos, "Byzantine and contemporary Greek Orthodox approaches to Islam," trans. George C. Papademetriou, *Journal of Ecumenical Studies* 33:3 (Fall 1996), p. 512. The Orthodox Christian view of Islam is well presented in the following works: Methodios Fouyias, *The Hellenic Pedestal* (in Greek) (Athens: Nea Smyrna, 1994); Gregorios D. Ziakas, *History of Religions. B. Islam* (in Greek) (Thessalonike: P. Pournaras Publications, 1991); Anastasios Yannoulatos, *Islam: A General Survey* (in Greek) (Athens: Ethne kai Laoi Publications, 1983). Also Anastasios Yannoulatos, *Various Approaches to the Other Religions* (A Historical Outline) (Athens: Poreufthendes, 1971), p. 32-48.
4 Yannoulatos, "Byzantine and contemporary Greek Orthodox approaches to Islam," p. 527.
5 N. M. Vaporis, ed., *Orthodox Christians and Muslims* (Brookline, Massachusetts: Holy Cross Orthodox Press, 1986), p. 1. The papers of this historic symposium were published in this volume. I was chairman and organizer of this conference and had the great pleasure of meeting many Orthodox Christian and Muslim scholars including Professor Mahmoud Ayoub. I was greatly impressed with his humility and deep wisdom.
6 A report by R. Marston Speight, "Orthodox Christian-Muslim Symposium," *Journal of Ecumenical Studies* 22:2 (Spring, 1985), p. 434.
7 Metropolitan Damaskinos Papandreou in *Episkepsis* 17:368

(November 6, 1986), p. 18. In this issue, a detailed report is given on pp. 14-18. These consultations of Muslims and Christians are listed by Metropolitan Damaskinos Papandreou in *Episkepsis* 27:532 (June 6, 1996), pp. 17-18.

8 *Episkepsis* 27:532 (June 30, 1996), p. 18.

9 See a full report on this conference in the *Episkepsis* 20:411 (15 January 1989), pp. 4-8. The papers are available in typescript; "The Fifth Muslim-Christian Consultation: Peace and Justice Texts, Commentaries, Discussions" (Chambésy-Geneva: Orthodox Center of the Ecumenical Patriarchate, September, 1989), vol. 1, pp. 239; (April 1990), vol. 2, pp. 185.

10 A detailed account of the academic consultations is given in *Episkepsis* 20:426 (October 1, 1989), p. 4-10.

11 *Episkepsis* 24:494 (July 31, 1993), pp. 14-26. The papers were published as *Youth and the Value of Moderation. Proceedings of the Muslim-Christian Consultation held in Amman, Jordan* (Amman: Royal Academy for Islamic Civilization Research, July 1994), no. 161, p. 272.

12 George C. Papademetriou, "The Sixth Muslim-Christian Consultation," *Theologia* 69:2 (1998), pp. 373-80, and a detailed report in *Episkepsis* 25:510 (October 31, 1994), pp. 6-17.

13 *Episkepsis* 27:532 (June 30, 1996), pp. 10-21. The papers from this conference were published as *The Educational Systems in Islam and Christianity: Proceedings of Muslim-Christian Consultation* (Amman, Jordan: The Royal Academy for Islamic Civilization Research, January 1997), no. 180, p. 169.

14 *Episkepsis* 28:545 (November 28, 1997), pp. 4-23.

15 *Episkepsis* 29:563 (November 30, 1998), pp. 11-24.

16 For an excellent and detailed article on all the dialogues between Orthodox Christians and Muslims, see Prof. Gregorios Ziakas, University of Thessalonike, "The Ecumenical Patriarchate of Constantinople and the Dialogue with Islam," in: *Phanari: 400 Chronia* (Istanbul: Ecumenical Patriarchate, 2001), pp. 575-713 (Greek), pp. 714-725 (English). Another excellent article is by Gary Vachicouras, "Tribute to Metropolitan Damaskinos for his Pioneering Contributions to the Dialogue of the Orthodox Church with Judaism and Islam." For a historical description of the relations of the

Christian East and the Arabs, see Ziakas's profound study, "The relation of the Greek thought to the Christian East and the Islamic traditions," *Scientific Annals of the Faculty of Theology – School of Pastoral and Social Theology* 5 (1998), pp. 82-99.
17 For example, Georgios Patronos, "Jesus as a Prophet of Islam: Christological and Eschatological Approach to the Qur'an" (in Greek), *Ekklesiastikos Pharos* 69 (1992-1995), p. 9 (English translation included in this volume).
18 Yannoulatos, *Islam*, p. 338.

The Ecumenical Patriarchate of Constantinople and Recent Dialogue with Islam

Gregorios D. Ziakas

Translated by George C. Papademetriou

The Ecumenical Patriarchate of Constantinople, as the Great Mother Church of all Orthodox Christians, is the guardian not only of the Orthodox faith but also of the unity and peace of the world, for which the Patriarchate addresses daily prayers to God. Therefore, the Ecumenical Patriarchate considers the study of non-Christian religions as very significant and promotes dialogue by the Orthodox Christian Church with the peoples of other living religious traditions, particularly with Islam.

The dialogue of friendship and mutual understanding between peoples and religions, a dialogue deriving from the universal meaning of the redeeming work of Jesus Christ, is a work of great importance. Dialogue minimizes distances and creates the presuppositions that enable mutual understanding, respect, and peaceful coexistence of the peoples. By studying universal religious experience and through a dialogue between peoples and religions, the Ecumenical Patriarchate contributes substantially not only to the promotion of world unity, human rights, and freedom, but also to a deeper, basic knowledge of the human being.

For this reason the Great Mother Church, inspired by a sense of Jesus Christ's love and responsibility towards the human person and all of human society – near or far – is at all times present to the world to testify to truth, love, and hope. The presence of the Mother Church, during this crucial period of international reclassifications and experimentations, is evolving into a more active and manifold service. Thus, the Ecumenical Patriarchate is beginning an even closer dialogue with the religions of the world, especially with Islam. Nowadays, this dialogue is dynamically promoted by the blessings and the initiatives of the Patriarch himself. In his enthronement speech (November 2, 1991), His Holiness, Patriarch Bartholomew I, on the one hand, stressed the meaning that the unity of the Orthodox Christian faith has for the unity and peace of the world; and, on the other hand, he emphasized the great duty of the Church toward humanity. This duty consists of a dialogue with the great world's religions and of the preservation of the universal spiritual and moral values that dignify the human being. This is why the Ecumenical Patriarchate considers dialogue with Islam both necessary and indispensable.

The dialogue with the Islamic world has a distinct and vital importance for the Orthodox Christian Church. Islam is our direct, immediate neighbor, and the "East" is not foreign to us. For fourteen centuries now, the Orthodox Christian faith and Islam have coexisted and lived together in close connection with each other.

The Ecumenical Patriarchate, based on the bonds of the past, opens itself to a new dialogue with Islam, according to the contemporary demands of our times. In general, the dialogues that the Patriarchate holds jointly with Islam can be outlined in four categories:

1. Local and regional dialogues (bilateral, between Muslims and Christians, or trilateral, among Muslims, Christians, and Jews);

2. Dialogues that the Patriarch conducts during his official travels through the Christian and Islamic world of the East, or during his official visits to Europe and the European Parliament, where he becomes an ambassador of peace between east and west, between Christianity and Islam;

3. For the last decade, the Ecumenical Patriarchate has been organizing a particular kind of dialogue with international implications, focusing on the protection of our natural environment. (This dialogue is very important for the life, cooperation, and peaceful coexistence of the Christian and Islamic peoples living in the Balkans, the Black Sea, and the Eastern Mediterranean countries.);

4. Academic dialogues of an international character between Islam and the Orthodox Church, which are organized with the blessing of His Holiness, the Ecumenical Patriarch, by the Orthodox Centre of the Ecumenical Patriarchate in Chambésy-Geneva, and conducted under the auspices of His Eminence, Damaskinos, Metropolitan of Switzerland.

Dialogues, Local and Regional

The Ecumenical Patriarchate organizes or participates in conferences of local and regional character, in which issues of religious, humanistic, social, and ecological nature are discussed. His Holiness, the Ecumenical Patriarch, takes part in these conferences – either in person or through his representatives – and actively promotes a dialogue of mutual understanding and friendship among Christians, Muslims, and Jews.

This is due to the cosmopolitan spirit of Istanbul, a city in which – and under various favorable or, at times, unfavorable conditions – Muslims, Christians, and Jews have long lived together.

Organization of Conferences

1. Peace and Tolerance

The 1994 conference, jointly organized in Istanbul by the Ecumenical Patriarchate and the New York-based organization, Voice of the Conscience, on the subject of Peace and Tolerance, was of great importance for Eastern Mediterranean peoples, the peoples of the Black Sea, and for the peoples of the Caucasus area.

Within the framework of this conference, the Patriarch (overwhelmed at that time by the ongoing drama in Bosnia, the Caucasus, and other regions of the Near East, especially Palestine) invited leaders of the three monotheistic religions to declare, as children of Abraham, their will to cooperate in order that mutual understanding, tolerance, and peaceful coexistence would predominate in the world.

The conference elaborated the famous "Bosporus Declaration," condemning all kinds of war, but particularly war in the name of religion.

The Patriarchal committee set the following guidelines for these meetings: mutual cognizance in an academic level; religious freedom; and the need to undertake joint action in the fields of altruism, education, and contemporary social problems.

2. Symposia, in Myra of Lycia, in honor of Saint Nicholas

Of great importance to communications between Muslims and Christians are regional symposia, organized in Myra of Lycia (southwestern Turkey) by the Ecumenical Patriarchate, with the cooperation of the local authorities. These symposia are held in honor of Saint Nicholas, patron saint of seamen, who is respected by Muslims and Christians alike. These symposia have been held since 1982 and have taken place almost yearly, on the Feastday in memory of Saint Nicholas (6th December).

Participation in bilateral conferences, local and regional, and international meetings

The participation of the Ecumenical Patriarchate – by the Patriarch himself or by his representatives – in bilateral or trilateral conferences, local and regional, is another activity that contributes substantially to the peaceful cooperation of Muslims and Christians and, furthermore, promotes the great vision of world peace.

1. The Ecumenical Patriarchate routinely extends congratulatory messages on the great Muslim feasts (*Id al-fitr* or *Seker bayrami, Id M-adha* or *gurban bayrami*).

2. Communications and dialogues are held with leading personalities of Muslim and Turkish societies. Through these, the Ecumenical Patriarchate promotes a fundamental, contemporary necessity: a dialogue of friendship and solidarity between the two religious traditions and peoples.

3. The relationship of the Patriarch with important people of Islamic and Turkish societies, especially with journalists and writers, has resulted in invitations for him to participate in a series of conferences that promote relations between the Orthodox Church and Islam. The Patriarch, who was respectfully invited to take part, delivered inspired speeches and messages during the following conferences:

a. The symposium "Eternal Mediation," (*Ebedi Risalet*), which was organized by the newspaper *Zaman* on October 22, 1995 in Istanbul;

b. The symposium "Tolerance and Moderation," which was organized during the period October 4-7, 1995, in Istanbul, under the auspices of UNESCO and with the cooperation of the University of Galatasarai, Istanbul;

c. The "Appeal" for universal peace by the Universal Fraternity, a conference held on November 1, 1995, in Istanbul, by the Institution of the Great Mevlana (*Dunya Kardeslik Birligi Mevlana Yuce Vakfi*);

d. The Patriarch delivered a speech to the opening session of the "Dialogue of Civilizations and Religions," which was held by the Municipality of Istanbul, on March 7, 1998, in the Congress Hall of Cemal Resit Rey. He made reference to two ways that the faithful of the two religions must follow in order to be guided to useful conclusions, i.e. the ways of peaceful coexistence and peaceful mutual understanding;

e. The "Inter-Religious Dialogue of the Second Council of Religious Affairs of the Turkish Republic." Patriarch Bartholomew, who was invited to participate by the Presidency of the Supreme Council of Religious Affairs of the Turkish Republic, went to Ankara on November 24, 1998, and participated in the work of the Second Council of Religious Affairs (*Din gurasi*), convoked by the Administration of Religious Affairs (*Diyanet*) of the Turkish Republic, from November 23-27, 1998. The Ecumenical Patriarch's speech, a theological and philosophical exploration of the necessity of inter-religious dialogue – especially between Christianity and Islam – was heard with great interest by the densely packed audience at the Council;

f. The Patriarch was also invited to deliver a speech on the central theme at the "Tolerance in the Ottoman Empire" conference, which was organized by the Foundation for the Strategic and Social Research of the Marmara Association, on July 12, 1999, in Istanbul. He stressed in a thorough and discerning manner that the forms of tolerance that prevailed during the Ottoman Empire era demand, in our time, completion and transformation into real freedoms that do justice to the human being;

g. At a Symposium on the 700th anniversary of the

foundation of the Ottoman Empire, organized in Istanbul by the Association of Journalists and Writers, on September 21, 1999, with the theme "The Art of Coexisting," the Patriarch stressed that the main element of the art of coexisting is love. The broader the love, the happier the coexistence;

h. One recent and distinguished opportunity for the Patriarch to participate in the dialogue of friendship between Islam and Christianity was his eminent presence in the International Symposium on "Abraham as a symbol of faith and bond of unity among the three monotheistic religions." The symposium was organized by the Association of Journalists and Writers of Turkey and was held first, April 13-14, 2000, in the renowned ancient cities of Harran and Edessa (Urfa) – the latter a city where the Patriarch had lived in the past – and then, from April 15-16, 2000, in Istanbul. His acclaimed speech during the inauguration of the symposium at the ancient historical area of Harran, in the presence of many officials and crowds of people who had arrived in great numbers, caused a great sensation and was extensively covered by the Turkish mass media.

i. "Religions, Faith, and Tolerance," another symposium that the Patriarch was invited to attend and address, stressed the great significance, for world peace, of dialogue among the three monotheistic religions. This symposium was organized with under the auspices of the Turkish religious communities in Izmir, from May 12-13, 2000.

Official Representations of the Ecumenical Patriarchate in International Congresses

The Ecumenical Patriarchate also engages in dialogue with the other two monotheistic religions, by its participation through, official representatives, in various bilateral (between Christianity and Islam) or trilateral (among Christianity, Islam, and Judaism) international conferences around the world. The most important of these are the following:

1. Orthodox Christian-Muslim Symposium. Boston, USA, March 17-19, 1985.

2. Three Religions: A commitment for Peace. University of Alcala de Henares, Madrid, Spain, November 23-30, 1994.

3. Various Conferences of European Churches.

4. The Mediterranean Society: A Challenge for the Three Civilizations? An informal dialogue among Islam, Judaism, and Christianity, Toledo, Spain, November 4-7, 1995, organized by the European Union Committee *Cellule de Prospective*, to discuss the presuppositions of cooperation and peaceful coexistence among the peoples of the three great monotheistic religions and civilizations of the Mediterranean area.

5. The Dialogue among the Three Monotheistic Religions: Toward a Culture of Peace, jointly organized by UNESCO and His Majesty King Hassan II of Morocco, Rabat, February 14-16, 1998.

6. Bethlehem 2000, organized by the UN Committee on the Exercise of the Inalienable Rights of the Palestinian People, February 18, 1999. His Holiness, the Ecumenical Patriarch, was represented by a pioneering

personality in the field of inter-religious dialogues, the Metropolitan of Switzerland, Damaskenos.

THE PATRIARCH AS AN AMBASSADOR OF PEACE BETWEEN EAST AND WEST, CHRISTIAN AND ISLAMIC WORLDS

Within the scope of his pastoral service and the realization of the Church's work in the world, His Holiness, Patriarch Bartholomew I, visits various provinces of the Ecumenical Throne all over the world and makes brotherly visits to the Orthodox Churches and the Old Eastern Christian Patriarchates. He also visits people of the other religions, especially the people of Islam, with the hope of fostering mutual understanding, benevolent cooperation, and peaceful communication and coexistence. These official tours and visits of the Patriarch to all centers of the world afford him opportunities to communicate, in the spirit of the love of Jesus Christ, with all people who seek the truth and God, and to listen to the voices of their hearts. These Patriarchal communications with the world constitute a broader dialogue of the Church with the entire human society, especially, however, with the world of Islam, and make the Patriarch an ambassador of peace between East and West, North and South. It is in this spirit that the Patriarch participates in international gatherings such as the European Parliament, UNESCO, and others, and undertakes initiatives toward the solution of those burning issues and problems that occupy all of human society, such as hunger and misery in the Third World, ecological concerns, and many others.

The Patriarch, the Old Eastern Christian Patriarchates, and the World of Islam

In 1992, His Holiness, Patriarch Bartholomew commenced a series of official visits abroad, in order to strengthen the Ecumenical Patriarchate's bonds and communications with both the Christian Churches of the East and West and with the peoples of the East and Islam. By visiting the East, the Patriarch had the chance to find himself among the Christian and Islamic people and open up his heart, the heart of Jesus Christ's great Mother Church, to all people of God, Christian, Islamic, and Jewish.

The Patriarch has said that the peoples of the East and the Third World are our brothers and sisters, that they are flesh of our flesh, and that our duty is to love them and care for them, for the improvement of their lives, material and spiritual, and for their dignity and honor. His words have had a great impact on his audiences and left the people to whom he spoke with vivid memories of his visits to the East.

The Patriarch as an Ambassador of Peace between East and West, the President of the Commission of the European Union, and the European Parliament

The aforementioned love and affection of the Orthodox Eastern Church toward the peoples of the East and the West, the South and the North, together with the responsibility of the European Union to comprehend, care, and offer their aid to alleviate their material and spiritual needs, were declared by the Patriarch during his May 1993 visit as an official guest to the President

of the Commission of the European Union, Mr. Jacques
Delors, and later in April 1994, to the Seat of the European Parliament in Strasbourg, where he delivered a
momentous speech to the MPs and to the peoples of Europe. The Ecumenical Patriarch's message makes us reflect that, if there is a "space" in which the spiritual limits of Europe are not defined by its geographical limits,
then this should be the "space" of Orthodoxy. The intellectual life, beauty, and civilization of Orthodoxy extends to the countries of the Near and Middle East, thus
manifesting the Church's particular interest and care for
these peoples. The Patriarch declared, while addressing
his speech to the European Parliament, the vision of the
Orthodox Church for the unity of all Christian Churches as well as for the unity of the entire world, for the
preservation of all human values and rights.

*The Patriarch and the Sixth International Conference on
Religion and Peace World Assembly, Riva del Garda, Italy,
November 3-5, 1994*

The Patriarch's outstanding participation in the
Sixth World Conference on Religion and Peace World
Assembly reveals to us the concern and responsibility
of the Church toward human society, for peace, liberty,
and justice among peoples.

DIALOGUES FOR THE PROTECTION
OF GOD'S CREATION AND THE
IMPROVEMENT OF THE ENVIRONMENT

Of particular significance for the prosperity, cooperation, and peaceful coexistence of the Christians and Muslims of the area around the Black Sea and the Eastern Mediterranean are the conferences on ecology, which the Ecumenical Patriarchate has organized over the last decade for the protection of the divine creation and the sanctity of life. These efforts, which have enjoyed the warm personal interest and care of His Holiness, Patriarch Bartholomew, included:

1. The establishment of the date of September 1st of each year as a day of prayer for the protection of the natural environment;

2. Ecological conferences organized at the island Chalki (Turkey), with the cooperation of the World Wildlife Fund For Nature. His Royal Highness, Prince Philip, the Duke of Edinburgh, attended some of these conferences;

3. Establishment of the Ecological Institute of Chalki on June 13, 1999, to promote dialogue between Christians and Muslims for the protection of the natural environment of the Balkans, Black Sea, and Eastern Mediterranean countries;

4. International on-board symposia.

The first of these was held from the September 21-25, 1995, in conjunction with the Orthodox Jubilee for the 1900th Anniversary of the writing of the Book of Revelation by John the Evangelist, on the island of Patmos, Greece, where all the Orthodox Churches participated. The vessel carrying the Patriarch and the other participants sailed from Istanbul and, via Kusadasi, arrived at the port of Patmos. From Patmos, the Patriarch sent a message of peace addressed to Muslim friends and to the entire world, a message that derived from the eschatological hope of the Revelation for the renovation and recapitulation of the Creation.

The second on-board international ecological symposium was very important for the peace of the Christian and Islamic peoples of the Black Sea and the Eastern Mediterranean. With a theme of "Religion, Science, Enviroment of the Black Sea," it took place October 19-20, 1997. The vessel, under the auspices of Ecumenical Patriarch Bartholomew and the President of the Commission of the European Union Mr. Jacques Santer, sailed from Trabzun and, after cruising the Black Sea with calls to the ports of Batum, Novorosisk, Yalta, Odessa, Costanza, Varna, and Istanbul, finally sailed into the harbor of Thessaloniki.

The third on-board ecological symposium took place on a vessel sailing the river Danube October 16-25, 1999, and was very important for the life and peace of the Christian and Islamic peoples of the countries through which the river flows, and for the countries bordering the Black Sea.

INTERNATIONAL ACADEMIC DIALOGUES WITH ISLAM

Inspired and visionary dialogues between Christians and Muslims have been jointly organized by the Orthodox Center of the Ecumenical Patriarchate in Chambésy-Geneva, Switzerland (directed by Metropolitan Damaskinos of Switzerland) and the Royal Academy for Islamic Civilization Research in Amman, Jordan (the *al Albait* Foundation, directed by Prince

Hassan bin Talal). To date, nine conferences have taken place.

The first conference was held at the Orthodox Center in Switzerland in 1986 and explored "Authority and Religion in the traditions of the two faiths and in contemporary reality."

The second was held in Amman in 1987, with the subject, "Models of Hisrorical Co-existence between Muslims and Christians and their Future Prospects."

The third was held in the Orthodox Center, in Chambesy in 1988, and addressed "Peace and Justice in the traditions of the Two Monotheistic Religions."

The fourth was held in Istanbul in 1989, on the subject of "Religious Pluralism," to emphasize that the co-existence of peoples of a variety of religious traditions in the same geographical region is a source of enrichment for their spiritual traditions, rather than a cause for conflict.

The fifth conference, after the nightmare of the Gulf crisis, was held in Amman in 1993, to discuss "Youth and the Values of Moderation," and presented a spontaneous and moving testimony to the special importance of the role of religion in appeasing the spirit of conflict and in propounding the value of moderation in the relations between nations.

The sixth was held in Athens in 1994, on the important topic of "Education for Understanding and Cooperation."

The special importance of the subject of education was also outlined in the seventh conference, held in Amman in 1996, to discuss "The philosophy of educational systems in Islam and Christianity."

The eighth conference was a genuine landmark in the dialogue between Christians and Muslims. Held in Istanbul, June 3-7, 1997, "Perspectives on Cooperation and Participation between Christians and Muslims on the Eve of the New Century," drew the participation of many Christians and Muslims. The inaugural speech by the Ecumenical Patriarch made a great impression on the audience, because he expressed in clear terms the vision of the Church for a world without frontiers, in which the justice of God and human values will prevail, since what unites us is greater than what divides us.

Finally, the ninth conference was held in Amman, November 10-12, 1998, and focused on the topic, "Muslims and Christians in Modern Society: Images of the Other and the Meaning of Citizenship." The meaning of co-citizenship in modern society remains current and vital, and calls us to proceed to further mutual Christian-Islamic efforts for its realization.

Conclusion

Summarizing the manifold dialogues of friendship that the Ecumenical Patriarchate holds today, with a particular sense of responsibility to the world of Islam, we can see that the great Mother Church, inspired by the love of Jesus Christ toward humanity, is at every moment present in the world with its charismatic life and blesses the human being in the quest for the truth.

CODA: HOW AN ORTHODOX CHRISTIAN MONK SAVED THE LIFE OF A MUSLIM PRINCE

George C. Papademetriou

In 1951 Father Theodosios Makkos saved the life of Prince Hussein, who later became king of Jordan. This is a remarkable story of friendship of a simple monk and a king, a Greek Orthodox Christian and a Muslim.

Father Theodosios was born in Smyrna, Asia Minor, present-day Turkey, on July 11, 1913. He became an orphan at an early age and was reared by his grandmother and aunt. He had a burning desire to become a monk and serve the Church in the Holy Land. He came to Palestine in 1928 and remained there until his death, in 1991, at the age of 78. He served the Church of Jerusalem with great devotion at various places and positions for 63 years. In his last 50 years he was the spiritual father and resident priest at the monastery for women, Saints Mary and Martha, sisters of Lazarus, in Bethany, a suburb of Jerusalem.

While in Palestine, Father Theodosios befriended King Abdullah. In July 1951, the king made a pilgrimage to the holy shrine of Omar at Jerusalem with his grandson Prince Hussein. The prince was a very young man at that time. While in Jerusalem, King Abdullah was assassinated. Father Theodosios was present, accompanying the king. He immediately took the young prince under his cassock (*rasson*) and brought him to the Greek Orthodox Patriarchate of Jerusalem. The prince was hidden there. Father Theodosios reported to the Patriarch the tragedy of the assassination of King Abdullah and was greatly concerned for the safety and life of the young prince. The Patriarch, before the rebels cut off the phones, placed a call to the Jordanian authorities that the young prince was alive and hidden in a safe place in the Orthodox Patriarchate. The Jordanian government sent appropriate officials to the Patriarchate and took the young prince under the protection of Jordan.

After this episode, Prince Hussein was always indebted to Father Theodosios for saving his life. He often visited Father Theodosios in the monastery in Bethany. When the prince later became king he continued to have close relations and visit Father Theodosios at the monastery. Father Theodosios was able to enter the king's palace at any time. He helped numerous people by giving his good word to the king.

The king requested the Patriarch to elevate Father Theodosios to the episcopate. Father Theodosios was elected by the synod three times to be elevated, but he refused the honor. Nevertheless he chose to remain a simple monk to serve the nuns at the monastery of Martha and Mary. He was well known throughout the region for his love and charity for all people without regard of religion or race. He loved all people without distinction and dedicated to charity and the service of justice.

When I was in Jerusalem for the month of January 1986 on a mission of study and dialogue with Jews and Muslims, I had the honor of meeting Father Theodosios. I visited him in the monastery and he told me the story of how he saved the king's life. He also told me that whenever the king greeted him, as a sign of respect, the king opened his palm for Father Theodosios to kiss, whereas the other people kissed the back of the king's hand.

Father Theodosios dedicated his entire life to protecting the holy shrines and the people of Palestine that he loved so much. This is a great example for all people to follow, that is, to love and protect the life of all regardless of religious affiliation, nationality, or race. All people are people of God created in His image. All should try to emulate Father Theodosios's example of love and respect for others.

REFERENCE

A Summary of Islamic Beliefs

George C. Papademetriou

One objective of this present study is to introduce Islam and its faith to Christians. Islam is rapidly growing in numbers (estimated at over one billion followers) and many Christians in America and elsewhere live as neighbors and go to the same schools with Muslims. For this reason, it is important to give Christians a correct understanding of the Islamic religion that will allow productive and peaceful interaction and coexistence in a democratic society that guarantees freedom to all people.

The "ideal society of God" for Muslims is the Islamic society governed by the *Qur'an*. All aspects of life are expressed in harmony with Islamic law. In this ideal society there is no distinction between religious and political organization of the state or religion. For Islam, there is no distinction between the holy and the secular. For this reason, all human actions must be done according to the law of God.

The religion taught by Muhammad known as "Islam" means submission, a name coined by Muhammad himself to indicate the complete surrender and obedience due to Allah. The use of the term "Muhammadanism" is offensive to Muslims, who do not espouse the belief that Muhammad is God. Rather, he is the messenger of God who re-instituted the commitment of Abraham and called all people to "submit" or "surrender" to God the Merciful. The basic creed of Islam is that, "God is one and Muhammad is His messenger."

FOUNDER

The founder of Islam is Muhammad or Abu al-Qāsim Muhammad ibn `Abd Allāh (570-632 CE). His father, Abdullah, died before Muhammad was born and his mother died before he was six years old.[1] His paternal grandfather brought him up and looked after him. Later it was his uncle, Abu Talib, one of Muhammad's first followers.

In his early years, Muhammad was a shepherd and camel driver. In 595, he married the wealthy widow Chadidscha who was sixteen years older than he was. They had two sons who died early and four daughters. One of his daughters, Fatima, married Ali, Abu Talib's son.

In 610, he climbed the mountain Erat near Mecca and lived in a cave. Here he experienced divine revelation. According to Sura 96 of the *Qur'an*, the Archangel Gabriel appeared to him on a regular basis to interpret the message of God. According to Islamic tradition, Muhammad saw in his vision that he was carried to Jerusalem, then, taken to the seventh heaven by the Archangel Gabriel. According to another tradition, he saw in his vision that he came from Mecca to Jerusalem by night and from there he was carried to heaven.

When Muhammad began to have these visions, he inaugurated the preaching of the message of God. The first person to believe in his prophetic mission was his wife.

Muhammad preached in the name of the revelation given to him by the Archangel Gabriel. He taught strict monotheism and condemned the Arabic paganism and idolatry. He initially converted twelve followers. However, his message was strongly opposed by the aristocratic class in Mecca, a city possessing the shrine of Ka'ba – containing the holy stone that fell from the sky – and a center of worship for the Arabs.

Muhammad, in spite of the opposition to his new religion, managed to reach the poor class of people, and established a religious community dedicated to his message. The population of Mecca was roused against him and his followers, and persecuted them violently. To avoid the danger, part of the first Islamic community was forced to seek refuge in the Orthodox Christian nation of Ethiopia. For ten years, the wealthy class of Mecca persecuted the Islamic community. Muhammad then turned to Medina where the residents were Arabs and three Judaic tribes.

In 611, 72 residents of Medina subscribed to Muhammad's message and became his followers. In 622, Muhammad decided to transfer the center of his functions to Medina. This year is called Hijra and is the beginning of the Islamic calendar.

Throughout these years, Muhammad was influenced by both Jewish and Christian teachings. In Medina, he worked through the monotheistic Jewish community to reach out to the larger social strata. But when the rabbis reacted negatively to him because of the Jewish converts to his message, he abandoned his peaceful means and used force. He started the warring method (*razzia*) against the caravans of Mecca. In 624, his followers battled the Meccans at Badr and emerged victorious. He proclaimed those who fell in battle as martyrs and divided the spoils among his followers. This gave them encouragement to proceed on to future successes.

In 627, the Meccans, assisted by the Bedouins, attacked Muhammad, massacred hundreds of men, women, and children, and destroyed the third tribe of the Jews in Medina. Muhammad, nevertheless, proclaimed that he represented the continuation of the Abrahamic tradition, and directed Muslims to face the Ka'ba in Mecca for prayer, rather than Jerusalem.

In 629, Muhammad engaged in a war with the Byzantines and was defeated. He began negotiations with the Meccans and eventually entered Mecca on a camel in 630. He went to the Ka'ba, ordered all pagan gods and idols to be cleared out, and proclaimed that the one true God – Allah – alone was to be worshiped.

Muhammad succeeded in extending his dominion over the entire Arabic peninsula and brought all the Bedouin tribes within his political and religious camp. He proclaimed holy war (*jihad*) against pagan idolaters, Jews, Christians, and Persians. Mecca was proclaimed "holy land" and non-believers were forbidden to enter.

Muhammad died in 632. He did not leave a political will, but said that the most competent of his followers was to succeed him in the political and religious leadership. Abū Bakr (573-634) was his first successor, known as caliph. In 634 Abū Bakr died and Omar became the second caliph. In 644, another close associate of Muhammad, Othman became caliph. Ali ibn Abu Talib, Muhammad's son-in-law became the fourth caliph in 656. He had two boys, grandsons of Muhammad and the only male successors to the prophet.

The Qur'an

The Sacred Book of Islam is called *Qur'an* (sometimes given in English as "Koran"), "which manifests the truth about all things."[2] It is the voice from on high, the message from God, the Word of God given to Muhammad by the Archangel Gabriel. It consists of 114 chapters or *suras*. In the beginning, the *Qur'an* was an oral tradition that was committed to memory. During Muhammad's life, sometimes verses were written out on palm leaves or on stones, and later were transcribed. The oral word of the *Qur'an* was collected by the second caliph, Omar, and committed into writing. The Authorized Version was established by his successor, Othman. This version remains still today the authorized word of God.[3]

The *Qur'an*, as the revelation of God, is the light that illuminates the way of the faithful to God. It says, "It is He who brings down clear revelations to His servant, so that He may lead you out of darkness into the light."[4] Muhammad, the messenger of God, received the light of revelation, "so He may lead the faithful who do good works from the darkness to light."[5] It is written that, "This Book is a veritable proof from your Lord, a guide and a blessing to true believers,"[6] and also, "And now we have revealed this Book with our blessings ... a veritable sign has now come to you from the Lord: a guide and a blessing."[7] The *Qur'an* must be obeyed if one wants to find favor with God, who says, "For to you we have revealed the Book which manifests the truth about all things, a guide, a blessing, and good news to those who submit to Allah."[8]

All actions that are in harmony with the *Qur'an* are good and holy. The Qur'an, as the revealed word of God, dictates all political and religious practices. For that reason, the Qur'an is the fundamental constitution of every Islamic society

In addition to the *Qur'an*, the Hadith is a source of authority in Islam. The Hadith is the oral tradition of the life and activities of Muhammad. The first to systematically collect the Tradition was Buchari (d. ca. 870). Others who made such collections were: Muslim (d. ca. 875); Ibn Madscha (d. ca. 886); Abu Dawood (d. ca. 888); Tirwidi (d. ca. 892); and Hasal (d. 915). Although the Tradition represented in these collections claims to go back to the time and life of Muhammad, they cannot today be verified as authentic.

THE FIVE PILLARS OF ISLAM

The Islamic community (known as the *Umma*) is guided by the *Qur'an* to live a life in harmony with the will of God. The basic requirement for a Muslim to live in the community is the observance of the five "pillars," which govern life according to Islamic faith and ethics.

The first pillar is *shahāda*. Though there is no formal

creed in Islam, this could be considered one. It is the confession of faith in the One God and in the prophetic office of Muhammad. This is a common affirmation of faith required of all Muslims and recited daily: "There is no god but God. Muhammad is the messenger of God." Islam is absolute devotion and submission to the one God and His will: "Obey Allah and the apostle that you may find mercy."[9] Again, it is written, "have fear of Allah ... Obey Allah and His apostle, if you are true believers."[10] Consequently, one cannot be a Muslim without accepting this *Quranic* truth.

The second pillar of Islam is *salât*, or prayer. The sacred law of Islam requires each believer to pray five times a day: at dawn, noon, afternoon, evening and before darkness at night.

In prayer, the believer enters into love and communion with God and fellow believers who join together in prayer. The communal prayer at noon on Friday is at the mosque, where the imam guides the believers in prayer. This communal prayer creates the atmosphere of "brotherhood," and is a duty required by the *Qur'an:*

> Believers, when you are summoned to Friday prayers, hasten to the remembrance of Allah and cease your reading. That would be best for you, if you but knew it. Then, when the prayers are ended, disperse and go in quest of Allah's bounty. Remember Allah always, so that you may prosper.[11]

The third pillar is *zakât*, charity, or works of love for the poor. It is a kind of tax, based on a certain percentage of one's annual income, set aside for the welfare of the indigent population of Islamic society. Alms are prerequisite to being "cleansed and purified."[12] The *Qur'an* says, "Attend to your prayers and pay the alms-tax. Allah shall reward your good works. He is watching over all your actions."[13] And also, "Believers, give in alms of the wealth you have carefully earned and of that which we have brought out of the earth for you, not worthless things which you yourselves would only reluctantly accept. Know that Allah is self-sufficient and glorious."[14] Alms given to the poor will be rewarded: "Whatever alms you give shall rebound to your own advantage, provided that you give them for the love of Allah. And whatever alms you give shall be paid back to you in full; you shall not be wronged."[15] And further on, "Those that have faith and do good works, attend to their prayers and pay the alms-tax, will be rewarded by their Lord and will have nothing to fear or to regret."[16]

The fourth pillar is *Sawn,* fasting during the month of Ramadan. This commemorates the occasion when Muhammad received the *Qur'an.*"[17] In Islam, fasting means not eating anything from dawn to sunset: "Eat and drink until you can tell a white thread from a black one in the light of the coming dawn. Then resume the fast till nightfall."[18]

The fifth pillar is the *hajj,* pilgrimage to one or more of the three primary holy places: the Ka'ba in Mecca, a city that Islamic tradition says was built by Abraham; the Mosque of the Prophet (first mosque to be built) in Medina, containing Muhammad's tomb; and, Jerusalem, where the Dome of the Rock was built (685-91) on the place from which Muhammad ascended to heaven. The *Qur'an* says, "Exhort all men to make the pilgrimage. They will come to you on foot and on the backs of swift camels; from every distant quarter they will come to avail themselves of many a benefit and to pronounce the name of Allah over the beasts which He has given them."[19] And again, "make the pilgrimage and visit the Sacred House for His sake."[20]

Pilgrims wear white robes and process seven times around the sacred rock of the Ka'ba and kiss the central dark part of the rock. This rock is believed to be a meteorite that has fallen from heaven as a sign to man, coming from God, of an eternal covenant that binds man to worship the only true God and no other God.[21]

The pilgrimage is required of all Muslims and strengthens communion with God and the desire of the believer to be part of the devoted religious community – the *Umma*. This gathering in Mecca, at the Ka'ba, brings together all the brethren in an international unity of all the Muslim community. Those who make the pilgrimage thereafter receive the title *hajj* or pilgrim.

COMMUNITY LIFE

For Muslims the *Umma*, the ideal "community of God," is an Islamic society that unites under Allah all people and all aspects of human life. The most important characteristics of members of this community are the fear of God and obedience. Obedience to divine law is what binds all followers of Islam together and creates the *Umma*. The *Qur'an* says, "You are the noblest nation that has ever been raised up for mankind. You enjoin justice and forbid evil. You believe in Allah."[22] And again, "The true believers, both men and women, are friends to each other. They enjoin what is just and forbid what is evil. They attend to their prayers and pay the alms-tax and obey Allah and His apostle. On these, Allah will have mercy. He is mighty and wise."[23]

In this "community of God" there is no distinction between religion and the state, between human and divine law. But there is a clear distinction between the holy and the profane, between the religious and the secular. All human acts, either political or religious, as long as they are in harmony with God's law, revealed in the *Qur'an*, are good and holy. The *Qur'an* contains the basic duties of the faith and actions for all the followers of Islam. The *Qur'an* dictates for each individual believer to live in harmony with this revealed law and abide in it from the cradle to the grave. One lives happily in eternity if he avoids even for a moment conflict with the religious law set forth in the *Qur'an*.

The fundamental demand of the Quranic law upon individual believers and upon society is that they follow the "light" of God:

> It is He who brings down clear revelations to His servants, so he may lead you out of darkness into the light. Allah is compassionate and merciful to you.[24]
> Believe then in Allah and His apostle and in true light, which we have revealed. Allah has knowledge of all your actions.[25]

The *Qur'an* is both the light of God and the law of God, and articulates clearly the divine commandments and our duties to God:

> Momentous signs have come to your Lord. He that sees them shall himself have much to gain, but he who is blind to them shall lose much indeed.[26]
> This (the *Qur'an*) is an admonition to mankind and a blessing to believers.[27]

The believer who follows the "revelation" of the

Qur'an and its laws stands in the straight path. He obeys God, and does the will of God; he succeeds in this life and, in the future life, he avoids condemnation and judgment and enjoys eternal happiness in paradise.

JIHAD

Jihad has become commonly understood in the West as "holy war." However, *jihad* in the Islamic tradition has two meanings: war against the enemies of Allah and His people; and, secondly, the inner spiritual struggle against evil passions. Internally, *Jihad* is a struggle in the path of God against evil. Externally, it can be warfare to expand Islam to non-Muslim territories or to defend the Islamic faith from the enemies of evil and is therefore a struggle against polytheism in order to bring its adherents into line with Islam.

Today, some Muslim scholars interpret *jihad* as witnessing to the faith in the world. Islam is a missionary religion and, as such, imposes this as a duty for all Muslims.

The mystics of Islam, however, interpret *jihad* primarily as a struggle against inner passions, that is, as an inner spiritual warfare. The objective is to overcome the evil disposition of the passions.

There are some sects of Islam that explicitly interpret *jihad* as "holy war." Kharji, an extremist sect of Islam, maintains that *jihad* is the sixth pillar of the faith dictated by Muhammad. This sect teaches that the community or the state must wage *jihad* against the unbelievers at all times and in all places. It is, they claim, the duty of all individual believers to fight the evil world (understood to be the non-Muslim world) and bring it to submit to Islam. This is the current view and practice of those characterized as "fundamentalist" Muslims. The *Qur'an* says to fight those who do not believe in God and who do not acknowledge the Religion of Truth: "Fight against such of those to whom the Scriptures were given as believe neither in Allah nor the Last Day, who do not forbid what Allah and His apostle have forbidden, and they do not embrace the true faith, until they pay tribute out of hand and are utterly subdued."[28] Those who die in a jihad promoting Islam are promised the noble fruits of martyrdom, eternal life in Paradise: "You must not think those who were slain in the cause of Allah are dead. They are alive, and well provided for by their Lord; pleased with His gifts and rejoicing that those whom they left behind and not yet joined them have nothing to fear or to regret; rejoicing in Allah's grace and bounty. Allah will not deny the faithful their reward."[29]

The Islamic community is called upon to unite against all nations and religions to subject them to Allah in order to root out evil and establish Islamic justice throughout the entire world. As is attested by modern scholars, "Jihad in Islam is a collective obligation of the whole community transcending location and nationality. It binds and unites all believers together against all other religions and political ideologies."[30]

OTHER BELIEFS OF ISLAM

The *Qur'an* refers to the creation both of man and of angels. With regard to man, it says, "We created man from dry clay, from black, molded loam, and before him Satan from smokeless fire. Your Lord said to the angels: 'I am creating man from dry clay, from black molded loam. When I have fashioned him and breathed of My spirit into him, kneel down and prostrate yourselves before him.'"[31]

Muslims believe in good and evil angels. The good angels are guardians of the believers to lead them in doing good deeds. They also believe in Satan that misleads people to do evil. Only in the Islamic community is one safe and delivered from fear of the evil machinations of the devil.

Islam promises that those who do good works in this life will be rewarded with the resurrection of the body and eternal life in paradise, while those who do evil in this life will reap punishment:

> Woe to those who serve other gods besides Him, who give no alms and disbelieve in the life to come. As for those who have faith and do good works, a lasting reward awaits them.[32]

SUNNI AND SHI'A

As noted earlier, Muhammad did not leave a "successor" to lead the new religion after his death. As a result, thirty years after his death his followers were divided into opposing camps. On the one side, there were the Sunni who stood for the tradition (*sunna*) of Muhammad. On the other side, there were the Shi'a who followed Ali ibn Abu Talib, who was the prophet's cousin and son-in-law. This difference of historic leadership, rather than one of doctrine, still divides these two main branches of Islam.

For the early Shi'ites, the Muslim leader had to be a descendant of the Prophet. For this reason, they supported Ali and his wife Fatima, Muhammad's daughter, as true successors. Even now, the leader must be a trusted *wasî* who has a personal inner knowledge of the prophet's life that allows him to be an authentic interpreter of the divine message. The *imam* is the "successor" of Muhammad. The *imam* is a spiritual functionary who interprets the Muslim revelation and legacy. As the leader of the Shi'a, the *imam* is considered to be a man with a spiritual charisma to preach and interpret the message of God. Shi'ites look back to Twelve Imams, beginning with Ali.

On the other hand, the Sunnis, or the orthodox Muslims, hold that the successor of Muhammad must be elected by consensus and must be the *Khalipha* (caliph) who governs the Muslim society. This leader is considered the protector of the religion of Islam and implements Islamic religious law (*Shari' a*) in society. The Sunnis believe that the first four caliphs, who succeeded Muhammad and were his descendents, ascended as caliphs by consensus and were "rightly guided." They ruled before the Sunni-Shi'a split.

NOTES

1 The most important source of the life and activities of Muhammad were written by Ibn Ishaq (died ca. 767) under the title *The Life of the Prophet*, translated into English by A. Guillaume (1955). The *Qur'an* "Muhammad" Sura 47 in *The Koran*, translated with notes by N. J. Dawood, Penguin Books (1974), p.123. All references from the *Qur'an* in

this study will be made from this edition unless otherwise stated. See also, K.D. Georgoules, "Mousoulmanismos" (in Greek) *Religious and Ethical Encyclopedia* (Athens: Athanasios Martinos Publisher, 1966), vol.9, p. 113ff. See also the excellent study by Gregorios D. Ziakas, *The Islamic Teachings on Man* (in Greek) (Thessalonike, 1979). This study is well documented and very helpful to me in writing this paper.

2 Sura 16:89, *Koran*, p. 310.

3 *Koran*, pp. 10-11.

4 Sura 57:9, *Koran*, p. 107.

5 Sura 65:10, *Koran*, p. 386.

6 Sura 7:203, *Koran*, p. 263.

7 Sura 7:56,57, *Koran*, p. 440.

8 Sura 16:90, *Koran*, p. 310.

9 Sura, 3:132, *Koran*, p. 310.

10 Sura 8:1, *Koran*, p. 314.

11 Sura 62:9, *Koran*, p. 105.

12 Sura 9:103, *Koran*, p. 131.

13 Sura 2:110, *Koran*, p. 343.

14 Sura 2:67, *Koran*, p. 362; Sura 107:1-7, *Koran*, p. 28.

15 Sura 2:73, *Koran*, p. 363.

16 Sura 2:77, *Koran*, p. 364.

17 Sura 97:1-5, *Koran*, p. 27.

18 Sura 2:187, *Koran*, p. 351.

19 Sura 22:28, *Koran*, p. 403.

20 Sura 2:196, *Koran*, p. 352.

21 Sura 7:17 1, *Koran*, p. 160.

22 Sura, 3:110, *Koran*, p. 417.

23 Sura 9:71, *Koran*, p. 328.

24 Sura 57:9, *Koran*, p. 107.

25 Sura 64:8, *Koran*, p. 89.

26 Sura 6:104, *Koran*, p. 435.

27 Sura 45:20, *Koran*, p. 131.

28 Sura 9:29, *Koran* p. 323.

29 Sura 3:169, *Koran*, p. 422.

30 A. J. Abraham and George Haddad, *The Warriors of God: Jihad (Holy War) and Fundamentalists in Islam* (Bristol, Indiana: Wyndham Hall Press, 1989), p. 30. See also Gregorios

D. Ziakas, *History of Religions, B Islam* (in Greek) (Thessalonike: P. Pournaras Press, 1991), p. 379. Also Cyril Glasse, *The Concise Encyclopedia of Islam* (San Francisco: Harper and Row, Publishers, Inc., 1991), pp. 209-210.
31 Sura 15:26, *Koran*, p. 243.
32 Sura 41:8, *Koran*, p. 159.

Appendix:
Recent Activities
of the Ecumenical Patriarchate
in Muslim-Christian Dialogue

Brussels Declaration

December 20, 2001

"The Peace of God in the World"
Toward Peaceful Coexistence and Collaboration
Among the Three Monotheistic Religions:
Judaism, Christianity, and Islam

Grateful to God for this opportunity to come together, we, the participants of this inter-religious meeting, have gathered at the invitation of His All Holiness Bartholomew, the Ecumenical Patriarch, and His Excellency Romano Prodi, President of the European Commission, in Brussels, Belgium, on 19-20 December 2001. Mindful of the horrific terrorist attacks of September 11th in the United States of America, and equally mindful of the existing conflicts in various regions of the world, we have considered in a spirit of good will and sincere disposition the positive contributions of Judaism, Christianity and Islam to the present condition of humanity. It is precisely on the basis of our respect for the diversity of our religions that we engage in this dialogue. Based on these discussions, we, therefore, strive to fulfill our common responsibility to proclaim together "The Peace of God in the World" as embodied within the teachings of our respective religions.

1. The will of God is for the peace of heaven to reign on earth. The peace of God is not the mere absence of war; it is the gift of abundant life. There is indeed an immediate and inseparable connection between peace and justice. Thus we pray constantly for peace to prevail in the world and for peaceful living together among the faithful of all religions in our modern, multicultural, and multi-ethnic global society.

2. Recognizing that, in the history of humankind, members of religious communities have committed crimes, we express our regret and repentance. We nevertheless affirm that extremists do not reflect the teachings of these religions, and therefore religious beliefs are not responsible for the acts of adherents that are committed either by transgression or by misinterpretation. This is why we reaffirm the statement of the 1992 Berne Declaration and the 1994 Bosphorus Declaration that "a crime committed in the name of religion is a crime against religion."

3. One major role of religion is to bring the peace of God into the world on a local and global level. It is the responsibility of religious leaders to prevent religious fervor from being used for purposes that are alien to its role.

4. A fundamental common element of our mono-theistic religions is faith and confidence in the good, human-loving, compassionate and merciful God. The offer of God's love is open to all human beings for free acceptance and without constraint, regardless of race, ethnicity, culture, or gender.

5. The response to God's invitation by the believer is achieved through faith, which is expressed through prayer, love, good works, respect for the other, and in contributing to a just society and social order. Indeed, the essence of each religion is manifested best by those who are pure of heart.

6. All of our religions consider justice and peace as gifts and blessings from God, and as duties of every human being to one another. None of them approves of violence, terrorism or ill-treatment of human beings. All of them disapprove of religious justification of violent and inhuman actions, which do not conform to the spirit of peace and justice, of peaceful cooperation and of respect for the dignity of the human person.

In view of these truths:

7. We emphasize the need to address causes of local and regional tensions, especially in the developing world. Injustices do exist, and we respect the efforts of those who strive to redress them. Nevertheless, this is not a justification for evil that would destroy innocent human life. Hence the call, in all of our religions, is to bring peace with freedom, justice, and human rights.

8. We unanimously reject the assumption that religion contributes to an inevitable clash of civilizations. On the contrary we affirm the constructive and instruc-

tive role of religion in the dialogue among civilizations.

9. We urge those who shape public opinion to avoid putting at risk the good relations and peaceful cooperation of all people through the projection of extremist religious views as representative of authentic religious belief.

10. Rejecting all forms of discrimination, we support the principles of mutual respect, reciprocity, human rights, religious freedom, peaceful coexistence, and multi-religious cooperation.

11. We appeal to all of the leaders of the peoples of the world to make every effort toward the peaceful resolution of conflicts. In the spirit of peaceful coexistence, we call for an end to the violence in the Middle East and for a return to the peace process. We therefore pray that wherever there are clashes, people will come to enjoy peace with justice. Our conviction is that all moral, political, and financial resources should be used to improve the integral development of all human beings and nations.

12. In solidarity, and sustained by our respective spiritual resources, we commit ourselves to cooperate in efforts that lead to peace in the world. To this end, we address a joint appeal to all men and women of goodwill in all walks of life, and particularly to those whose religious and political positions carry the responsibility to work for the benefit of the common good, to be convinced of this call to peaceful collaboration.

13. In unity, solidarity, and love, with the prayer that our efforts will lead to "The Peace of God in the World," we commit ourselves and call upon our re-

spective religious communities:

a. To engage educators, members of the media, policy-makers, and other individuals, as well as institutions in civil society, in order to enhance understanding of religious communities and their beliefs, and to familiarize them with these communities' respective historical, cultural, and religious heritages worldwide. With specific regard to education, this calls for the elimination from textbooks of prejudicial and discriminatory statements or references concerning religions, cultures, and ethnic groups.

b. To support ongoing and new inter-religious and cross-cultural initiatives, including youth initiatives, in as many regions as possible throughout the world. Mindful that discriminatory behavior is learned rather than innate, we commit ourselves to educating our spiritual leaders and faithful in the ways of peace, mutual respect, and trust.

c. To continue our dialogue and encourage all efforts to promote collaboration among our three religions, as manifested by the participants of this meeting.

d. To foster communication networks that promotes the exchange of views and ideas on a regular basis.

FINAL REPORT AND RECOMMENDATIONS
OF THE 10TH SESSION OF THE MUSLIM-
CHRISTIAN DIALOGUE CONFERENCE

Manama, Kingdom of Bahrain
October 28-30, 2002
We thank God Almighty for what He bestowed upon us, by availing us of the chance to hold this dia-

logue conference between Muslims and Christians, which was hosted in Manama, the capital of the Kingdom of Bahrain, following a proposal by His All Holiness The Ecumenical Patriarch Bartholomew I which was met by acceptance from His Grace Sheikh Hamad Bin Issa Al-Khalifah, King of the Kingdom of Bahrain. The Conference passed a resolution that the Gracious Royal Address delivered by His Majesty before the participating delegations shall be regarded as an official document of the Conference and, accordingly, shall assume an international legal status.

For the purpose of fruitful cooperation to achieve peaceful coexistence on earth at all national, regional and international levels, and because of the basic and effective role of religion and scholars of religion in establishing the bases of justice, security and peace with such bases emanating of the religious teaching embodied in divine scriptures and texts for the protection of the human self from all types of aggression the endanger the essence of its existence or distort its security and safety, this dialogue conference was convened to establish these bases called for by the divine scriptures and texts to achieve peaceful coexistence on the levels of individuals and communities, locally, regionally and internationally.

This session was held from the 28th to the 30th of October, 2002, under the title "The Role of Religion in Peaceful Coexistence," under the patronage of His Excellency Sheikh Abdullah Bin Khalifa Al-Khalifah, Minister of Justice and Islamic Affairs in the Kingdom of Bahrain representing His Majesty King Hamad Bin

Issa Al-Khalifa, King of the Kingdom of Bahrain.

In nine working sessions, the papers, commentaries and discussions targeted the three topics of the Conference, namely:

1. Principles of Peaceful Coexistence at the Local Level

2. Principles of Peaceful Coexistence at the Regional Level

3. Principles of Peaceful Coexistence at the International Level.

The Muslim and Christian participants agreed on the following principles according to their respective religious tradition:

1. Affirmation of their belief in the one God, in such a practical way that elevates the behaviour of individuals and communities to an ideal ethical standard.

2. Their strong condemnation of anyone who defames prophets and messengers because they believe that such defamation is contrary to belief in the One God who sent these prophets and messengers to guide mankind.

3. Affirmation of their belief that regulating life cannot be effected apart from religion that charts the path of righteousness for mankind. Thus the participants affirm their commitment to religion's values, ethics, and principles to achieve peace, justice and cooperation among mankind.

4. They affirm that belief in God means, by necessity, standing with what is right everywhere, and siding with human dignity and prosperity.

5. Their condemnation of anything that abuses the rites and sacred matters and places for Muslims and Christians, and their intent on rooting mutual respect in this regard.

6. Affirmation that justice in all its forms is the basis of peace and peaceful coexistence, and that injustice in all its forms is a major cause for enmities, wars and terror in all their forms.

7. Affirmation that usurpation of rights and abuse of sacred places and prosperity are among the great dangers that threaten world peace and peaceful coexistence, and drag the world to war and its aftermath of destruction and misery.

8. Recognition that the human being was honored by God and preferred to all other creatures, and that he has recognized rights on which divine regulation concur, they believe that depriving people of these rights constitutes an international danger and threatens world peace and peaceful coexistence.

9. Affirmation that terrorizing those living in peace and civilians in any form of assault and intimidation is an act of terror that is not condoned by any divine teaching.

10. That respect of agreements and conventions is a sacred duty in all regulations in order to assure security and achieve peaceful coexistence.

11. That individual acts cannot constitute a verdict on religion, no religion or nation should be accused or indicted as a result of acts committed by its adherents.

12. That religion should not be used as a shield or pretext for usurping property or aggression against

people in Jerusalem and all sacred places in other parts of the world.

13. That the right to resist is guaranteed in all divine teaching for those who are oppressed and are under attack; moreover, divine teachings consider self defence and resisting the occupying force a sacred duty.

Building on all of the above mentioned ideas, the participants recommend:

First: The necessity for opening constructive dialogue among all divine teaching and beliefs to achieve the necessary cooperation to establish the principles of international peace of coexistence, and to achieve security and safety for individuals and communities.

Second: That there is no clash among civilizations, and that all divine teaching aim at achieving man's happiness and establishing security and peace on earth.

Third: Calling on the international community to denounce terrorism that targets and horrifies civilians and innocent people and assaults them and their properties.

Four: Condemning occupation and usurping of rights and property and the abuse of sacred places, irrespective of any motives or justifications.

Five: Condemning forcefully the occupation of Palestinian land and all acts of aggression and abuses in Palestine and in other parts of the world, and calling on the international community to intervene in a responsible and practical manner to implement international resolutions.

Six: Calling on the United Nations and UN Security Council to interfere in a practical way to end the political crises that lead to damaging wars in all countries.

Seven: Calling on international decision makers to interfere to end massacres against minorities in every country in the world to establish peace and security and achieve peaceful coexistence.

Eight: Calling on the leaders of nations to support adjustment and comprehensive development programmes that are in the interest of their citizens and to work towards achieving a better life for their citizens.

Nine: Denouncing unjust discrimination in all its forms, and affirming the necessity for achieving the principles of human rights, and calling for greater cooperation between religions to materialize peaceful coexistence individuals and communities.

At the end of the Conference, and after listening to the speech delivered by His Excellency Sheikh Khalifa Bin Hamad Al Khalifah, Assistant Undersecretary of the Ministry of Justice and Islamic Affairs in the Kingdom of Bahrain and Vice Chairman of the Organizing Committee of the Conference, in the closing session of the Conference, the participants recommended that this speech be included in the Conference documents which will be documented internationally to avail the ideas in them the chance to materialize.

The participants also recommended the establishment of a permanent joint secretariat for Muslim-Christian dialogue, between the Kingdom of Bahrain and the Ecumenical Patriarchate.

BAHRAIN DECLARATION

October 28-30, 2002

On the conclusion of the 10th Session of the Muslim-Christian Dialogue Conference held in Manama, Capital of the Kingdom of Bahrain 28-30 October, 2002.

In accordance with the directives of His Majesty Sheikh Hamad Bin Issa Al-Khalifah, King of the Kingdom of Bahrain, and in response to a proposal by His All Holiness The Ecumenical Patriarch Bartholomew I, and to enhance cooperation between Muslims and Christians on the road to reinforcing peaceful coexistence and international cooperation between them, and exchanging views on contemporary issues of mutual importance to establish a mutual base of understanding between believers from both religions, to achieve peaceful coexistence on three levels: local, regional and international, and to lay the foundations of world peace that are based on the common basis embodied in the values matrix that combines the divine message of Islam and Christianity.

By hosting the 10th Session of the Muslim-Christian Dialogue Conference in accordance with its rooted belief in the importance of dialogue on all levels, Bahrain, calls all peoples and nations to work on reinforcing the dialogue methodology in search of peaceful coexistence and the negation of violence; it also calls for exchanging views on contemporary issues in the service of humanity and for achieving security and happiness for mankind, and sparing mankind the dangers of conflict, reminding all peoples and nations at the same time of the noble principles embodied in both messages of Islam and Christianity for the achievement of mutual coexistence, the respect of religious and national specificities, encouraging constructive cooperation and supporting the efforts of Muslim and Christian scholars and intellectuals in crystallizing bases of peaceful coexistence and respect for the other, in accordance with the teachings of Islam and Christianity.

And building on the aims of this Conference in which Muslims and Christians assembled for constructive purposeful dialogue, the participants assert the following :

1. Continue with dialogue, and encourage efforts aimed at cooperation for achieving peaceful coexistence.

2. Cooperate, after the Inter-religious Dialogue, in healing the traumatic experiences of the historic past, by taking concrete initiatives addressed to the local society, so as to remove negative prejudices and to foster respect among their faithful for the particularity of other religious traditions.

3. Work together in an international perspective on modern interreligious dialogue to promote the idea of peace with freedom and social justice and to extend protection for human rights to relations between peoples and nations on a global scale.

4. Realize that violence breeds violence, and suppression breeds animosity and hatred, so concerned authorities should stand up to tackle violence through constructive dialogue rather than repression.

5. Highlight religion's principles, tolerance and mercy to mankind and give the real image for its purposes which were drawn to achieve happiness for mankind and establish security, safety and peaceful

coexistence on earth.

6. Respect national, religious and cultural specificities for each society.

7. Remove obstructions that stop people from understanding properly and correctly their religion.

8. Urge civil society organizations in every community to assume their role in protecting individuals from confused intellectual invasion, and protecting them mentally, psychologically and ethically from the negative aspects in this regard.

9. Care for the rights of the human being and to work towards realizing his security and safety by making sure that concerned authorities are doing what they are entrusted with in this regard.

10. Spread the right understanding of Islam and Christianity to all concerned individuals through education and mass media a correct method that reverts to authentic accepted sources of each religion for information on that religion.

The participants and organizers of the Conference are delighted to convey their heartfelt feelings of gratitude and appreciation to His Majesty Sheikh Hamad Bin Issa Al-Khalifah the King of Bahrain for his support to the Conference, in spite of his compelling engagements, in accordance with His Majesty's belief in the necessity of supporting the spirit of cooperation, understanding and love among nations and peoples.

The participants also highly commended the spirit of fraternity, mutual harmony, love and objectivity that characterized their Conference, expressing their appreciation to the people and government of Bahrain for the hospitality extended to them. The participants and organizers also expressed their gratitude to His Excellency Sheikh Abdullah Bin Khaled Al-Khalifah, Minister of Justice and Islamic Affairs in the Kingdom of Bahrain who patronized the Conference representing His Majesty Sheikh Hamad Bin Issa Al-Khalifah King of the Kingdom of Bahrain, His Grace Bishop Emmanuel of Reghion, Director of the Office of Interreligious and Intercultural Relations of the Ecumenical Patriarchate, to all Muslim and Christian scholars and intellectuals for their papers, commentaries and discussions during the Conference, and to all chairpersons and members of the committees working in the preparations for this Conference.

May God Almighty grant success to mankind in the road to righteousness and wisdom.

ADDRESS OF HIS ALL HOLINESS
ECUMENCAL PATRIARCH BARTHOLOMEW

The Islamic College, Libya
September 11, 2003

"The Necessity of Inter-Religious Dialogue –
The Relationships between Christianity and Islam"

Reverend Religious Representatives,
Dear Students,
It was with great joy that we accepted the invitation by your historic country to visit you and speak within the framework of inter-religious dialogue between the

religions of Christianity and Islam. We come with two identities. We come as a simple fellow human being, and as the first in order among equal bishops of the Orthodox Christian Church, Presiding Hierarch of the Orthodox Church of Constantinople.

We bring you the wholehearted and friendly greetings both of our Modesty personally, and also on behalf of the Church to which we belong and which we represent. We also express from this podium our warm thanks to the World Islamic Call Society and its General Secretary, the Rev. Dr. Mohammad Ahmed Al-Sherif, and to all the honorable members of the Executive Council of this Society, for the invitation to speak before you about the timely and important subject of inter-religious dialogue.

This is not the first time that we have dealt with this issue; and of course neither is this the first time that you have heard about it. The World Islamic Call Society, from the time of its very foundation, included in its constitutional goals the realization of inter-religious dialogue, and has conducted at least one official dialogue with the Vatican, as the representative of the Roman Catholic Christian Church. This resulted in such remarkable mutually agreed-upon pronouncements as "no compulsion should be used on persons or societies in the name of religion." That dialogue also came to the remarkable conclusion that antagonism should be replaced with co-operation as a subject of preaching. At the same time, the Ecumenical Patriarchate, which we head, has co-operated with others to organise numerous international academic inter-religious meetings and conferences with the participation of representatives of the major religions. During these conferences, specific subjects have been examined, and mutually accepted decisions have been taken. Some of them have already become universally recognized by the global community, such as the Bosphorus Declaration, according to which "every crime in the name of religion is a crime against religion."

Humanity currently finds itself in a situation where the necessity of dialogue as a method of solving conflicts and problems in every area of human life has become clear. The co-existence of members of different religions is increasing and they interact now in a uniquely direct way, due to the recent advances made in the mass media and means of transportation, and to the immigration of followers of one religion to countries where another religion predominates.

Moreover, the establishment of numerous international organizations, first of which was the United Nations, has led representatives of different peoples with different religions and civilizations into the halls of international conferences and to the tables of bilateral or multilateral negotiations, to find solutions to several issues. This has resulted in increased familiarity between peoples and a greater tolerance for their respective religious and cultural preferences and peculiarities.

Thus, both the unofficial dialogue that has been conducted on a personal level between followers of both of these two great religions and of others, and also the frequent high-level international meetings, have prepared hearts and minds for a more official dialogue comprised of spiritual leaders and scholars of religion. Such a dialogue would aim to clarify the many centuries-old misunderstandings about the true content of the world's religions. It would also aim to preserve, and not to prohibit out of religious reasons, the possibility of peaceful co-operation between peoples of different religions.

Cohabitation between Christians and Muslims, especially in the Mediterranean region, has been the rule for centuries, and has made these groups of people familiar with each other, created friendships and co-operations, facilitated discussions and exchanges of views, and has given rise to mutual understanding. In particular, both Arabic- and non-Arabic speaking Christians alike, have lived in the Arabic world together with Muslims, and the literature of both religions has greatly benefited as a result.

Moreover, in the countries of Syria (which hosts the Orthodox Patriarchate of Antioch in Damascus), Lebanon, Jordan, Palestine (which is the ancient See of the Orthodox Patriarchate of Jerusalem), and others, the percentage of Christians within the Muslim majority is remarkable. This centuries-long daily interaction, cohabitation and co-operation between both the simplest and the most erudite members of the community, and the elevation of individuals from both religions to high positions in government, has made people spiritually interested in a more responsible and substantial dialogue.

For sure, exchanges of information about the teachings and spiritual experiences of both religions have taken place throughout the centuries, and indeed still take place within communities. But it is also true that the nature of faith, and especially of Christian and Muslim faith, contains a high degree of absoluteness, which sometimes becomes intensified so as to prevent followers of one religion from converting to another.

This has resulted in an increase in apologetic works, works whereby the superiority of one religion's claim to truth is set over and against the other's. In cases like these, the discussion highlights oppositions and differences, and does not lead to peaceful mutual understanding, but rather to mere logical argumentation. However, there also exist progressive minds who consider faith in God as a strong connection between these two religions. These people, without equating the religion with the other, are more interested in discovering the deeper message of God that both religions contain within themselves, instead of focusing on the differences that exist between them. This does not imply indifference to the faith, nor minimalism regarding its substantial elements, nor syncretism; it only implies having a friendly attitude towards the person who believes and worships in a way different from ours, because this person is within God's sight on their personal spiritual path. The depth of the soul, where this journey takes place, is a holy and inviolate place, where no coercion can exist, for God himself grants us the time for the lengthy and barely discernible inner workings of faith.

The call for a more profound investigation and for a friendly attitude that leads to an end to conflict is not recent. Many centuries ago, the poet Jalālud-Dīn Rūmi wrote in his poem called "The Religious Conflict":

The blind face a dilemma when they worship,
While the powerful on the one and on the other side stand established:
Every place is happy with its way.
Only love can make their conflict stop.
Only love comes to help when you call for help against their arguments.

Accordingly, we have not come to set our arguments against yours in the framework of conflict. We have come in a spirit of love, in response to your kind invitation, so as to get to know you and to offer you our desire for inter-religious dialogue.

Dialogue is born of speech, equality and mutual respect of those who engage in it. When equality is absent, the speech of a superior to his subordinate becomes a commandment, and that of a subordinate to his superior becomes beggary, praise or cajolery.

When a relationship of hostility persists between those who communicate, speech becomes contradiction. Cases such as these are spiritual disputes where a mere logical victory of the one over the other is the goal—this cannot be called dialogue.

When one party in a discussion is not interested in receiving something from the other, and instead wants only to give, it is not dialogue that results, but rather monologue. What a tragedy it is that many people engage in mere monologue, while thinking that they conduct a dialogue! This is a common phenomenon, and from the spiritual point of view is more repugnant than contradiction; in arguments between people who openly disagree, there exists at least a kind of communication. The one who responds to what he is told tries to understand his interlocutor and to present his objection to the other's views. But the person who conducts a monologue, even if he has heard the other, has not thought about what he has heard, neither does he truly respond, but instead says whatever he initially intended to say, indifferent to what he has been told. Some describe this as the dialogue of the deaf, behavior that does not deserve the name of dialogue.

True dialogue is a gift from God to humankind. According to St. John Chrysostom, Archbishop of Constantinople in the 4th century A.D., God Himself is always in dialogue with humans. God speaks through the Prophets and the Apostles, and He also speaks through His creation. The heavens declare the glory of God, exclaims the holy Psalmist, and who is able to listen with understanding to the silent words of the created beings, is blessed.

Dialogue is most necessary and useful for the interaction of men! It is so useful that God Himself uses it when He speaks in various ways to man, and when He listens to man's prayers. Life would be impossible without dialogue. It is through dialogue that a mother communicates with her children, teaches them, participates in their joy and pain, comforts them, encourages them, listens to their difficulties and eases their way to maturity. It is through dialogue that a teacher cultivates knowledge, that a preacher of the faith catechises, solves enquiries, bears burdens, and serves the believer. Dialogue promotes science, broadens horizons, communicates feelings, changes emotions, reveals truths, dissolves illusions, abolishes prejudice, cultivates relationships, forges bonds, and makes the human person what he is. Speech is only justified when it is truly responded to, and true response to speech is dialogue.

The speech of God, reflected in the speech of humans, constitutes a fitting example of dialogue. For there is no place for coercion in religion, and ultimately faith cannot be obtained through threats, but is rather encouraged by gentle persuasion.

The person who refuses to engage in dialogue will always remain spiritually poor. He suffers from the illusion of self-sufficiency and the horror of insecurity. He sees only by the light of his own eyes, and refuses to enrich himself with what the eyes of others have seen; he listens only through his own ears, and refuses to hear what the ears of others have heard. If he starts down a wrong way, he is unable to change direction, for he does not speak with anyone who can show him the right way.

Dialogue is safe and beneficial because it does not eliminate the responsibility, held by each member of the conversation, to form a considered opinion. Whatever subject arises in the course of a conversation, the participant listens carefully, examines and evaluates it, and then either accepts or rejects what he has heard. Consequently, dialogue does not upset the convictions of the one who engages in it; it does not alter his convictions against his will, but only when he himself decides to polish them.

Dialogue between followers of our two religions is

indeed both necessary and beneficial.

Let us now make a small attempt to engage in theological inter-religious dialogue.

The Christian faith teaches that Jesus Christ is the Son of God. The Koran states that God does not have a son. There appears to be a clear contradiction between these two teachings. But is this really so?

Christian dogmatics affirms that no matter what we positively say about God, it is in the end never possible to define God, because God is beyond every definition. God is unknowable and incomprehensible by our weak human mental powers. Therefore, concepts of God are but anthropomorphic icons of Him. They aid our limited ability to fully understand Him, but we must always bear in mind that every human conception of God is inferior to what He really is. We know only a part, as the Apostle Paul says. Consequently, the identity of Jesus Christ as the Son of God expresses a reality, though not as understood by the simple person, who associates this reality with his relationship with his son. Because of this simplification, Christian teaching also uses another expression to describe Jesus Christ. It calls him the Incarnate Word of God, the One-Who-Became-Flesh. The Gospel of John begins by declaring, "In the beginning was the Word, and the Word was with God, and the Word was God." It adds that "the Word became flesh and dwelt among us," that is, became human and lived among men.

It is easier for human logic to accept that God "possesses Word," that is, He is able to express Himself; a god without the capability for self-expression is not an acceptable god. However, the use of the term "Word of God," and especially "incarnated," together with the term "Son of God," enlightens more lucidly the reality of "Jesus Christ." However, none of these terms, separately or in combination, could ever define this reality exactly.

This is why Holy Scripture and the writings of the great ecclesiastical thinkers use many other terms for the Word of God, such as "Wisdom of God," "Light of Light," "Son of Man" and others by which they try to express angles or rays of a reality that exists above human understanding and logic.

The ideal is always superior to the expressive ability of the human mind. That an expression is understood as being unable to convey a given reality in its entirety is not a cause of scandal for the sincere Christian, for he knows the apophatic or negative character of cataphatic or positive theology. In every positive expression about the divine realities there necessarily exists an apophatic element, one that affirms the insufficiency of human logic to define them, and that something inexpressible must lie beyond expressions.

From everything we have said, it is clear that for the thinking man, Christian or Muslim, the belief that God does not have a Son on the one hand, and the belief that Jesus Christ is both the Incarnate Word and Son of God on the other, may not be as essentially opposed as they seem. For Christians do not accept that Jesus Christ was born of God in the same way that the children of humans are born. They can thus respond with agreement to the Muslim who refuses to believe something so crude, and can affirm that the issue goes deeper, to the true relationship of the Word of God with God, and to the Incarnation of the Word.

Mohammed the Conqueror of Constantinople asked the Patriarch of the time, George or Gennadios Scholarius, about this issue. The Patriarch replied that for us Christians it is out of the question that the Word of God does not possess substance. So we Christians believe in a Word of God who is substantial, and from this point of view we call him Son of God, without of course implying a father-son relationship identical to the human one.

From this short but representative analysis, we see that dialogue, when engaged in with good will and deep knowledge of the issues leads, if not to agreement, then at least to mutual understanding and rapprochement, to the removal of misunderstandings that have sometimes prevailed for centuries, and to the realization that those who seem opposed to us are not always necessarily so. Therefore, before we say that we disagree on a specific issue, we must investigate it more deeply. This is so we might realize with surprise that we agree, even if it does not seem so, or that we are very close to agreeing.

Something else that causes disagreement and conflict, not only between different religions but also within the same religion, is to treat a part of the truth as it were the whole truth.

It is has been shown that human logic cannot express everything. There are thoughts and experiences and objects for which no specific words or expressions exist. Consequently, human beings are driven to use images or comparisons. For example, it is said that at the time of Christ's Transfiguration, His clothes became "white as the light," although light is not exactly white. During the ascension of St. Paul to a world totally unlike our earthly one, he ascended "unto the third heaven" and heard "unspeakable words," and none of his readers, except perhaps for very rare exceptions, have any experience of what the third heaven or the unspeakable words are like. Consequently, each member of his audience, or each one of his readers, though he might have an inkling of what he who expressed himself in this way wanted to communicate, nevertheless does not understand everything. In cases like these, if we consider the small piece of the truth that we can understand as comprising the whole truth, we will be led into serious misunderstandings and disagreements. Moreover, when we unhesitatingly insist that we possess the right and correct understanding, we are led into those conflicts and divisions that every religion experiences. We of the Orthodox Church accept that the Church correctly interprets Christian teaching as expressed through the Holy Synods, made up primarily of its hierarchs and other erudite and righteous believers. The Roman Catholic Church accepts that the Pope infallibly expresses the truth when he speaks *ex cathedra*. The majority of Protestant churches believe the truth is expressed through each congregation or even through each individual believer separately. This leads to ambiguity in the faith, to the relativisation of everything.

The correct path is not of course the relativisation

of everything, but rather the acknowledgement that the abilities of the human mind are limited. The person who understands his and other men's mental insufficiency is peaceful and humble and conciliatory towards his fellow human beings who might understand a particular truth in a different way than he. He chooses what he considers the most correct view according to his best judgment, or according to the judgment of the Church or the religion to which he belongs, but he does not condemn those who with good intentions have chosen another view. And he always prays to God that the deeper meanings of the holy texts might be revealed to everyone, because many times they are not disclosed at the first reading.

This brings us to a third point, which is concerned with the interpretation of the word of God within the context both of the conditions in which it was expressed and of the people to whom it was addressed, and also within the context of the spiritual situation of today's believer.

We all know that many commandments of God are provisional, concerned with a specific place and time, advisable actions within the context of the conditions of a specific people. If we attempt to enforce today commandments that were handed down long ago, without making the necessary distinction, we will act against the will of God. For though it is written in the Old Testament that God commanded the extermination of a certain person or nation, this does not allow us today to exterminate a person or nation, believing that we thereby fulfill the will of God. Unfortunately, many people cite verses from Scripture written long ago for other people in other circumstances, in order to justify their misguided actions, or to lead astray their fellow human beings, who might not have knowledge enough to resist them.

Special attention must be paid to the level of spiritual progress of the believer for whom the commandment has been given. It is evident that what has been commanded of the faithful solitary ascetic, who is completely dedicated to God, is not always similarly valid for the householder, who lives within society. There certainly exist commandments that are equally valid for all people, but there also exist commandments given to the beginners on the road to virtue, as there exist pediatric nurses who are suited only for infants. Similarly there exist infant words and childish words and words for spiritual maturity. It is the duty of every era to investigate which of the earlier commandments remain valid. For we must distinguish the universal will of God, valid for all people of every era, such as charity, faith, and the like, from the provisional commandments of God, such as specifically how acts of charity are to be performed. This does not mean that the essential will of God changes, but that since we humans are changeable, our approaches to the will of God change according to our spiritual situation. That is another reason for humility and peace, for just because the followers of one religion interpret the will of God in one way, and other followers of the same or of another religion interpret it in a different way, this does not mean that one of them must be wrong, or that everyone is equally wrong. Someone spiritually more advanced than someone else may understand God's will differently. And as we have no other judge besides our own often-untrustworthy self to determine who is right, we ultimately are held responsibility for our choice.

Of course there are religious leaders who lead the faithful, but each person himself chooses the religious leader he wants to follow, and is responsible for his choice. All this means that we need discretion, that it is a mistake to be fanatical and to condemn our fellow human beings who might think or believe in a way different from ours, and that dialogue is necessary for mutual understanding and for peaceful co-existence and co-operation.

Despite the absoluteness that provides the foundation for every religious faith, inter-religious dialogue is also necessary because as our knowledge of other religions increases, so too does our understanding of our own religion. Finally, a better understanding of our own religion and of one or several other religions helps us to better understand what God expects from humankind, and to better see the weaknesses or inaccuracies that may lie beneath our beliefs. Certainly not every believer is able to undertake such comparisons, for he might not have the knowledge or the necessary wisdom. Specialized spiritual knowledge and experience are called for, and this is why the top representatives of each religion conduct inter-religious dialogues today. In this way suspicions of proselytizing are avoided, a high level of discussion is maintained, and fears of compromising elements of one's faith and of one's affection for one's fellow speaker, who belongs to a different religion, prove unjustified. We say this because unfortunately the less educated of believers are not only unqualified to participate in inter-religious dialogue, but they also hold those who participate in them in suspicion, doubting their religious honesty and integrity.

This is why we explicitly declare that inter-religious dialogue does not take place either for participants to enter into alliances with members of other religions, or for them to badger others into conceding to their beliefs. They take place rather for the cessation of religious intolerance, for the triumph of mutual understanding, and for the establishment of certainty in the good intentions of both sides, respectful of each person's cultural background and freedom of religious choice.

During the 14th century A.D., a dialogue was conducted between the great Christian theologian and saint, Archbishop Gregory Palamas of Thessalonike, and distinguished representatives of Islam. Of course they did not entirely agree, but one of the representatives of Islam stated that for him the time should come when mutual understanding between followers of the two religions would exist. St. Gregory agreed to this statement, and wished that time would come soon. Today we are able to wish, and we do wish wholeheartedly, for this to be fulfilled in our days.

We thank you for your patience and your kindness in listening to us. And we wish you every blessing from God.

Address of His All Holiness
Ecumenical Patriarch Bartholomew

The Abant Platform in Washington, D.C.
April 19-20, 2004

"Islam, Secularism, and
Democracy: The Turkish Experience"

Esteemed Panel Members,

Participants,

Host Committee and Distinguished Guests,

In addressing you and opening the discussion on
a subject of such intimate and far-reaching concern to
us, we think back to the two recent tragic terrorist attacks in Turkey and the words of the Prime Minister of
Turkey Recep Tayyip Erdoğan, who said, shortly afterwards:

> "I cannot bear it when terrorism and Islam are spoken of in
> the same breath… the Religions of the Book want to protect
> life, not destroy it. In Islam, those who take human life are
> acting as if they are blowing up the House of God."

These words resonate an attitude that goes to the
heart of Turkish Islam, the nature of the secular state
and the principles of democracy. They reflect the profound changes that have taken place recently in Europe and Turkey regarding Islam.

Today, The European Union has some 15 million
Muslims; three million of who are Turkish. While its
history and culture is interwoven with Europe, contemporary Turkey faces one of the most profound
challenges - its accession to the European Union. Tur-

key is, after all, the only Muslim society that came in close contact with and embraced the ideals of the Enlightenment and the French Revolution. In the Ottoman Empire the State took precedence over religion and Turkish Islam remained open to the influence of mystical traditions. While embracing the notion of the modern national State, it resisted incessantly and in so many ways the ideology of Political Islam. As a result, Turkey is unique because there is a harmony between traditional Turkish Muslim values and secularism. As a matter of fact, Turkey is "Islamic *and* secular" rather than "Islamic *but* secular."

The Turkish model shows that the interaction of Islam and the modern world need not be on a collision course. The results of Atatürk's goal for Turkey to join what he called "Universal Civilization" have been impressive, with greater opportunity and better conditions than in many countries where government and Islam remained conjoined.

But the roots of secular Turkish Islam go even deeper into the social fabric of the country. Turks themselves are committed to the secular path and a democratic future. Even if there was a period of divergence when the State promoted Islam vis-à-vis the challenges of the Cold War, today the desire is to fulfil the Copenhagen criteria and join the European family of nations. Thus, Turkey is getting itself ready to join the European Union.

Like European identity, American identity cannot be seen in terms of geography or even within the narrow bounds of a specific history and culture. It has a wider context and has to do with espousing the same set of fundamental values and principles - human rights, religious freedom, tolerance and the rule of law - which are mutually shared by many nations. Turkey readily subscribes to and closely identifies with these values and has repeatedly proclaimed its commitment to apply them equally to all its citizens regardless of race or creed.

In Turkey, Christians, Muslims and Jews live together in an atmosphere of tolerance and dialogue. We wish to mention the work of Fethullah Gülen, who more than 10 years ago began to educate his believers about the necessity for the existence of a dialogue between Islam and all religions.

The Turkish model of Islam seeks the legitimisation of all religions and the freedom to choose now and forever without coercion from the State, whether with religious or secular leanings. In other words, the Turkish model envisages Islam as occupying in the Islamic societies the same position that religion does in the Western World today; a world far removed from the concepts of Jihad and Crusades.

Turkey shaped its modern identity out of a struggle with the new political order at the advent of nationalism and it is being tested again today with the emergence of the Post-Cold War era at the advent of a new geopolitical reality, unlike any we have known in the past.

The incorporation of Turkey and the Turkish model into the European Union may well provide a concrete example and a powerful symbol of mutually beneficial cooperation between the Western and Islamic worlds and put an end to the talk of a clash of civilizations. This, in turn, would be a true strengthening of Europe and the European Ideals that converge with the values of "the Religions of the Book" spoken of by the Prime Minister of Turkey.

Today, we have before us an even greater challenge – to truly break down the wall between East and West, between Muslims and Christians, between all religions, all civilizations and all cultures, to bridge the great divide and recognize our common humanity and common values. *This is God's model for the world.*

We must continue this journey together, East and West, North and South to that appointed time and place in God's Kingdom.

May the peace of God be upon each and every one of you, upon all participants and upon all who strive and struggle in love for unity, peace and justice.

ADDRESS OF HIS ALL HOLINESS ECUMENICAL PATRIARCH BARTHOLOMEW

The International Conference in Vienna, Austria
November 16, 2005

*"Islam in a Pluralistic World:
Cultures in Conflict and Dialogue"*

Your Eminences,
Your Excellencies,
Learned Sirs,

Distinguished Professors,

Beloved fellow participants

We would like to thank His Excellency, Wolfgang Schlüssel, Federal Chancellor of Austria, and Her Excellency Ursula Plassnik, the Federal Foreign Minister of Austria, as well as the Austrian Organization for the Middle East for inviting our Modesty to participate in this International Conference on *"Islam in a pluralistic world."* We thank you even more for offering us the floor to express our thoughts on this topic, especially from the point of conflict and dialogue of cultures.

We congratulate wholeheartedly the honorable Austrian Government for this beautiful initiative to convene this International Conference and to invite distinguished representatives of the Muslim world from many countries and nuances. Such gatherings prepare the way for the peaceful cooperation of the peoples; bring cultures to proximity toward one another and the faithful of the various religions to a convincing communication, that all human beings as individuals face the same problems in life, and that they ought to help, instead of instigating and persecuting one another.

Therefore, we were delighted and we consider worth emphasizing the initiative of His Excellency, the President of Austria to invite the representatives of the Muslim communities of Austria to congratulate them on the occasion of the past feast day of the Ramadan. It is through such initiatives that they are becoming part of the social life of the entire Austrian family. This factual dialogue extracts the people who have different religious beliefs than the majority from their isolation and it prepares them for mutual respect, understanding and acceptance of one another.

We have expressed ourselves many times for the dialogue and the possibility of the coexistence of the peoples who come from different cultural traditions. We are glad that once again an opportunity is given to us to repeat in the presence of so many select personalities our unswerving conviction that if we so desire, if our hearts accept it, we can coexist in peace and profitable cooperation, despite the difference of religion among us.

We wholeheartedly greet the prominent Muslim brothers who participate in this meeting, some of whom we have met in other similar conferences, during which all together, them and us, try to infuse the world with the spirit of reconciliation and peaceful coexistence among all. We are in dispute with the spirit of enmity and conflict between all people and every culture, a dispute of course that is of a peaceful nature on our behalf. And we believe that the two cultures, namely the Christian and the Islamic, about whom we converse mostly these three days, have within them strong the elements of peaceful coexistence.

It is well known that the Koran, the Sacred Scripture of Islam, defines explicitly that the Christians and the believers of Judaism, the so-called monotheists, must not be forced to become Muslims. In general it says that religion is not forced upon anyone. Furthermore, it describes the Gospel as an *"illuminating book"* (Ch. 3, verse 184), and it recognizes that the Christians are those who are mostly disposed to love the faithful (Ch. 5, verse 82). Therefore, there is no religious reason according to the faith of Islam for disputes and conflicts between Christians and Muslims. There are of course differences in faith and conviction, but Islam does not exalt them to reasons for conflict.

The conflicts between Christians and Muslims that are mentioned in history have their roots in politics and not in religion. Every time religion has been used for inciting enmity and misfortunes, it has been a case of taking advantage of the ignorance of the masses and misleading them into actions of intolerance and fanaticism. If we examine these cases with a clear and healthy mind we see that they are unjustifiable.

Respectively, Christianity that is unalloyed by political goals and views, has respect for the freedom of the Muslims to have their own faith regarding God. I do not believe that we have to insist on this issue, for it is generally accepted. There have been of course enmities and acts of violence committed by Christians against Muslims, but not due to the Christian religion; these acts were due to ignorance, or corruption and weathering of its commandments. The Koran ascribes the favorable attitude of the Christians towards the Muslims to the fact that the Christians have priests and monks, namely people who live and experience truly the immense Christian love to all fellow human beings.

Under these circumstances there are no religious reasons that would justify a violent conflict of the Christian and Muslim cultures. Regarding the opinion that had been expressed, publicized, and become known to the entire world on the inevitable violent conflict of the aforementioned cultures we say that it is not valid, inasmuch so it refers to religion as reason for such a supposedly expected and supposedly unavoidable conflict. If the aspirations of the nations and the geopolitical correlations lead to isolated or generalized conflicts of the Muslim and Christian peoples, or of some of them; and if the politicians mobilize religions for the reinforcement of the idea of otherness and of the hostile attitudes of one nation against the other is a totally different issue and irrelevant to the true nature of religion. Moreover, war and other hostile conflicts and actions between people who belong to the same general religion, but to other denominations, as for example are the cases of the Orthodox of Serbia and the Catholics of Croatia, or the Muslim Sunnites and the Muslim Shiites, are convincing witnesses that the real reasons for these conflicts are not the differences in religious beliefs, but claims on other worldly matters. And that is clearly proven and manifested by cases in which people who belong to the same exact religion are in conflict. That is a phenomenon that appears many times in history.

We see then that there are no religious reasons for the realization of the aforementioned prophesized conflict. But even if there were reasons for such a conflict, then it is our duty, as religious leaders of both religions to try and prevent such an outcome. A fundamental way of settling any national, economic, ideological, or other differences of every other nature is the development of a serious and fair dialogue between the parties involved.

Dialogue resolves superstitions and biases, contributes to the mutual understanding and paves the way for finding a peaceful solution to all problems. The most important though result of dialogue is the fact that it brings the conversing people closer to each other and reveals to those involved the true personality of their counterparts in the dialogue. The personality of each one, the content of their psychic world, defines one's attitude on various issues. Fear and suspiciousness are ill advisors, and can only be ostracized by getting to know people better on a deeper level and by cultivating good and truly friendly relations. Deep and meaningful relations will either affirm the honesty, or possibly the dishonesty of one's colloquist.

Furthermore, the dialogue constitutes an opportunity for us to self-transcend our limits and to see the facts and our ideas from the viewpoint of our fellow person in dialogue. This procedure frees the spirit from the partiality that existed so far in approaching the issue. There is however, a risk within this opening up to the viewpoint of the other. And this risk results from the possibility of reaching the conclusion that the way we used to view and evaluate certain things and situations needs to be reviewed. There is no greater risk than to accept the fact that our spiritual foundation has some cracks and that these cracks are the reason that our foundation is collapsing, or even that our foundation is weaker in certain points, or that it is less beautiful and perfect than the foundation of the person we are in dialogue with.

Many people have such strong convictions that

they would rather sacrifice their own life than change them. Now, the following question is raised: Do we, by mentioning this, introduce instability and variability of one's faith? No, we do not introduce any such concept. We introduce only a closer examination, a continuously deeper permeation of the truth. Those who examine truth closer, come to the conclusion that many times ideas, which up to a point seemed contradictable and ruled one another out, are in fact harmonized.

Let us give an example. It is written in the Gospel that *"whoever desires to save his life will lose it"* (Mt 16:25). It's as if the person who wants to save his or her own life, must accept to sacrifice it, for life is only won when it is sacrificed, and not when it is preserved from danger with petty feelings and fear of loss. The contradiction is obvious and the acceptance of this paradox goes against our rationality. However, according to the testimonies of those who survived in the concentration camps, the people who loved their life and who tried to protect themselves from dangers were losing the battle of life, whereas, incredibly enough, those who survived were the ones who had voluntarily accepted their sacrifice.

According to the understanding of those who have indulged in the matters of philosophy, the contradiction and contraposition of many ideas does not correspond to the truth. The famous pre-Socratic philosopher Heraclitus writes about Hesiod that he is known as the one who has knowledge about many things, for day and night he did not differentiate because both were one and the same.

«Διδάσκαλος δέ πλείστων Ἡσίοδος,

Τοῦτον ἐπίστανται πλεῖστα εἰδέναι,
Ὅστις ἡμέρην καί εὐφρόνην οὐκ ἐγίνωσκεν,
Ἔστι γάρ ἕν.»
"Teacher of most men is Hesiod,
They are sure he knew most things,
A man who did not yet recognize day and night,
For they are one."

If someone wants to support the claim that night and day is one and the same thing, then what is needed is great spiritual courage and the transcendence of what is generally acknowledged by the average person. If however, we read a little deeper into it, we will be convinced that Hesiod was right, and that those who were mocking him for not being able to tell the evident difference, namely that night (according to the majority) is different than day, were in error. How many are the things for which people nowadays disagree and quarrel about, whereas if they took the time to read a little deeper into them, they would see for themselves that their deeper existence, the suppressed voice of their conscience recognizes that the phenomena which appear to be dividing, do not necessarily constitute an impediment for peaceful coexistence.

Certainly, a bright ray of light shone in the very depths of the soul of that Palestinian father who donated the organs of his young son who was murdered by Israeli solders, to an Israeli hospital to be transplanted indiscriminately to either a Jew or a Palestinian. This ray of light revealed to him the truth, namely that all the people are brothers, despite the fact that innumerable myriads of our fellow men and women today believe unfortunately that they differ radically from one another, and that therefore they cannot coexist peacefully with them. If night and day is one and the same, then why isn't Jew and Greek, slave and freeman, male and female, human being and human being of any race, language and religion one and the same thing?

Ancient Greeks distinguished themselves for their ability to take knowledge and ideas from their fellow people and to develop them without the fear that by doing so, they would actually downgrade or undervalue their own convictions. The rapid and inspired development of the ancient Greek spirit during the classic age is due also to their character. It was their character that allowed them to intercross their ideas with the ideas of other peoples and civilizations, and with great discernment to take on and reform all that was good and outside of Hellenism into a new composition.

This freedom of spirit is found in the foundation of every spiritual progress. We believe that wherever there is the Spirit of God there is also freedom. The danger that lies within spiritual freedom is not worth taking into account if compared to all the good that this freedom has to offer. Unfortunately though, as we have already mentioned, many of our fellow people construct a spiritual and ideological stronghold, and shut themselves inside its walls to safeguard their spiritual wholeness and integrity. Nevertheless, despite their efforts, the time will come when they will realize that the more they safeguard themselves against the spirit of new ideas, the more stressful will their life become, because the infiltration of these ideas is such that no obstacle is able to hinder their entrance into the hearts of the people.

We have to clarify that a closer and deeper examination of the truth does not necessarily imply a change of religious affiliation. This might be possible in some cases, and the human right that all people have to change their faith should be respected. But when we speak of a closer and deeper examination, we mean the improvement of the way a person thinks and perceives the relations of things, thus the more explicit awareness of truth.

In the Greek ecclesiastical language we use the word "μετάνοια," which literary means the shift of the mind, of our mentality, and therefore according to the Church Fathers this is necessary even to those without sin.

It is this shift of mentality that the dialogue helps realize, and that is why we hope that due to the repeating dialogues we will succeed in the better closer and deeper examination of those truths, which facilitate the peaceful coexistence of the people. For the differences between them are much smaller than the difference between day and night, and if Heraclitus was here with us today, he would not hesitate to tell us that the people who think they are different from the others are one; that we are one.

During these three days we had the beautiful opportunity to talk with one another peacefully, and to listen to the distinguished speakers developing their positions on important issues that are created by the coexistence or cooperation of Christians and Muslims. What should be highlighted is the development of the issues regarding the position of the Christians in the Muslim countries, and the position of the Muslims in the Christian countries. It seems that the position of the Christians in certain Muslim countries is susceptible and needs important improvement, so that the Christians will be able to enjoy in them the equivalent rights and possibilities as the Muslims in Christian countries do.

It was only a week ago that we had in our see the second Conference on the topic of "Peace and Tolerance," which declared among other things the respect for life by the proverbial expression "Live and let live," the respect for human rights, especially the rights of Minorities, and for religious tolerance, and it also condemned terrorism and violence. Furthermore, it also pointed out the Christian saying *"blessed are the peacemakers, for they will be called Children of God,"* as well as the Muslim saying *"Allah summoneth to the abode of Peace."* We finally expressed our gratitude to God, for He gave us the opportunity to verify our decision to cooperate for the increase of peace, justice and human dignity.

It is therefore necessary that we move towards that direction, beyond the disabilities of the past. The impartial and incorruptible history has of course registered behaviors of Christian nations and Governments that are incompatible to the Gospel, as well as behaviors of Islamic nations and Governments that are incompatible to the Koran. The time has come to act for God. We shall both converge to what the will of God commands for all. Those who have opened their hearts to God feel that the merciful and loving God is not pleased by bloodshed, but by peace, which is the ultimate good and divine present. Christians and Muslims greet one another using the word peace. And it is with this greeting and with this wish that we will end our speech.

Peace be unto you. Peace be unto the world.

Joint Press Release
of the Ecumenical Patriarchate
and the World Islamic Call Society

Athens, Greece
December 13, 2008

Dialogue between Islam and Christianity
Launch of Inter-Religious Training Partnership Initiative

The Ecumenical Patriarchate and the World Islamic Call Society have launched the Inter-Religious Training Partnership Initiative. This will provide joint training opportunities for young imams, priests, theologians and students of respective Muslim and Christian Orthodox communities. The Inter-Religious Training Partnership Initiative will train participants to use inter-religious dialogue as a tool to facilitate peace and reconciliation. The aim is to learn and share good practice from around the world and to look within the respective faiths for guidance.

The Initiative commenced with a three day Seminar (December 11–13) held in Athens that included over 65 participants who came from all the Autocephalous Orthodox Churches and the Islamic communities of

North Africa, Europe and the Middle East.

In 2009 the Ecumenical Patriarchate and the World Islamic Call Society will organize two training courses. The first training course will focus on inter-religious mediation by empowering young people with the skills to facilitate dialogue; and broaden the awareness of the importance of cooperation between Christians and Muslims in North Africa, Europe and the Middle East. The second training course will concentrate on communication and media strategies with the aim of making the dialogue more visible.

Through the Inter-Religious Training Partnership Initiative the Ecumenical Patriarchate and the World Islamic Call Society will establish a network of trust for future religious leaders to support their counterparts at the local and global levels.

Media will be used to reach out to people who are involved in Christian-Muslim initiatives.

Selected Bibliography

Ayoub, Mahmoud Mustafa. *Islam: Faith and Practice*. Ontario: Open Press, 1989.

Ayoub, Mahmoud Mustafa. *Islam: Faith and History*. Oxford: Oneworld Publications, 2004.

Cragg, Kenneth. *The House of Islam*. Belmont, California: Wadsworth, 1975.

Cragg, Kenneth and R. Marston Speight, eds. *Islam from Within: Anthology of a Religion*. Belmont, California: Wadsworth, 1980.

Cutsinger, James, ed. *Paths to the Heart: Sufism and the Christian East*. Bloomington, Indiana: World Wisdom, Inc., 2002.

Dawood, N.J. *The Koran*. New York: Penguin Books, 1974.

Denny, Frederick. *An Introduction to Islam*. New York: Macmillan, 1985.

Esposito, John L. *Islam and Politics*. 4th ed. Syracuse, New York: Syracuse University Press. 1995.

Esposito, John L., ed. *Oxford Encyclopedia of the Modern Islamic World*. 4 vols. New York: Oxford University Press, 1995.

Esposito, John L. *Islam: The Straight Path*. rev. 3rd ed. New York-Oxford, Oxford University Press, 2005.

Gibb, H.A.R., and J.H. Kramers. *Shorter Encyclopedia of Islam*. Ithaca, New York: Cornell University Press, 1953.

Gibb, H.A.R., and J.H. Kramers, et al. *The Encyclopedia of Islam*. 2nd ed. Leiden: E. J. Brill, 1954.

Goddard, Hugh. *A History of Christian-Muslim Relations*. Chicago: New Amsterdam Books, 2000.

Haddad, Robert. *Syrian Christians in Muslim Society*. Princeton, New Jersey: Princeton University Press, 1970.

Haddad, Yvonne Yazbeck. *Contemporary Islam and the Challenge of History*. Albany, New York: State University of New York Press, 1982.

Massignon, Louis. *The Passion of al-Hallaj: Mystical Martyr of Islam*, 4 vols. Trans. H. Mason. Princeton, New Jersey: Princeton University Press, 1983.

Nasr, Seyyed Hossein. *Three Muslim Sages: Avicenna, Suhrawardi, Ibn 'Arabi*. Cambridge, Massachusetts: Harvard University Press, 1964.

Nasr, Seyyed Hossein. *Sufi Essays*. London: Allen and Unwin, 1972.

Nasr, Seyyed Hossein. *Islamic Life and Thought*. Albany: State University of New York Press, 1981.

Nicholson, Reynold A. *Rumi: Poet and Mystic*. London: Allen and Unwin, 1950.

Nicholson, Reynold A. *Studies in Islamic Mysticism*. Cambridge: Cambridge University Press, 1973.

Omar, Irfan, A. ed. *Islam and Other Religions: Pathways to Dialogue, Essays in Honor of Mahmoud Mustafa Ayoub*. London, New York: Routledge, 2006.

Parrinder, Geoffrey. *Jesus in the Qur'an*. New York: Oxford University Press, 1977.

Peters, F. E. *Allah's Commonwealth: A History of the Near East 600-1100 A.D.* New York: Simon and Schuster, 1973.

Peters, F. E. *Children of Abraham*. Princeton, New Jersey: Princeton University Press, 1982.

Rahman, Fazlur. *Islam*, 2nd ed. Chicago: University of Chicago Press, 1979.

Rahman, Fazlur. *Islam and Modernity: The Transformation of an Intellectual Tradition*. Chicago: University of Chicago Press, 1982.

Sachedina, Abdulziz. *Islamic Messianism*. Albany: State University of New York Press, 1981.

Smith, Wiofres Cantwell. *Islam in Modern History*. Princeton, New Jersey: Princeton University Press, 1957.

Vaporis, N. Michael, ed. *Orthodox Christians and Muslims*.

Brookline, Massachusetts: Holy Cross Orthodox Press, 1986.

Voll, John Obert. *Islam, Continuity and Change in the Modern World*. 2nd ed. Syracuse: Syracuse University Press, 1994.

Watt, W. Montgomery. *Free Will and Predestination in Early Islam*. London: Luzac, 1948.

Watt, W. Montgomery. *The Faith and Practice of all-Ghazali*. London: Allen and Unwin, 1953.

Watt, W. Montgormery. *Islamic Philosophy and Theology*. Edinburgh: Edinburgh University Press, 1962.

Watt, W. Montgomery. *Islam and Christianity Today*. London: Routledge and Kegan Paul, 1983.

Wolfson, Harry Austryn. *The Philosophy of the Kalam*. Cambridge, Massachusetts: Harvard University Press, 1976.

Contributors

Patriarch Bartholomew is Archbishop of Constantinople, New Rome, and Ecumenical Patriarch. He provides spiritual guidance to millions of Orthodox Christians worldwide, including many who live in majority-Muslim countries. He was named 11th among the world's 100 most influential people by *Time* magazine and was awarded the United States Congressional Gold Medal for his efforts to promote human rights and religious tolerance. He has also been recognized by the United Nations as a Laureate Champion of the Earth for his pioneering work to protect the environment, and is affectionately known as "the Green Patriarch."

Mahmoud M. Ayoub is a Faculty Associate at the Duncan Black MacDonald Center of the Hartford Seminary in Connecticut. Previously, he was a Professor and director of Islamic Studies in the Department of Religion at Temple University, in Philadelphia. He helped devise and launch a graduate M.A. level program in Muslim-Christian relations and comparative religion for the Centre for Christian-Muslim Studies at the University of Balamand in Lebanon. Since 1999, Dr. Ayoub has participated in the United States Department of State's program, serving as one of its ambassadors to various parts of the Middle East and Southeast Asia, commenting on American society and institutions, inter-religious dialogue, and Islam in America.

Marios P. Begzos is Professor of Comparative Religion on the faculty of theology at the University of Athens. He has published over 15 books and 300 articles on such topics as philosophy, Byzantium, and Islam. His writings have appeared in Greek, German, English, and French, and have been translated into Hungarian, Chinese, and Italian. Dr. Begzos is a lay theologian of the Greek Orthodox Church.

Samira Awad Melki holds a Licensenciate in Theology from the Institute of Saint John of Damascus and a Master's Degree in Christian and Islamic Studies from the Centre for Christian-Islamic Studies, both at the University of Balamand, Lebanon. She has written on ethical issues and on common issues in Eastern Christianity and Islam, such as the image of Mary and prophethood. She has represented the Orthodox Archdiocese of Tripoli at a number of conferences and ecumenical meetings.

George C. Papademetriou is Professor Emeritus of Theology and Director of the Library at Hellenic College/Holy Cross Greek Orthodox School of Theology in Brookline, Massachusetts. He has written and lectured extensively on comparative theology, Saint Gregory Palamas, and philosophy of religion. In addition to his research and teaching, he has been actively engaged in inter-religious trialogue among Christians, Muslims, and Jews. Rev. Dr. Papademetriou was the faculty organizer and chairperson of the first International Muslim-Orthodox Christian Dialogue on the campus of Holy Cross in 1985.

George Patronos is a Professor Emeritus of Theology at the University of Athens. Dr. Patronos has written 33 books and 200 articles on the theological and cultural interactions among Hellenism, Judaism, Islam, and Christianity. He wrote on topics such as Hermeneutics and theology of the New Testament, Eschatology, and Missiology. He has worked with Archbishop Anastasios Yannoulatos in African missions, and is now working with Patriarch Bartholomew in Asian missions.

Radko Popov is an Orthodox Christian living in Bulgaria. He studied theology in Bulgaria and Christian-Muslim relations and dialogue at Hartford Seminary, Connecticut. He has written several articles on Christian-Muslim relations for national and international publications, and produced over 600 religious programs for the BBC World Service, London. Recently, Professor Popov published the book *Jesus Christ in the Qur'an* – the only book on the subject in the Bulgarian language.

Anastasios Yannoulatos has been Archbishop of Tirana and All Albania since 1992, where he has sought to reestablish the Orthodox Autocephalous Church of Albania. He founded the international Orthodox Missionary Society in Athens (1971), which focused on several African nations; directed the *Apostolike Diako-*

nia of the Church of Greece (1971-75); served as vice president of Syndesmos (1964-77); and has edited the missionary review *Panta ta Ethnoi* (All Nations) since 1981. A longtime member of the Commission of World Mission and Evangelism of the World Council of Churches, he was its first Orthodox Moderator (1984-91), and presided at the 1989 San Antonio World Mission Conference. He has written eight books, including *Islam: A General Survey*.

Gregorios D. Ziakas is Professor Emeritus of Comparative Religion at Aristotle University, in Thessalonike, Greece. Dr. Ziakas is the foremost Islamicist in Greece. He has written extensively on Islam, Orthodox Christian-Muslim relations, and Eastern religions.

Index

Abraham
  and Hagar, 117–18, 127, 128
  and lineage of the prophets, 21, 33, 69, 171, 254, 256
  mentioned, 9, 137, 234, 260
  as symbol of faith and bond of unity amongst monotheists, 9, 238
  and the Maqam Ibrahim "The Black Stone," 127–29
Abu al-Qāsim Muhammad ibn 'Abd Allāh. *See* Muhammad
Abubacer (Ibn Ṭufayl), 81
Abū Bakr, 29, 256–57
Abu Dawood, 138, 258
Abukarra, Theodore (Bishop of Charan), 147, 149–50
Abu Talib (uncle of Muhammad), 254, 265–66
adhkar (remembrances), 185
Against the Jewish and Saracene Heresies, 149–50
Alameddine, Suleiman Selim, 183–85
al-Kindī. *See* Kindī, Abū Ya'qūb al-
angels
  creation of in the *Qur'an*, 264
  Gabriel, 21–22, 123, 254–55, 257
  Muslim belief in good and evil of, 265
  as servants of God, 25, 27

as witnesses in the *Qur'an*, 120, 165
Antichrist
  as person in Islamic eschatology, 29
  used as accusatory term, 116–17, 151–52
Aquinas, Thomas, 41, 94
Aristotle
  Averroes's commentaries on corpus of, 96–98, 102–3
  Avicenna's interpretations of philosophy of, 89–90
  al-Kindī's synthesis of thought of with Neo-platonism, 81–82
  Neoplatonic transformation of by al-Fārābi, 87
ascesis, 203, 204
Ata ur-Rahim, Muhammad, 18–19
Athenagoras, 9
'āttihad, 204–5
Avenpace (Ibn Bājjah), 81
Averroes (Ibn Rushd)
  commentaries on Aristotelian corpus by, 96–98
  criticism of the *falsafa* by, 98
  Greek philosophical influence on views, of, 102
  impact on Western philosophy by thought of, 102–3
  interpretations of Aristotle's

menical Patriarchate and the World Islamic Call Society, 312–13

Judaism
according to *Qur'anic* history of Islam, 18
Biblical foundation of Islam and teachings of Christianity and, 78
conversion of Chiones to Islam from, 58–60
need of Islam to distinguish itself from Christianity and, 138–39
requests for miracles from Muhammad by believers in Christianity and, 124–25

Ka'ba in Mecca
explained as holy site, 255, 256, 260
sacred stone of, 127–29, 143n.29, 255, 261
See also icons and images; worship
kalima, 26
Kassianos, Abba, 165–66
Khalipha, 266
Kharji, 263–64
al-Kindī, Abū Ya'qūb
Christian influence upon, 86
synthesis of Aristotelian and Neo-platonic philosophy by, 81–82
theological/philosophical reconciliations of, 83–86
thinking of al-Fārābī contrasted with, 86, 88

Last Judgment, 28–29, 34, 69
Logos of God
Christian and Muslim views

of compared, 25–28, 61–65, 153, 162
compared with Moses role as "trusted servant," 70
Qur'an expression of critiqued John of Damascus, 120–21, 127
Qur'an expression of used for dialogue with Gennadios, 157

Makkos, Theodosios, 247–49
Malik, Abd al-, 113
Manicheans, 41, 115
Manuel II, Paleologos (Emperor), 151, 155
Margolioss, 187
Mary
and Jesus's virginal birth, 5, 16, 20–23, 34, 58, 64, 70, 165
Muslim views of, 8, 27, 121
Massignon, 186–87
mass media
coverage of dialogues of between Islam and Christianity, 238
need for education to influence effect of, 220, 273, 281
potential of, 284, 313
Mecca
John of Damascus's knowledge of, 128, 134
and the life of Muhammad, 134, 254–56, 260–61
Medina, 255, 256, 260
Melkites, 112, 141n.2, 5
Meyendorf, John
on breath regulation and prayer, 193–94
and Chiones, 59
Miller, Elliot, 192–93
miracles
Black Stone of the Ka'ba and,

45020726R00210

Made in the USA
Lexington, KY
15 September 2015